Chinese Capitalism and the Modernist Vision

In the past fifty years, the experience of the Chinese economy has continually challenged the assumptions of laissez-faire economics. It has sustained a strong growth rate, changed the structure of international economic relationships and has become critical to many multinational corporations. Now, it appears to be on the verge of becoming a new economic superpower. This book addresses the structure and dynamics of the Chinese economy, examining in depth the connection between growth and the particular version of Marxism that has been adopted by the Communist Party of China.

Satyananda J. Gabriel offers one of the most comprehensive analyses of the contemporary Chinese economy, covering industry and agriculture, rural and urban enterprises, labor power and financial markets, and the process of integrating the Chinese domestic economy into global capitalism. *Chinese Capitalism and the Modernist Vision* identifies the current transition in China as a historic passage from state feudalism to state capitalism that will significantly alter both the internal political and economic dynamics of China and the global political economy.

Satyananda J. Gabriel is Associate Professor of Economics at Mount Holyoke College, USA and Academic Coordinator of the Rural Development Leadership Network.

Routledge Studies in the Growth Economies of Asia

1 **The Changing Capital Markets of East Asia**
Edited by Ky Cao

2 **Financial Reform in China**
Edited by On Kit Tam

3 **Women and Industrialization in Asia**
Edited by Susan Horton

4 **Japan's Trade Policy**
Action or reaction?
Yumiko Mikanagi

5 **The Japanese Election System**
Three analaytical perspectives
Junichiro Wada

6 **The Economics of the Latecomers**
Catching-up, technology transfer and institutions in Germany, Japan and South Korea
Jang-Sup Shin

7 **Industrialization in Malaysia**
Import substitution and infant industry performance
Rokiah Alavi

8 **Economic Development in Twentieth Century East Asia**
The international context
Edited by Aiko Ikeo

9 **The Politics of Economic Development in Indonesia**
Contending perspectives
Edited by Ian Chalmers and Vedi Hadiz

10 **Studies in the Economic History of the Pacific Rim**
Edited by Sally M. Miller, A.J.H. Latham, and Dennis O. Flynn

11 **Workers and the State in New Order Indonesia**
Vedi R. Hadiz

12 **The Japanese Foreign Exchange Market**
Beate Reszat

13 **Exchange Rate Policies in Emerging Asian Countries**
Edited by Stefan Collignon, Jean Pisani-Ferry, and Yung Chul Park

14 **Chinese Firms and Technology in the Reform Era**
Yizheng Shi

15 **Japanese Views on Economic Development**
Diverse paths to the market
Kenichi Ohno and Izumi Ohno

16 **Technological Capabilities and Export Success in Asia**
Edited by Dieter Ernst, Tom Ganiatsos, and Lynn Mytelka

17 **Trade and Investment in China**
The European experience
Edited by Roger Strange, Jim Slater, and Limin Wang

18 **Technology and Innovation in Japan**
Policy and management for the 21st century
Edited by Martin Hemmert and Christian Oberländer

19 **Trade Policy Issues in Asian Development**
Prema-chandra Athukorala

20 **Economic Integration in the Asia Pacific Region**
Ippei Yamazawa

21 **Japan's War Economy**
Edited by Erich Pauer

22 **Industrial Technology Development in Malaysia**
Industry and firm studies
Edited by K.S. Jomo, Greg Felker, and Rajah Rasiah

23 **Technology, Competitiveness and the State**
Malaysia's industrial technology policies
Edited by K.S. Jomo and Greg Felker

24 **Corporatism and Korean Capitalism**
Edited by Dennis L. McNamara

25 **Japanese Science**
Samuel Coleman

26 **Capital and Labour in Japan**
The functions of two factor markets
Toshiaki Tachibanaki and Atsuhiro Taki

27 **Asia Pacific Dynamism 1550–2000**
Edited by A.J.H. Latham and Heita Kawakatsu

28 **The Political Economy of Development and Environment in Korea**
Jae-Yong Chung and Richard J. Kirkby

29 **Japanese Economics and Economists since 1945**
Edited by Aiko Ikeo

30 **China's Entry into the World Trade Organisation**
Edited by Peter Drysdale and Ligang Song

31 **Hong Kong as an International Financial Centre**
Emergence and development 1945–1965
Catherine R. Schenk

32 **Impediments to Trade in Services**
Measurement and policy implication
Edited by Christopher Findlay and Tony Warren

33 **The Japanese Industrial Economy**
Late development and cultural causation
Ian Inkster

34 **China and the Long March to Global Trade**
The accession of China to the World Trade Organization
Edited by Alan S. Alexandroff, Sylvia Ostry, and Rafael Gomez

35 **Capitalist Development and Economism in East Asia**
The rise of Hong Kong, Singapore, Taiwan, and South Korea
Kui-Wai Li

36 **Women and Work in Globalizing Asia**
Edited by Dong-Sook S. Gills and Nicola Piper

37 **Financial Markets and Policies in East Asia**
Gordon de Brouwer

38 **Developmentalism and Dependency in Southeast Asia**
The case of the automotive industry
Jason P. Abbott

39 **Law and Labour Market Regulation in East Asia**
Edited by Sean Cooney, Tim Lindsey, Richard Mitchell, and Ying Zhu

40 The Economy of the Philippines
Elites, inequalities and economic restructuring
Peter Krinks

41 China's Third Economic Transformation
The rise of the private economy
Edited by Ross Garnaut and Ligang Song

42 The Vietnamese Economy
Awakening the dormant dragon
Edited by Binh Tran-Nam and Chi Do Pham

43 Restructuring Korea Inc.
Jang-Sup Shin and Ha-Joon Chang

44 Development and Structural Change in the Asia-Pacific
Globalising miracles or end of a model?
Edited by Martin Andersson and Christer Gunnarsson

45 State Collaboration and Development Strategies in China
The case of the China–Singapore Suzhou industrial park (1992–2002)
Alexius Pereira

46 Capital and Knowledge in Asia
Changing power relations
Edited by Heidi Dahles and Otto van den Muijzenberg

47 Southeast Asian Paper Tigers?
From miracle to debacle and beyond
Edited by Jomo K.S.

48 Manufacturing Competitiveness in Asia
How internationally competitive national firms and industries developed in east Asia
Edited by Jomo K.S.

49 The Korean Economy at the Crossroads
Edited by MoonJoong Tcha and Chung-Sok Suh

50 Ethnic Business
Chinese capitalism in Southeast Asia
Edited by Jomo K.S. and Brian C. Folk

51 Exchange Rate Regimes in East Asia
Edited by Gordon De Brouwer and Masahiro Kawai

52 Financial Governance in East Asia
Policy dialogue, surveillance and cooperation
Edited by Gordon De Brouwer and Yunjong Wang

53 Designing Financial Systems in East Asia and Japan
Edited by Joseph P.H. Fan, Masaharu Hanazaki, and Juro Teranishi

54 State Competence and Economic Growth in Japan
Yoshiro Miwa

55 Understanding Japanese Saving
Does population aging matter?
Robert Dekle

56 The Rise and Fall of the East Asian Growth System, 1951–2000
International competitiveness and rapid economic growth
Xiaoming Huang

57 Service Industries and Asia-Pacific Cities
New development trajectories
Edited by P.W. Daniels, K.C. Ho, and T.A. Hutton

58 Unemployment in Asia
Edited by John Benson and Ying Zhu

59 Risk Management and Innovation in Japan, Britain and the USA
Edited by Ruth Taplin

60 Japan's Development Aid to China
The long-running foreign policy of engagement
Tsukasa Takamine

61 Chinese Capitalism and the Modernist Vision
Satyananda J. Gabriel

Chinese Capitalism and the Modernist Vision

Satyananda J. Gabriel

Routledge
Taylor & Francis Group
LONDON AND NEW YORK

First published 2006
by Routledge
2 Park Square, Milton Park, Abingdon, Oxon OX14 4RN

Simultaneously published in the USA and Canada
by Routledge
270 Madison Ave, New York, NY 10016

Reprinted 2006

Routledge is an imprint of the Taylor & Francis Group, an informa business

Typeset in Times New Roman by
Newgen Imaging Systems (P) Ltd, Chennai, India
Printed and bound in Great Britain by
Biddles Ltd, King's Lynn

British Library Cataloguing in Publication Data
A catalogue record for this book is available
from the British Library

Library of Congress Cataloging in Publication Data
A catalog record for this book has been requested

ISBN 10: 0-415-70003-5
ISBN 13: 978-0-415-70003-0

To Ella I. Gabriel, for providing intellectual and spiritual support and without whom this would not have been possible

and

Bishara Cloudthunder Resnick Gabriel, whose ceaseless questions and optimism served as both inspiration and catalyst.

Contents

Acronyms

ACFTU	All-China Federation of Trade Unions
AESA	Association of Economic and Social Analysis
AMC	Asset management company
BHP	Broken Hill Proprietary
CMEA	Council for Mutual Economic Assistance
CPC	Communist Party of China
FDI	Foreign direct investment
GDP	Gross Domestic Product
GLF	Great Leap Forward
GPCR	Great Proletarian Cultural Revolution
HRS	Household Responsibility System
IPO	Initial public offering
JSC	Joint stock cooperative
NPL	Non-performing loan
OECD	Organization for Economic Cooperation and Development
PBC	People's Bank of China
PLA	People's Liberation Army
PRC	People's Republic of China
RMB	Renminbi
RSCE	Rural state capitalist enterprise
S&L	Saving and loan
SME	Small and Medium Enterprise
SOE	State-owned Enterprise
SRE	State-run Enterprise
SV	Surplus Value
TVE	Township–Village Enterprise
WTO	World Trade Organization

1 Theory matters

As an important part of the intellectual heritage of China's postrevolutionary leadership, Marxian theory is one of the factors shaping (via public policies and practices) Gross Domestic Product (GDP) growth, averaging nearly 10 percent per annum for almost a quarter century, including the years of the Asian economic crisis of 1997–98. Neoclassical orthodoxy cannot explain this growth, indeed would have (and did) predict something considerably less spectacular (Todaro 1977). For the entire span of this extraordinary growth, many orthodox economists predicted disaster just around the corner (Zheng 1997; Wolf *et al.* 2003). Many continue to argue that policy makers in China are making serious mistakes, not moving fast enough to "liberalize" the Chinese economy and failing to recognize the limitations of state intervention. Neoclassical orthodoxy has proven inadequate to the task of either making sense of the dynamics of the Chinese economy or the complex decision-making processes within the Chinese leadership (and bureaucracy). This failure is, in part, the consequence of an underlying logic and methodology in orthodox economic theory that presumes simplicity, homogeneity, and stasis where complexity, heterogeneity, and dynamic change in social processes, institutions, economic agents, and theories (including the type of Marxian theory that informs Chinese public policy) must be recognized to grasp the conditions driving the type of dynamic economic growth occurring in China. Just as critically, this failure in orthodox theory extends to its inability (due to the specific nature of the neoclassical form of essentialism, with its foundation in a simplistic notion of decision-making and minimalist view of social and environmental context) to recognize the dramatic nature of the internal transformation in Chinese society or the global implications of that transformation. This is a transformation that touches every aspect of social life and the natural environment. It is not just the Chinese economy that is in transition. The transformations in economic relationships shape and are shaped by simultaneous transformations in cultural processes, including preferences, notions of the self, and understandings of the nature and role of the market; political processes, including internal rules governing the Communist Party of China (CPC), the differential authority of local versus national government, laws relating to property and contract law (and related rules governing transactions); and environmental processes, including transformations in the physical terrain of China, extraordinary growth in air transportation (in total numbers of aircraft and the speed at which they move people and objects), diversion and control of flood waters, and construction of the world's largest dam.

In order to open up the theoretical exploration to a wide range of factors shaping the nature of transition in China, to avoid prejudging the nature of the interaction of these factors (there are no deterministic relationships), and to engage directly the concepts that have shaped the CPC (past and present), this text is grounded in post-structuralist Marxian theory. Grounding the text within Marxian theory makes it possible to simultaneously produce an internal (within the broader Marxian tradition) critique of the logic of the current leadership of the CPC and to make this logic more transparent, generating a better understanding of the current transformation of the Chinese social formation. It is understood that such an analysis is a necessary step in making sense of public policy formation, which contributes to understanding the dynamics of economic and social interaction in the Chinese social formation. Economic growth has taken place in the context of internal struggles within the CPC over Marxian theory and practices and the ultimate rise of a version of modernist Marxism, strongly associated with Deng Xiaoping, to prominence within the party and state bureaucracy.

Thus, one of the premises of this text is that theory really does matter. Theory matters both in terms of producing knowledge of the society (theory acting as epistemological lens shaping what is or is not perceived, as well as the relationships between perceived objects or processes) and as one of the many determinants of the society (theory as the source of effects that, along with other factors, constitutes reality). In other words, explaining the dynamics of Chinese social transformation requires an understanding not only of economic and political processes, but also cultural processes (of which theory is a sub element).

Post-structuralist Marxian theory

The Chinese social formation is shaped by the complex and ever changing effects of the social and environmental processes comprising it and the social and environmental processes occurring outside of the political boundaries of China. Indeed, the notion that social and environmental processes can be clearly distinguished as constituted inside China or outside China is problematic, given the interaction of processes across politically defined boundaries. This is a point that has relevance to the ultimate conclusion of the text. Nevertheless, the text provides an elaboration of a wide range of these internal and external influences, providing social analysts and students with a starting point for making sense of the dynamics of transition/development of the People's Republic of China (PRC).

The approach of this text is to use a post-structuralist version of Marxian theory,[1] grounded in the ontology and epistemology of overdetermination[2] and utilizing class concepts shaped within and by a long history of debates over Marxism and modernism, to construct this complex understanding of China. This approach does not presume that any aspect of the political, economic, cultural, and environmental configuration of processes within China is more important than any other or that any of these processes is insignificant to understanding the whole. And this includes class processes. In an overdetermined universe, the issue is not whether this or that array of factors is significant, but instead to make clear the particular manner in which the significance of factors or processes is manifest at any given moment in the social formation. This approach is contrasted to that of determinist theories, both Marxian and non-Marxian, used to explain transition in China.

Modernist Marxism

By contrast, determinist theories separate reality into significant and insignificant factors and exert hegemony over other theories in providing a singular explanation (Truth) of social dynamics.[3] Classical Marxism is grounded in a deterministic logic by which history is understood as following a predetermined, linear, and irreversible path toward a telos (communism as end point of historical evolution). This underlying teleology is the basis for understanding transitions, in general, and the transition currently underway in China, in particular. A version of classical Marxism, associated most closely with Zhou Enlai, Deng Xiaoping, Jiang Zemin, and, most recently, Hu Jintao, has become prevalent among the CPC leadership, cadre, and state bureaucrats. As previously indicated, this version of classical Marxism, which is simply described herein as modernist Marxism, was shaped in the cauldron of internecine struggles within the CPC. In particular, the conflict between modernist Marxists and Maoists resulted in a gradual shift of the modernists away from the Stalinist model, where socialism translated into directly coercive tactics by state functionaries to secure conditions for communist party rule, the centralization of control over surplus labor and related value flows, and the inviolability of state ownership, toward a more liberal version of modernist Marxism where incentives replace coercion, control over surplus value (SV) is largely decentralized from the central government to localities, and state ownership loses the status of necessary condition for defining China as socialist.

Socialism

The modernist position on socialism is not as far removed from its origins within orthodox Marxism as some might think. The most orthodox Marxian definition of socialism posits it as a society *in transition* from capitalism to communism. In this particular conception, the term "socialism" refers not so much to a distinct social formation as it does to a nebulous *transitional state* with mixed features from both capitalism and communism. Paul Sweezy, one of the leading figures in American Marxism, once described socialism as "a way station on the journey from capitalism to communism" (Sweezy and Bettelheim 1971: 123). Socialism, as transitory stage on the teleological road to communism, is of an undetermined duration. There is no clear-cut delineation of the path this transition should take such that one can determine at any given point in time where along that path a society might fall. Sweezy indicated that the transition would take "not years or even decades but . . . a whole historical epoch, or perhaps even more than one historical epoch." This understanding of the duration of the socialist phase is important in making sense of the modernist Marxist reforms. The modernists perceived the Maoists as impatient and unrealistic in their view that the transition to communism could be brought about in a relatively short period of time. Indeed, the so-called "Great Leap Forward" was, from a Maoist perspective, designed to thrust China directly into communism, without the necessity of passing through a capitalist phase, although its implementation may not have been consistent with that point of view. The modernists were and are more orthodox in their Marxism. Their teleology is both rigid and follows a time frame similar to that articulated by Sweezy. In their worldview, China must fully develop capitalism *before* communism is possible. Socialism is, for the modernists, defined by the leadership role of the vanguard party-state in managing the transition, particularly orchestrating the adoption of "advanced" technologies and related social relationships. The modernist Marxist leadership believes that the Maoists were romanticists who failed to recognize "historical necessity." "Modern" technology and the social relations of capitalism are such a historical necessity:

> There is no fundamental contradiction between socialism and a market economy . . . the overriding task in China today is to throw ourselves heart and soul into the modernization drive. While giving play to the advantages inherent in socialism, we are also employing some capitalist methods – but only as methods of accelerating the growth of the productive forces. It is true that some negative things have appeared in the process, but what is more important is the gratifying progress we have been able to achieve by initiating these reforms and following this road. China has no alternative but to follow this road.
>
> (Deng 1985)

The modernist point of view has a long lineage in orthodox Marxism, as Lenin demonstrated in his statement that "Socialism is inconceivable without large-scale capitalist engineering based on the latest discoveries of modern science" (Lenin 1960). The technological determinism at the root of modernist Marxism tends to displace class analysis. Exploitation, whether capitalist or feudal, cannot only exist within the context of socialism, so defined, but can be encouraged by a "vanguard party," as part of the overall push to adopt "modern" technologies. This is particularly the case where it is understood that effective deployment of hard technology, in the form of material artifacts, requires a coherent structure of social relationships.

Class matters

Theoretical concepts, such as socialism, are used to bring certain aspects of reality into focus, to produce these aspects as objects of analysis. All concepts are necessarily composites of other concepts. The definition of the concept in question is overdetermined by the definitions/understandings of these other concepts. The modernist understanding of socialism exposes their understanding of class. Class becomes an epiphenomenon of the exercise of state power. Communist party control of the state defines the social formation as socialist and is sufficient to answer all questions related to class. Class transition is determined by development of the productive forces (technology), which under socialism is the responsibility of the vanguard party.

Charles Bettelheim criticizes the sharp modernist turn within the post-Mao CPC, the displacement of "class struggle" at the site of production and appropriation (the Maoist road) with intellectual debates ("class struggle" of a different type?) over theoretical issues and public policy. Bettelheim questions the party's continuing commitment to Marxism, as he understands it:

> Lin Chin-jan speaks of the "fundamental" completion of the socialist transformation of ownership and declares that, as a result of this "fundamental" completion, the class struggle has to develop mainly on the ideological and political fronts. Lin Chin-jan thus deletes *that which is decisive, namely, the struggle waged by the workers themselves with a view to transforming the labor process and production and, thereby, production relations*. He advocates substituting class struggle as this developed during the Cultural Revolution (a struggle concerned with different forms of the social division of labor) a "struggle of ideas," a struggle between "modern ideology" and the vestiges of "old" ideas. This abandonment of the class struggle implies the transformation of Marxism into its opposite.
>
> (1978: 71–72, italics in original)

The modernist notion that struggles over the actual processes reproducing class relations is no longer necessary has a kind of familiar ring to it. It resonates on a similar frequency to arguments that the rise of the liberal democratic state and capitalism represent the "end of history." In the modernist vision, history may not yet have reached its denouement, but the dominance of the communist party has all but guaranteed that such will be the case eventually. Not the end of history but the end of struggle over one of the prominent aspects of history, class relationships and the forms of exploitation they engender.

Bettelheim rejects modernist Marxism and bemoans the failure to produce a class analysis of China:

> While the absence of a class analysis of present-day China constitutes an obstacle to a full understanding of the changes which have come about in class relations during recent years, it is also – and this is a much more serious matter – one of the reasons for the failure of the revolutionary line. One cannot transform class relations in a revolutionary way if one does not know what these relations are. Lacking this knowledge, a ruling party can only, in the end, maintain the status quo while endeavoring to "modernize the economy."
>
> (1978: 94)

This text represents an attempt to answer Bettelheim's challenge. The starting point for carrying out this class analysis of the Chinese social formation and the transitional path from which it reached this present moment is to revisit the underlying concept of class. The concept of *class* delineates a particular subset of social relationships. In this text, class defines the relationship by which distinct human beings engage in the performance, appropriation, and distribution of surplus labor. This concept of class process is most closely associated with the version of Marxist social critique and analysis that has been elaborated, as a tool for the analysis of social transformation, by Stephen A. Resnick and Richard D. Wolff in the journal *Rethinking Marxism*. While all forms of Marxian analysis, including modernist versions, use the concept of class, there are significant differences among Marxian theorists over the proper way to conduct class analysis. Some Marxian theorists have focused on property ownership relationships as the key determinant of transitions from one form of class society to another – property ownership is viewed as determining transitions in the mode of production, appropriation, and distribution of surplus labor (or the fruits thereof). Others have focused on political (power) relationships as the determinant of class transitions. And the modernist Marxists have focused on the forces of production (technology) as the determinant of transitions in class relationships.

The concept of class process is the entry point into social analysis for post-structuralist Marxian theory, and the understanding of transition as complexly determined (rather than the outcome of essential determinants) comes out of the post-structuralist ontology within which this concept of class process is deployed. This ontology is grounded in the concept of overdetermination. The term "process" implies a constellation of events, which can occur in sequential order and/or simultaneously, that produce a specific state of being: the state of being exists only in so far as this constellation of events continues to be reproduced. Process, therefore, implies movement, a continuous reproduction of conditions (events) for the existence of a specific state of being. Process dies when the movement/reproduction dies. In general terms, a transition occurs when one set of processes is displaced by another set. The notion of transition in an entire social formation implies that a focused-upon set of processes (entry point into analysis) has undergone a fundamental transformation. The terms feudal, capitalist, and communist are applied as adjectives describing a particular set of social relationships by which surplus labor is performed and appropriated. A shift from the prevalence of one class process to that of another is described as a class transition. It is precisely this class transition that is at the roots of the much debated concept of socialism (whether with or without Chinese characteristics).

All processes (and therefore all transitions) are overdetermined, in that each is the result of the effects of other social and environmental processes, not one of which is *the* determinant. Thus, post-structuralist Marxian theory embraces property ownership, political (power) relationships, and technology as determinants of class processes and transitions from the prevalence of one class process to another, but no factor or subset of factors is considered as sole determinant(s). Therefore, there can be no one-to-one correspondence between any particular type of property ownership, power relationship, or gestalt of technologies and a particular class process or transitional path; given that class process and transition are shaped by a complex interaction of all social and environmental processes. Sometimes a particular type of property ownership will, in the context of other social and environmental processes, shape the existence of a particular class process and transitional path, and at other times this type of property ownership will not produce this result, in the context of a different gestalt of other processes.

Class process is, then, a unique social process – the production, appropriation, and distribution of surplus product – which exists as the overdetermined effect of other processes. In the course of human history, a number of different social arrangements have linked direct producers who perform surplus labor to the appropriators of such surplus labor. Marxian theorists have identified five different class processes (five different ways in which surplus labor may be produced and appropriated): slave, ancient, feudal, capitalist, and communist. Each type of class process is overdetermined by a matrix of different and changing social and environmental processes. Each type of class process can exist if and only if a suitable matrix of processes exists and therefore generates the conditions for its existence. The possibility for favorable conditions to disappear, as the existing matrix of social and environmental processes changes, constitutes the potential for crisis in the life of the class process. Nevertheless, the possible arrays of processes that can, in combination and interaction, produce favorable conditions for the existence and reproduction of any given class process is multiple, producing variant forms of that class process. In other words, the existence of class process X is not dependent on a singular matrix of social and environmental processes Y, but rather can be reproduced under a number of different such matrices. This point is critical to understanding the conclusions reached in this text regarding the class processes discovered to have been prevalent both prior to and following the post-Mao reforms.

A post-structuralist view of transition recognizes that social formations are always changing, always in some kind of transition, precisely because the matrix of processes comprising the social formation is always changing. Indeed, transition and development are different words for the same pervasive and unending changes in the complex matrix of social and environmental processes. All societies are in transition, in a state of development. Transition/development does not follow any necessary pattern, linear or otherwise. This is not to say change is random. Transition/development is constituted by the logic of the interaction of countless social and environmental processes producing a trajectory of change that is always partially seen and understood in social analysis. To gain even partial insight into transition requires narrowing the focus to some aspects of the social formation. It is in focusing our theoretical lens on certain conceptual elements of the social formation that qualitative difference in social formations, across both time and space, may be identified and analyzed, allowing for the recognition of transition from one type of social formation to another.

The Marxian focus on class provides an entry point into such identification and analysis. For many Marxian theorists, transition is precisely understood as transition from one type of class society to another. In the framework adopted in this text, the adjective used in the description of class societies (ancient, feudal, slave, capitalist, communist) will be based on which of the numerous class processes present in the social formation is prevalent. This identification and analysis of the transitions from the prevalence of one class process to that of a different class process is understood as relevant to all manner of phenomena, including the quality of life in that society, the state of the natural environment (globally), and the nexus connecting that society to other societies.

In order to test the hypothesis that China has undergone several class transitions *since* 1949 (the year that marks a revolutionary change in the Chinese state), class process must be more carefully defined. This will allow us to test the possibility that different class processes have been prevalent at different times in the life of this social formation and to then analyze the impact of these class revolutions/transitions. This is facilitated by returning to the definition that Marx laid down – class as the appropriation and distribution of surplus labor (in direct labor form, product form, or value form). The appropriation of surplus labor is an event marked by the socially determined transfer of the fruits of productive labor from the laborer to the appropriator(s). The distribution of surplus labor is marked by the secondary transfer of those fruits to other economic agents. Resnick and Wolff describe class process in the following passage:

> It (the fundamental class process) is defined as the process of producing and appropriating surplus labor. Laborers are understood to do a certain amount of labor sufficient to produce the goods and services their current standard of living requires. Marx calls this "necessary labor." However, laborers in all societies perform more than necessary labor. They do what Marx calls "surplus labor." This surplus may be retained by the laborers, individually or collectively. Alternatively it may be appropriated directly and immediately by non-laborers. The latter case is Marx's precise definition of exploitation: when the class process involves non-laborers appropriating the surplus labor of others.
>
> (1987: 20)

Socialism with Chinese characteristics

Ironically, the rise to dominance of modernist Marxism within the CPC (and the larger party-state) has led to the religious assumption (faith-based) that class ceased to be relevant as a tool for internal analysis of Chinese society after the 1949 state revolution. While the Maoists fought to retain the relevance of class relations/processes, and used this as the basis of political practices and struggles, including the Great Leap Forward (GLF) and Great Proletarian Cultural Revolution (GPCR), the modernists have shifted the focus of theoretical work and policy away from considerations of class structures and toward their *deus ex machina*, technology, and a broader notion of modernization. For the modernist leadership, from Deng Xiaoping to Hu Jintao, acquisition and innovation of "advanced" technology is *the* necessary, if not sufficient, condition for the continued movement of Chinese society along the path of progress (toward the telos of communism). For the modernists, advanced technology plays a transcendental role in history, generally, and in the current transitional state, in particular.

This transitional state is described as "socialism with Chinese characteristics." In other versions of modernist Marxism, from Stalin and on, socialism was signified by communist party control over the organs of the state and state ownership of the major means of production (material technology and physical plant required for manufacturing and extractive industries). Given the presumption that socialism represents an advance along the path of progress, away from capitalism and toward communism, then it was anticipated that among the outputs of socialism would be other signs of progress. In particular, technological determinism has played a role in many types of modernism, including modernist Marxism. Thus, within modernist Marxism, the socialist-era sign of progress is not a reduction in the prevalence of exploitation (capitalist or otherwise), or even the relative egalitarianism of the Maoist era, but the realization of technological advance in the form of material artifacts, whether objects of consumption or means of production. And this technological advance is predicated on a certain type of social organization: in classical Marxism there is the assumption that the forces and relations of production must be synchronized. In the rigid teleology of classical Marxism there was the presumption that a great leap forward in social relations of production was doomed to failure and that all societies must necessarily go through the same stages of development under similar technological conditions. Ironically, this approach results in the displacement of class analysis, including the effect of exploitation upon social transformation and technological innovation. It is argued that this essentialism has contributed to the rise of a specific type of exploitative class process in the current period and to the increasing integration of the Chinese social formation into a larger global network of SV flows and related processes. In yet another irony, the modernist leadership in China took an odd philosophical turn when they appended the phrase "with Chinese characteristics" to the term "socialism." The resulting phrase "socialism with Chinese characteristics" aimed to retain much of the modernist narrative of movement along a linear path toward a telos and the necessary role of communist party rule in pushing the society along that path, but also "accidentally" opened the path to jettisoning the idea of fixed characteristics common to all manifestations of socialism. The phrase "with Chinese characteristics" decentered the notion of socialism and opened up the possibility of multiple socialisms. In other words, this was a postmodern moment within the modernist framework of the CPC leadership. China's unique circumstances, culture, and history are understood, in this phrase, to shape a completely different type of socialism from that imagined in classical Marxism or promoted by intellectuals in other communist parties or within the broader Marxian literature. No matter what the reason for this postmodern moment, it is understood to have unexpected consequences, some of which will be explored in this text. In other words, the text presents an analysis of the overdetermined relationship of the theoretical frameworks deployed by the

CPC leadership, particularly their form of modernist Marxism (as the frame for organizing political policy and practices, as one of the cultural influences on other aspects of social life, and including its postmodern moments), the transitional path of the Chinese social formation, and the meaning and impact of the globalization of the Chinese social formation.

Typology of class processes

In order to test for prevalence switching between class processes, it is necessary to define the difference between types of class processes. As previously indicated, the typical typology of class processes includes the slave, capitalist, feudal, ancient, and communist forms. These are class processes in so far as they involve the production, appropriation, and distribution of SV. The difference between the various class processes is the particular social arrangement that results in the worker performing the surplus labor (creating SV), and the appropriator taking possession of the fruits of that surplus labor. These social arrangements have been variable over time and place. The first three of these class processes (slave, capitalist, and feudal) are similar in that the performers of surplus labor, the person(s) who creates the surplus goods and services, is distinct from the person(s) who takes possession of those goods and services. This is precisely the definition of an exploitative class process.

The slave class process is distinguished from other class processes by the status of the direct producer as chattel: the direct producer is living capital, property that can be consumed in production, leased or sold, or otherwise treated as tangible property, to secure incremental increases in value for the owner. The performance of surplus labor by a slave and the appropriation of that surplus labor (or the fruits thereof) by someone other than the slave constitute the slave fundamental class process. The distribution by the slave master/appropriator of the surplus fruits of the slave's labor to secure conditions for the reproduction of slavery is defined as the slave distributive class process. Together the fundamental and distributive class processes are referred to as the slave class process. Variant forms of slavery have included the version in Pharaohnic Egypt where slavery was overdetermined by a highly centralized, bureaucratic regime with extensive state ownership of land and other means of production and antebellum United States where slavery was overdetermined by a relatively democratic, free market regime. While slavery has existed in China and may still exist in some unusual circumstances (as it does in many social formations), there is no evidence of the wide-scale prevalence of slavery today or at any point since the CPC came to control the Chinese state in 1949.

The feudal fundamental class process is defined as the production and appropriation of surplus on the basis of socially constituted ties of obligation of the direct producer to service a specific feudal appropriator qua lord. Feudal obligation presents the direct producer with a socially determined limitation on his or her ability to perform labor: to exist in the normal sphere of social life, he/she must perform surplus labor for the lord. The hegemony of the lord over the sphere of work life gives this social entity the power to appropriate this laborer's surplus labor or the fruits thereof. In essence, it is a rent the laborer must pay to exist and work as a normal human being. In return the lord grants the laborer access to social necessities. This relationship between feudal lord and feudal direct producer may be described as *feudal reciprocity*. This process, like all processes, exists in motion. In other words, the feudal fundamental class process exists only as long as feudal direct producers perform surplus labor and feudal lords appropriate this surplus labor or the fruits thereof. Additionally, the feudal lords/appropriators must secure some of the conditions necessary for reproduction of feudal exploitation by distributing surplus labor (secured from the feudal serfs/direct producers) to others. This process of distributing the surplus fruits of feudal labor is defined as the feudal distributive class process. Necessarily, the social and environmental conditions coincident with any instance of the feudal class process are always changing. Thus, the context of feudalism is always changing, creating continual variations in the form of the feudal society, including changes in the array of social agents who are linked to feudal exploitation by the feudal distributive class process. It is an important contention of this text that a form of feudal class process came into being *after* the 1949 Chinese revolution and is critically important to the nature of the current Chinese social formation and the transition it is undergoing.

The capitalist class process is distinguished by the unique wage–labor relationship by which surplus labor is brought into existence. Human beings sell their potential to do labor (their labor power) in a "market" where the number of possible buyers is large enough so as to allow some modicum of choice of employer. In other words, every worker is *free to choose* his or her employer. This definition indicates that capitalism, if it is to exist and be reproduced over time, requires a particular type of market, a free market in the buying and selling of labor power, and a particular type of ownership, the ownership of the fruits of the labor of an employed wage laborer by someone other than that employed wage laborer. However, capitalism is not reducible to either markets or ownership. There must be a *free market in labor power*, meaning that potential laborers must have the freedom to seek employment (for a wage) in an environment where there are choices about possible employers. There must be a political and cultural environment within which it is possible for someone other than the worker who created a product to take ownership of that product and to realize the SV embodied in the product. The worker is paid a wage, embodying a certain amount of economic value, in exchange for his or her giving up the right to own the fruits of his or her labor. He or she accepts this contract willingly and retains the right (the freedom) to quit his or her employment and seek employment elsewhere. As with the slave and feudal class processes, the capitalist class process can be decomposed into a capitalist fundamental and distributive class process. The latter is critically important to securing certain conditions for the reproduction of capitalism. One of the conclusions of this text is that the capitalist distributive class process (inside and outside of China) is shaping a particular type of "globalization" and provides a tool for understanding the impact of China's transition upon a global network of capitalist relationships.

Two nonexploitative class processes have been identified within Marxian theory: the ancient and the communist. The ancient class process[4] has been known by many names: productive self-employment, independent commodity production, the independent class process, petty mode of production, peasant class process, etc. Marx used the term "ancient mode of production" to refer to the self-appropriation of surplus labor by a singular direct producer. His use of the word "ancient" may have been a historicist moment in which it was presumed that the individualized self-appropriation, often associated with life in "ancient" Greece, was necessarily primitive or backward in some linear representation of the advance of class societies. Certainly this is how class terms, including the ancient mode of production, have been used in the literature. The use of the term "ancient" in this text is not meant to reproduce the historicist notion of class societies but to provide an alternative to it. The adjective "ancient" was retained in order to alter its meaning, to associate the term specifically with a class process that has no necessary place in a linear evolution of class societies, and by so doing to displace all historicist uses of the term "ancient" with a non-historicist use. In other words, not only is the ancient class process understood as relevant throughout times and spaces, but the same can be said of all social and environmental processes. The attempt to demarcate an "ancient" and a "modern" world, part of a historicist reading of human societies and the foundation for modernist theories, including modernist Marxism, is completely rejected within the post-structuralist framework. There is no need, then, to try to protect the historicist use of the term "ancient" by seeking to find an alternative to Marx's use of the adjective in his description of individualized self-appropriation of surplus labor in the concept of ancient mode of production.

Thus, the ancient class process represents an alternative to capitalism, feudalism, and slavery (where producers do not own the fruits of their labor) and to communism (where the individual producer is not the sole owner of the fruits of her labor). In the ancient class process, the worker does not sell her laboring potential on a market, nor does anyone else sell her laboring potential. The individual ancient producer is also the ancient appropriator and distributor. This form of nonexploitative production is understood as potentially relevant (and potentially prevalent) in all human societies. This form of class process has been a factor at every stage in the history of the Chinese social formation, including the present.

Finally, the communist class process occurs when the direct producers who perform surplus labor are also the collective first receivers and distributors of that same surplus. This collective appropriation of SV distinguishes the communist class process from the ancient class process and the nonexploitative nature of the appropriation distinguishes it from the slave, capitalist, and feudal class processes. The communist class process, as with all the other above mentioned class processes, is decomposable into a fundamental and distributive class process. As with other class processes, the communist class process can exist if and only if there are other, complementary social and environmental processes generated and reproduced in the society. In classical Marxism it has been assumed that communist parties would, upon achieving control over the state, carry out policies in accord with a transition to communism. It can be presumed that if this was the case there would be evidence of the establishment of conditions conducive to fostering the prevalence of communal appropriation and distribution of surplus labor (or the fruits thereof) or, alternatively, to find evidence that the conditions for the existence and reproduction of exploitative class processes are being undermined.

These class concepts provide the theoretical tools for not only testing for shifts in the prevalence of class processes and the consequences of such shifts but also allows for evaluation of the claim that China's current social formation represents "socialism with Chinese characteristics."[5] This is no minor point. The argument that contemporary China is a socialist society is the primary rationale for the CPC's control over the state. If socialism is understood as a class-based concept, such that movement away from exploitative and toward nonexploitative class processes is an important litmus test for the existence or nonexistence of socialism, then the aforementioned class concepts could be deployed in testing the claim that China is a socialist country. The contradiction this presents for the CPC leadership may not be permanently solved by the aforementioned postmodern amendment to their modernist framework. It may not be enough to simply claim a privileged understanding of the implications of "socialism with Chinese characteristics" such that it can continue to be argued that China is necessarily on the road to telos/communism/end of history so long as the CPC controls the organs of the state. The contradiction may be solved in any number of ways. The CPC may abandon modernist Marxism altogether, replacing it with an alternative modernist or non-modernist framework. The CPC could revert to more traditional modernist Marxism and restore those lost conditions that would satisfy, in the popular imagination, the idea that China is socialist. The CPC could even disintegrate (at least in its current manifestation as core of a party-state) and transform China into a multiparty democracy. As this text will demonstrate, the resolution to this and other problems is not solely up to the CPC leadership but will be shaped by the complex interaction of domestic and foreign institutions, shaped by and participating in a wide range of social processes, including class processes. This dynamic interaction includes the contemporary transition of the Chinese social formation from feudalism to capitalism, a transition which may lead to some surprises for all parties involved, including the CPC leadership.

Transition from feudalism to capitalism

As the noted historian Marc Bloch (1961: 447) wrote:

> Feudalism was not "an event which happened once in the world." Like Europe – though with inevitable and deep-seated differences – Japan went through this phase. Have other societies passed through it?... It is for future works to provide the answers.

Despite his essentialist notion of Europe (a shared delusion), he does allow for the possibility of locating feudal periods in other societies. How did Bloch define "Western or European feudalism" and can we extract from his definition the points common to a more generalized and class-based definition that can be used in exploring the possibility of transition into and out of feudalism in post-1949 China? Bloch identified a "subject peasantry" as one of the defining characteristics of feudalism, where we can understand "subject peasantry" to refer to rural, primarily agricultural, direct producers bound to the service of a particular lord. Although this was not the only characteristic Bloch identified, it is already possible to see the manner in which Bloch conflates the "subject" condition of feudalism, the condition of bondage to the service of a particular lord, with factors that were idiosyncratic to a particular instance of such bondage, but which are not necessary, in a more generalized sense, for such bondage to exist. Obligation to service a particular lord, the subject condition, does not require that the direct producer be agricultural or rural or located in the geographical space described as Europe. In terms of defining a feudal class process on the basis of the subject condition, the only requirement would be that the direct producer enters into a relationship, on the basis of the subject condition, such that he performs surplus labor for a feudal lord, who appropriates and distributes this surplus. Expanding Bloch's notion of the direct producer in this way allows for the possibility of all manner of direct producers, including industrial, urban, and non-European workers being classified as feudal. In a manner similar to the way in which the term "lord" has already been attached to a more generalized feudal relationship, the term "serf" can be understood narrowly as defining a feudal direct producer.

However, Bloch was not explicitly making use of the concept of surplus production, appropriation, and distribution in his definition of feudalism and, therefore, did not produce as narrow a (class-based) definition as the one described earlier. For Bloch, Western feudalism was defined in terms of a range of economic, political, and cultural factors, including the fragmentation (decentralization) of authority "leading inevitably to disorder." Bloch demonstrated his modernist tendencies by assuming a natural progression of the conditions of feudalism toward "disorder" or crisis. In this, Bloch has common ground with classical Marxism, which saw crisis inscribed in all forms of class society (except communism), including feudal society, leading inevitably to progression through a set of predictable stages toward the telos of communism. The idea that crisis is an inevitable consequence of feudalism is clearly at odds with a post-structuralist approach: if processes are overdetermined, then crisis must be overdetermined, a possibility but not an inevitability. Bloch weds this notion of innate crisis to the idea of "fragmentation" which is included in his definition of feudalism. This step has a corollary among those who define capitalism as necessarily requiring the presence of competition (another form of fragmentation). These parallel approaches to feudalism and capitalism beg a number of questions: How much decentralization or fragmentation is necessary to define feudalism? Similarly, how much competition is necessary to define capitalism? Why does fragmentation lead necessarily to crisis (and collapse)? The same question could be asked of classical Marxists who believe that competition necessarily leads to the falling rate of profit in capitalism and crisis. Perhaps some level of decentralization was a condition for the existence of the feudal form of surplus appropriation in certain locations in the geographical space now known as Europe.

However, why assume that this condition is always necessary? By narrowing the definition of feudalism to the class process, the recognition that explicit or implicit "contracts of individual subjection" (Bloch 1961: 248) form the basis for a unique feudal form of surplus appropriation, it becomes possible to identify variant forms of feudalism, some of which may fit Bloch's broader definition of "Western or European feudalism" (including instances not in the spatial region known as Europe or in the time period Bloch had in mind). Allowing for these variant forms of feudalism opens the door to instances of more centralized versions, including instances of a single feudal lord in a specific social formation, as well as instances where a centralized feudal authority behaves in ways not common to the more decentralized versions. For instance, it is widely recognized that the Catholic Church, in addition to its spiritual role, served as feudal lord over thousands of serfs spread across Europe and in other parts of the world, as well. The Church was a highly centralized bureaucratic structure within which its various domains were governed by church officials under the ultimate authority of the Pope. Because the Church was a sovereign entity, the form of feudalism that prevailed within the Church bureaucracy was a version of state feudalism. Church officials appropriated the surplus labor of feudal direct producers within its domains and distributed the fruits of that labor so as to reproduce feudal exploitation and the Church bureaucracy. However, the Church hierarchy also used its control over value flows to provide one of the most elaborate social welfare systems known in European feudalism. Overdetermined by its spiritual mission (a corollary to the socialist mission of the CPC), the Church "provided for the poor, the sick, widows, orphans, and abandoned children" (Genicot 1990: 96). The state feudalism of the Catholic Church came to include providing healthcare and education to rural direct producers on its domains (and others) in a manner that would find parallel centuries later in Maoist China.

Among Marxian theorists the issue has not been the absence of a concept of feudalism but the presence of an essentialized concept of feudalism. Marxian theorists have followed Bloch and other non-Marxian theorists in collapsing an array of political, cultural, economic, and even environmental processes into their definition of feudalism, removing the possibility of observing feudalism outside of certain very narrowly defined geographic and temporal spaces. The concept of a feudal class process, defined in terms of a particular type of production and distribution of surplus, has often been subsumed within an essentialized theoretical structure. The most serious form of essentialism has been a temporal one, one of the defining essentialisms of the modernist way of thinking, within which feudalism has been understood as a possible mode of production only within a bounded period on the calendar (although these boundaries are often fuzzy). Feudalism cannot be imagined beyond these boundaries and, in particular, has been understood as ceasing to be a relevant category for social formations of the "modern" period.

This is precisely the reason that one of the conclusions of this text may be difficult for some to accept, despite the evidence. During the GLF, in the late 1950s, a number of political, cultural, and economic processes came together to create a condition wherein direct producers, in both rural and urban China, were bound to serve the state, to produce a surplus for that state, and by which the state was bound to provide certain social welfare protections to those same direct producers and their families. The State Council was the specific body within the Chinese state that had ultimate power over the communes and state-run enterprises (SREs), including either direct control over the SV generated in those sites or the power to vest others (such as industry-specific bureaus) with such power, as well as the granting of title of commune or SRE director to members of the party-state. In other words, the State Council acted as the feudal lord over the direct producers in the communes and SREs. The ability of the State Council to vest its authority over surplus to others is critical to the reform process. This reform process led eventually to wide-scale decentralization in the location of appropriation and distribution, as well as the severance of lifetime bonds of feudal obligation between workers and enterprises. This top-down revolution against state feudalism was overdetermined by the rise of the modernists and their long struggle with the Maoists over the heart and soul of the CPC, strengthening of local resistance to the highly centralized power structure, and a wide range of other social and environmental conditions. These conditions shaped a complex and multistage process of revolutionary change in class processes that is described in detail in the following chapters.

The irony of finding that contemporary China has undergone a transition from feudalism to capitalism is that for many Marxian theorists, the transition from feudalism to capitalism has played a similar role to that of the Holy Grail in Christianity. The famous debates over this specific type of transition were fueled, in part, by a belief that uncovering the "law of motion" that led from feudalism to capitalism held the key to understanding the transition from capitalism to communism. This dynamic, if it could be understood, held the secret to the end of history (to the attainment of the telos). It would, therefore, be quite ironic if the essentialisms of time and place (or other similar essentialist interpretations of feudalism) make it impossible for present-day Marxian theorists to recognize and analyze contemporary transitions from feudalism to capitalism: transformations occurring within their own lifetimes and sometimes all around them.

In any event, this text has more modest objectives than the search for the Holy Grail of transition to the end of history. The post-structuralist approach leads to the conclusion that there is no telos at the end of the rainbow. However, this does not mean that the presence of feudalism in post-1949 China is inconsequential, just the opposite. The presence of state feudalism, the fragmentation of that feudalism during the early reform period, the transition to state capitalism, the more recent and still unfolding growth of private capitalism, and the rise of global capitalism are of the utmost importance to understanding contemporary China. And the implications of these changes are planet-changing.

For one thing, the presence of feudalism in post-1949 China provides the initial conditions for the type of capitalism that has emerged in that social formation. Understanding these initial conditions makes it possible to have a clearer sense of the contradictions of contemporary Chinese capitalism (a form of capitalism arising out of a form of state feudalism, the vestiges of which will linger and exert influence upon social relationships, institutional rules, and the shape of things to come), the potential for sustained economic growth, the possibilities for political transformation, and the nexus of social and environmental processes linking Chinese institutions with those in other social formations. As others have said, in various poetic ways, the past (including the immediate past) does not die but is absorbed into the present and paves the way to the future.

In the chapters that follow, this text will examine the structure of state feudalism that served as initial conditions of the post-Mao reforms and examine the changing institutions of the Chinese economy in transition, including SREs, township–village enterprises (TVEs), and reforms to financial institutions and markets. The text will explore disintegration in the social contract that had provided Chinese citizen-workers with an "iron rice bowl" of social welfare protections, the development of capitalist labor power markets, and agricultural reform. The text ends with an exploration of the role of Chinese capitalism (and the Chinese state) in globalization and the rapidly changing political, cultural, economic, and environmental landscape upon which humanity continues its collective evolution/transition.

2 Social contracts and the rural–urban divide

The nexus of the Maoist and modernist visions

> It used to be said that there were three great laws of dialectics, and then Stalin said that there were four. In my view there is only one basic law and that is the law of contradiction. Quality and quantity, positive and negative, external appearance and essence, content and form, necessity and freedom, possibility and reality, etc., are all cases of the unity of opposites.
>
> (Mao Zedong, speech at Hangchow in 1965)

There has been much debate over the philosophical idea of the social contract – a theory that states government is created and legitimized by the will (or coercion) of its citizens for their benefit.[1] In the Chinese social formation, the CPC made demands upon its citizens to accept the legitimacy of one party rule and in return promised protection from imperialist forces and social benefits. As Tang and Parish (2000) argue in their work, *Urban Reform in China*, the Chinese party-state entered into a social contract with the citizenry. Perhaps more to the point, they use the term "socialist" social contract, an expression which seems to be borne of the classical Marxian notion of socialism. It is this "socialist" social contract that is being transformed:

> The transformation involves a fundamental redefinition of the social contract the government has with society. The socialist social contract promised an egalitarian, redistributionist order that provided job security, basic living standards, and special opportunities for those from disadvantaged backgrounds. In return, the state demanded sacrifices in current consumption, a leveling of individual aspirations, and obedience to all-knowing party redistributors . . .
>
> The new, post-1978 market social contract makes a different set of demands and promises. In return for abandoning the ideal of communal egalitarianism and security of jobs and other benefits, the market contract promises that giving free reign to individualistic aspirations will produce better jobs and greater consumption. Freedom from communal dictates by all-knowing redistributionist party superiors will allow the economy to adapt readily to changing domestic and international markets. While some may be left behind, the growing economic pie means that the vast majority of people will benefit.
>
> (Tang and Parish 2000: 3–4)

Why is this implied social contract socialist? Why is it presumed that the new social contract/arrangements will give "free reign to individualistic aspirations" and what does this phrase mean anyway? The above use of the term "socialist" in describing the implied social contract is dependent upon the notion that state ownership of the means of production and control over the distribution of certain resources implies a necessary relationship between those phenomena and class relations. The possibility that the Chinese social formation, under this type of state ownership and distribution, might fit some alternative class definition, such as feudal, is not considered in their text. Of course, this is not unusual. There are a large number of texts that make a similar assumption and use the term "socialism" in roughly the same way. Nevertheless, if socialism is defined in class terms, then it is not sufficient to *assume* a one-to-one correlation between state ownership and/or state control over the distribution of certain resources and the appropriation and distribution of surplus in the society. It is necessary to deconstruct the myriad social processes overdetermining the type of surplus appropriation and distribution in order to reveal the underlying class process. The role of the state in participating in and/or providing conditions for the existence of that surplus appropriation and distribution are aspects that need to be considered in context. It is in this contextual deconstruction that the implicit social contract between the Chinese party-state and its citizens must be understood.

What is a social contract but the expectations that have been shaped historically about the behavior and rights of citizens? The expectation that the Chinese state would guarantee a certain level of subsistence to all citizens is not an objective or static phenomenon. It is the product of theories, including versions of Marxism (specifically, modernist and Maoist), and is always in flux as theories and other aspects of social life (and the natural environment) change. The Marxian concept of socialism influenced the idea that the post-1949 Chinese party-state, if it was to be recognized as legitimate, had to guarantee a certain level of subsistence as a right of citizenship. In turn it was understood that Chinese citizens would recognize the vanguard role of the CPC and the primacy of the party-state in matters of governance and economic allocation. This implicit agreement, forged within Chinese Marxism, provided the foundation for what Tang and Parish describe as the *socialist social contract*.

If the goal is to understand the complex dynamics that shaped the existence of and transition from the social contract discussed in Tang and Parish, it is not enough to essentialize the role of the state (or any singular social process) and then collapse the complexity of the social contract into that essentialism, producing the aforementioned notion of socialism as *the* answer to a series of unspoken questions and displacing class analysis which might provide an alternative answer to those questions. First, as is implied by Tang and Parish's use of the adjective "socialist" there are many different types of social contract (implicit or explicit obligations of the state to its citizens and vice versa). If there is a socialist social contract, then there must be nonsocialist social contracts and the distinction between these two subsets of social contracts must be made clear. But in order to make such a distinction the definition of socialist must first be made clear.

Is it sufficient to define the social contract between the CPC party-state and Chinese citizens as socialist because the CPC leadership claims that China is, by virtue of CPC control over the state, socialist? If not, then what is the basis of the adjective? Because social contracts (like private ones) are among the conditions for the existence (or nonexistence) of distinct class processes in the society then they are implicated in the process of transition/change/development of the social formation. As indicated by our prior discussion of the Marxian roots of the CPC use of the term "socialist," where socialism is recognized as a transitional stage between capitalism and communism, there is an implication that a socialist social contract creates obligations that contribute to moving the social formation away from capitalist (or feudal) class processes and toward communist social relationships. In other words, the social contract would need to contribute to the movement away from noncommunist forms of exploitation and toward democratically communal appropriation of the social surplus (appropriation and distribution governed by the direct producers or representatives that they have democratically empowered to act on their behalf). Was the so-called socialist social contract a condition for the existence of a transition from noncommunist to communist social relationships in China? The short answer is no. The social contract referred to as "socialist" was precisely the set of obligations and loyalties that are described in this text with the adjective feudal. In other words, it is argued herein that the social contract Tang and Parish are referring to would be better described as a *feudal* social contract. Rather than promoting a transition from noncommunist to communist social relationships, this social contract was an important condition for the existence of feudal exploitation in China and rather than serving as the foundation for a transition to communism, the feudal social contract contributed to conditions that have fostered a very different transition, the transition to capitalist exploitation, albeit the interaction of the feudal social contract and the transition to capitalist exploitation was one of thesis/antithesis: the attack on the feudal social contract as "inefficient," "wasteful," and "the source of disincentives to hard work and initiative" provided the catalyst for a new capitalist social contract that was understood as having exactly opposite effects.

But perhaps Tang and Parish's use of the term "socialist" is not connected to the CPC's use of the term. In other words, perhaps they are not using the term in a Marxian sense. There is an anti-Marxian meaning to the term: a counter to the Marxian notion that socialism refers to a transition from a society grounded in exploitation to a new type of nonexploitative society. Socialism, in this anti-Marxian context, refers to certain state interventions to provide for the well-being of the citizenry. In this context, the socialist social contract is simply the agreement by the state to engage in such interventions in exchange for the loyalty of the citizenry. If this is what they mean by socialism (government intervention to provide social services = socialism), then it brings to the foreground a theoretical problem. It is not uncommon for governments to provide social services to citizens and to expect loyalty (patriotism) of the citizenry in return. Indeed, very often the cultural mechanisms for reproducing the latter are built into the manner of provision of the former, such as flying flags at sites of social service production or requiring pledges of allegiance and so forth. Is it then the quantity of social services provided by the Chinese state that constitutes its particular social contract with the citizens as socialist? How is the boundary between socialist and nonsocialist social contracts to be determined? This seems impractical and without obvious theoretical merit. Indeed, the use of the adjective socialist in this manner is redundant, since all social contracts are, by definition, between governments, who provide certain services to the citizenry, and the people subject to that government.

The anti-Marxian notion of socialism is simply the reverse image of the anti-Marxian notion of capitalism: capitalism as market allocation, rather than capitalism as class process. In Marxian terms, the issue is not market allocation versus state allocation or administratively set prices versus prices negotiated between buyers and sellers, but the nature of the social arrangement by which one set of individuals perform surplus labor in the service of a different set of individuals. State provision of social services or state intervention in other types of resource allocation and use are not inconsequential – this is the reason the adjective "state" may be used in conjunction with class terms, for example state feudalism – but the presumption that specific types of state involvement in economic activities is *the* determinant of class is rejected.

The social contract and class processes are both overdetermined by varying types of market allocation and state allocation, which are not mutually exclusive phenomena, in any event, nor are they homogeneous practices. Market and state allocation are comprised of many common *administrative* practices, such as pricing and budgeting (setting output and input targets). The neoclassical vision of pricing as the outcome of *negotiations* between (private) buyers and sellers (even when one removes such unrealistic assumptions as atemporality, power asymmetry, and outcome certainty) is not the typical case in most contemporary transactions. On the other hand, supply and demand conditions influence the decisions of state agencies, corporations, and individuals alike, although the way in which this influence is manifest is dependent upon other social and environmental conditions. In other words, the simple fact of state involvement in the economy doesn't provide as much information as is frequently assumed in the literature.

In order to differentiate types of social contracts it is necessary to look elsewhere. Perhaps returning to the Marxian origins of the term, at least as it is deployed in China, would be helpful. As indicated earlier, the social contract described by Tang and Parish was none other than a subset of the conditions of existence of state feudalism in China, not simply because the state provided, by direct provision, many of the use values necessary to the subsistence of Chinese citizens in return for their loyalty but because such provision was directly linked to the performance of surplus labor by citizen-workers whose loyalty was expressed in being bonded to the state as the sole appropriator of that surplus labor. This is the point that Tang and Parish and many others seem to miss about the relationship between the Chinese state and citizen-workers.

In the chapters to follow, class analysis will be used to create a new mapping of the role of the Chinese state onto the terrain of a decidedly nonsocialist/noncommunist (in Marxian terms) social formation. This analysis delineates the collectivization in agriculture and nationalization of industrial enterprises as conditions for the existence of feudal class relationships between the party-state and a subset of Chinese citizen-workers. The feudal class process shaped all aspects of the social formation, including the social contract. The reverse is also true. Thus, post-structuralist Marxian analysis theorizes this metaphor of a social contract – a singular term connoting the obligations of the state to the citizenry and vice versa – as a relationship that shaped and was shaped by the prevalent class process. This reconstituted social contract is understood as an integral element in the bondage of workers to the service of the Chinese state qua feudal lord, and is therefore understood as a *feudal* social contract.

The new social contract embodied changes not only in economic relationships but also in cultural and political relationships, as well: social obligations are comprised of complex political and economic rules of behavior and response, interpreted by changing cultural notions. The social contract is not simply a "market" social contract, as Tang and Parish argue, but a social contract that is dependent upon new notions of state, market, individual, and so on. The transition to the prevalence of state feudal relationships in the late 1950s led to such changes in the social contract and the more recent transition to the prevalence of capitalist relationships is similarly leading to changes in the underlying cultural, economic, and political relationships embodied in the term social contract. In these terms, the concept of social contract embodies the notion of transformation/transition. The transitional social contract is that set of reciprocal relationships which fosters the shift from the prevalence of one class process to another. In the current period, this transitional social contract is conditioning the transformation of feudal direct producers into new social identities, including as capitalist wage laborers. In so far as it does the latter, the emergent social contract may be understood as a capitalist social contract, an implicit set of obligations by which Chinese citizens give up their dependency on the feudal state for many of the subsistence goods necessary for their social life in favor of gaining sufficient income to meet these needs by selling their labor power in the market. The state's reciprocity in this capitalist context is to create the conditions for capitalist exploitation, including fostering the growth of a labor market, the protection of property rights to technology and outputs, the development of financial markets, and so on.

The dismantling of the feudal bureaucracy in the reform period was a concrete manifestation of this break in the feudal social contract thereby simultaneously releasing formerly feudal direct producers into the capitalist labor market (into capitalist freedom) and terminating their feudal citizenship rights. This latter aspect of the termination of feudal reciprocity is what has been described as "breaking the iron rice bowl." The transition from feudal to capitalist social relationships in China has therefore resulted in a dual freedom: workers have been freed from the permanent employment obligation to a single feudal lord and the party-state has been freed from an obligation to support those direct producers and their families. From an alternative standpoint, the former is a condition for the existence of a new type of freedom: the freedom to seek employment in a capitalist labor (power) market. The latter represents the freedom from a wide range of state feudal social benefits/obligations, including lifetime employment, free healthcare, free education for dependent children, free housing for employees and their dependents, old age pension, and subsidized food allowances. To the extent publicly provided social services have survived the transition, their provision has been shifted to other noncentral government institutions (such as local governments, private enterprises, and individual households). And while Tang and Parish recognize and criticize the "personalized dependency" produced by the state feudal system in postrevolutionary China, the weakening and decentralization of social services provision has resulted in a new dependency – dependency on capitalist social relations for livelihood. Thus, the reforms did not end dependency but transformed the type of dependency that prevailed.

The iron rice bowl: feudalism with benevolent characteristics

As Maurice Meisner (1970: 265) pointed out: "Institutional forms, social habits, and patterns of thought and behavior that evolved over some three thousand years cannot be so easily disposed of – not even by the most iconoclastic revolutionaries." Once the teleological view of history is abandoned, it is reasonable to assume that the traditions of pre-1949 China would have influenced the choices made by the CPC leadership after the 1949 revolution. It is not, therefore, surprising to find evidence that the revolutionary leadership might have rediscovered economic forms from the past, including feudal exploitation and the imperial bureaucratic tradition that conditioned the existence of that form of exploitation. In other words, starting from a non-teleological standpoint, it is not difficult to perceive the institutional foundations of the postrevolutionary state-feudal bureaucracy in China, including the absolutist rule of the CPC, state ownership of land and other resources, legal ambiguities related to property rights, reliance on mass mobilization of obligatory labor service for infrastructure development, and the foundational role of a singular (though open to numerous interpretations) theoretical framework, in similar institutions of Imperial China:

> the emperor had absolute authority over his subjects and ruled the country through a bureaucracy system... the emperor, who claimed to be the son of heaven, owned the whole country and collected taxes. The property of his subjects was not guaranteed by any form of law... The legitimacy of the emperor came from Confucianism... In Confucianism, the family is the basic unit constituting the society. The state is organized as a huge family and ruled by the emperor as if he is an authoritarian father... The emperor rules his country through a bureaucracy system which is staffed with non-hereditary elite selected through imperial examinations...
>
> The economic base of traditional China was a huge number of peasants. They submitted taxes in physical forms of grain and fabrics to maintain the state bureaucracy. They were forced to provide labour service to build public

> civil engineering projects. When needed, they had to provide military service as soldiers of the imperial army. Although they were entitled to be the second highest social class in imperial China, because they were the base of the state, peasants were bound to the soil by the government through a neighborhood administration system, in which the large landlords ... were responsible for collection of taxes and fulfillment of labour services.
>
> (Shi 1998: 4–6)

In the post-1949 period the CPC mirrored the feudal past by acting as the "imperial" body of the state. The vanguard party served as the new absolutist authority overseeing a vast bureaucracy that would eventually come to directly appropriate surplus from millions of "loyal" subject-workers and redistribute the surplus so as to maintain the bureaucracy. The rules governing property were not much changed from the imperial regime. In other words, property ownership was rife with ambiguities and provided ample discretion for authorities to determine usufructuary rights. It was only recently that protection for private property was codified.

Rural direct producers played a critical role in generating social surplus in both imperial and revolutionary China. The CPC revolutionized rural production by abolishing feudal relationships after 1949 (and before 1949 in those areas where they had control) but then restored feudal relations during the GLF. The creation of the danwei system in state industrial enterprises was an innovative step that expanded feudal relationships from the countryside to the cities. Many cadre schools were set up to inculcate "revolutionary" and Marxist ideology in new recruits to the CPC. The version of Marxian theory that was promulgated encouraged young people to identify capitalist and feudal exploitation outside of the Chinese context, even as they were encouraged to view China as a "socialist" nation on the vanguard of revolutionary change in the world. The CPC, while spreading its vision of a socialist China, was simultaneously using its control over state power to organize corvee labor to improve and expand infrastructure. During the GLF, the involuntary mobilization of rural direct producers became more commonplace as the party-state moved to establish the conditions for feudal SV production. And while the peasantry was lauded as the "revolutionary masses" and the "teachers," they were coerced by and bound to the state through a system of household registration and, for a time, by so-called communes in which bureaucratic administrators were responsible for the collection and distribution of SV to the party-state, as well as the coordination of surplus labor in the service of the state. Nevertheless, the fact that the CPC depended upon Marxian theory and the ideology of socialism, rather than the ideology of Confucianism, meant that the social contract in the postrevolutionary context would include a far more generous array of social services than was common to any of the prerevolutionary social contracts or to most other versions of state feudalism, including the various manifestations of theocratic state feudalism, such as that of the Catholic Church, where social services were also quite common elements in the social contract.

While the Communist Party claimed in 1949 to merely have overthrown the political leadership of the "bourgeois" state – to have made a political revolution against a pro-capitalist state – and by so doing to have cleared the way for construction of "socialism," the actions that followed created a social formation shaped, in part, by the feudal class process, which was one of the vestiges of the past that the revolution was to have eradicated. The collectivization of agriculture, along with the hukou and danwei systems provided conditions for the existence and reproduction of a variant of the feudal class process whereby direct producers were obligated to perform surplus labor for a single lord – the party-state bureaucracy. The appropriation of feudal surplus labor became a bureaucratic function and direct producers were required to pledge their allegiance to this state/appropriator. In another of those strange historical ironies, the CPC was responsible both for adopting Marxism as the dominant ideology informing intellectual debates and legitimizing CPC rule and for the reestablishment of feudalism in the economy, albeit in a new variant form. As Meisner has pointed out:

> if the Chinese Communists bear the burden of "traditional China," they are also the bearers of other and more recent traditions. They carry, in their own particular fashion, the "Western" Marxist tradition – the tradition that was adopted rather than the one that was reluctantly inherited. And there is a third tradition, neither inherited nor adopted by Chinese Communists but of their own making – the Chinese Communist revolutionary tradition forged in the bitter wars and civil wars of the two decades... These two new "Chinese" traditions also bind and shackle in various ways, but they convey new values and proclaim a future different from that which the Confucian tradition of the more distant past would dictate.
>
> (1970: 265–266)

Meisner's point is not a minor one. The revolution in 1949 did, indeed, mark a significant break with the past. However, the reconfigured landscape of the Chinese social formation, with the party-state as the new imperial power, was not without some of the social processes (vestiges) of that past, albeit wrapped in the cloak of completely different sets of conditions of existence. As Meisner argues, the new social arrangements "also bind and shackle in various ways" and this text argues that, from the late 1950s until the end of the commune era, these "various ways" included ties of feudal bondage. Again, the social contract(s) that provided conditions for the existence of feudal bondage in CPC-led China was different from those of imperial China: the feudal social contract differed in the post-1949 Chinese social formation *vis-à-vis* other social formations whether in different historical periods in China or elsewhere in the global social formation. While the state feudal bureaucracy had its roots, so to speak, in the imperial feudal bureaucracy, changes in social and environmental processes, as well as the rise of the Maoist variant of Marxism, helped to constitute a variant of feudalism with a distinctive social contract between the party-state and its citizens, one which required the party-state qua feudal lord to be relatively benevolent (in many, if not most, social interactions with citizens) and provide a whole assortment of services to meet the basic needs of the feudal direct producers and their families, while at the same time requiring these direct producers to be obedient, to remain dependent on feudal relationships, and to perform the feudal surplus labor necessary to the reproduction of the feudal bureaucracy.[2] In this sense, the state feudal variant developed by the CPC-led party-state may have had more in common with the state feudalism of the Catholic Church in those domains within which the Church acted as a sovereign and state feudal appropriator. In both cases, the CPC-led party-state and the Catholic theocratic state, feudal exploitation is legitimized by a stated transcendental role of the state: in the former case, the party-state orchestrates the passage through the stages to communism and in the latter case, the Catholic Church acts as mediator between man and God and provides mortals with the proper rituals necessary to passage from Earth to Heaven. The feudal social contract under conditions where the feudal appropriator serves as state and transcendental midwife may require a more complex form of reciprocity to reproduce legitimacy: the reciprocity agreement is more likely to include a wide range of social services. In the case of the party-state these services included education, healthcare, housing, permanent employment, and old age pensions: the iron rice bowl.

These "social services" provided legitimacy to the party-state and motivated direct producers to continue performing feudal necessary and surplus labor. However, it is important to note that the social services necessary to reproduce that legitimacy and to motivate direct producers varied according to a wide range of characteristics, particularly demographics. In particular, the services necessary to gain the cooperation of rural direct producers, for example, was different from that required to gain the cooperation of urban direct producers (who enjoyed some social services not available to their rural counterparts), although in both cases these social service provisions raised the value of labor power above average levels prevalent prior to the 1949 revolution.

The differential treatment of rural and urban workers was shaped, among other factors, by prejudices predating the revolution of 1949. This differential treatment was also an attempt to address one of the contradictions of the revolution: the higher expectations and perceived greater threat of hostile organizing activities of urban workers. Despite a history of "peasant" revolts, rural direct producers were understood to be more docile and compliant than urban direct producers. However, favorable treatment of urban workers created more contradictions. One of the most celebrated contradictions was rural to urban migration. Higher value accorded to urban over rural labor, among other factors, has served as a catalyst for the movement of workers from rural to urban locales. A number of theorists, most notably Arthur Lewis (1955), have attempted to develop theoretical models explaining (in deterministic terms) this migration and its effects. However, migration of rural direct producers would threaten the continuation of feudal exploitation in the countryside. How could they keep them down on the farm (communes), once they have seen the cities (realized that life was better in the cities)? In addition, mass movement of workers to the cities could place downward pressure on the value of urban labor power (one of the effects that Lewis recognized), while simultaneously straining the urban infrastructure of housing, roads, water supplies, etc. Thus, not only could such movement create a crisis for feudal exploitation in the countryside, it could also potentially ignite a crisis among urban workers. The solution adopted by party-state officials was to codify the rural–urban divide, to take measures to block internal migration from the countryside to the cities.

To further complicate matters, the CPC had come to power largely on the basis of rural support and "peasants" were considered *the* core constituency of the party. Nevertheless, the pressures within the CPC to solidify control over and support from the urban direct producers, partly through the provision of low cost food, clothing, and other household products, as well a wide range of social services, generated policies that would eventually alienate large numbers of rural direct producers, whose surplus labor was used, in part, to provide these benefits for their urban comrades. Indeed, the decision to abandon productive self-employment as the primary class structure in rural China, which had been the case since the 1949–50 land reform, appeared incompatible with some of the objectives of the party-state. Ancient farmers and artisans in the countryside simply did not distribute sufficient surplus to the party-state to fund the social services and infrastructure required for both rural and urban residents, given the existing social contract, as well as to meet the larger modernization plans of the CPC leadership. Thus, the establishment of feudal communes may have been one response to these pressures, given the difficulties of raising sufficient public revenues via taxation of ancient farmers and artisans.

It is important to recognize that the innovation of state feudal relations in production was not incompatible with party policies, including notions of social contracts, precisely because, for the most part, these policies (and related social contracts) were not formulated in class terms. As discussed in Chapter 1, the modernist Marxist notion of socialism did not preclude the existence of exploitation but presumed that communist party rule (the party-state) was sufficient to confirm the socialist nature of the society. While the Maoists did speak in terms of class relations and class struggle and were influential in the decision to collectivize, the social contracts that prevailed made no commitment to democratize the appropriation of surplus labor but, rather, committed the party-state to provide basic subsistence and social services such that the standard of living and life expectancy of Chinese citizens would, on the average, improve. There is widespread agreement that party-state policies raised the level of urban *and* rural subsistence and life expectancy via major improvements in access to healthcare, education, and other social securities (Howard 1988; Selden 1988; Knight and Song 1999; Bramall 2000; Hussain 2003). Thus, the social contract that legitimized CPC rule had a positive impact on the lives of Chinese citizens but was, nevertheless, devoid of any commitment to democratizing the relations of production. It is ironic that the emergence of a feudal contract came, in part, out of the ideological commitment of the party-state to provide basic necessities to Chinese citizens, a commitment that was informed, to a significant extent, by Marxian theory. For some this relative egalitarianism reinforces the notion that

China was socialist, although other forms of state feudalism, such as the aforementioned Catholic Church version, have also been relatively egalitarian. The point is that this social contract did not negate the underlying form of exploitation. In other words, the various nonclass objectives of the CPC, including both the social contract and modernization, trumped any attempt at eliminating exploitation, which was, in Marxian terms, the ultimate rationale for communist party rule. The CPC required more public funding to meet these nonclass objectives than could be secured in the post-land reform environment of relative economic freedom for rural direct producers, creating a contradiction that was resolved by eliminating that economic freedom in favor of feudal exploitation. The fact that the CPC was willing to ignore class relationships in forging a "socialist" social contract grounded in feudal exploitation was, in fact, a signal that an eventual emergence of capitalist exploitation, with the CPC still in power, was possible, perhaps even predictable. This may, in a sense, provide partial explanation for Mao's continual assaults upon the party-state bureaucracy of which he was titular leader.

And it is clear that placing nonclass objectives at a higher priority than class objectives (or class struggle) was a continual source of tension within the party, particularly between the Maoists and modernists. The tensions within the CPC over the nature of the social contract was an important aspect of these internal struggles from the late 1950s, particularly given that the shift to feudal exploitation placed greater control over relative subsistence levels in the hands of state planners and administrators. Whether influenced by modernist or Maoist versions of Marxism, the CPC leadership would have been unified in wanting to transform the conditions of both urban and rural China, although they held opposing views on the role of the peasantry in shaping the future of China: within modernist Marxism the peasantry had traditionally been conceptualized as backward elements, while the Maoist version of Marxism celebrated the peasantry as no less a progressive force for change than the urban proletariat. Ironically, these two conceptions may have both provided theoretical support for the creation of the communes: the former recognizing the communes as a means for seizing control over rural surplus labor and the latter viewing the communes as a step forward toward communist (communal) appropriation of surplus labor. Although perhaps for different reasons, both versions of Marxism recognized collectivization as a progressive step in Chinese development.

Education policies, the rural–urban divide, and modernity

Another factor influencing the social contract was the rural–urban divide. In many ways China is two countries united by a single government: one rural and the other urban. The differential treatment of rural and urban residents seems ingrained in Chinese culture, a legacy of both romanticist and modernist notions of rural life and rural people. One area where this rural–urban split was evident was in educational policies. While pursuit of a communist ideal might have inspired an early emphasis on more egalitarian attempts to spread wide-scale educational knowledge among the entire population (as a precondition for a time when SV appropriation, as well as other aspects of social life, might be fully democratized), counter to the long existing prejudices against peasants, the reemergence of feudal exploitation shifted priorities toward policies the CPC leadership believed more conducive to meeting the immediate demand for higher SV extraction from the countryside. To the extent rural China was viewed as a potential source of resources that could be invested in urban industrialization or as a source of cheap agricultural goods to provide for (or lower the cost of) urban subsistence, attempts to equalize rural and urban educational standards or to provide for a basic education for every Chinese citizen might have been viewed as counterproductive. The demand for a higher surplus, coupled with the view that modernity required focusing attention on a minority of highly educated, typically urban, specialists would militate against applying scarce resources to basic education in the countryside. Despite the efforts of Mao and the influence of the Maoist faction with the party, the CPC followed the Soviet path in structuring education to meet nonclass objectives. As Chris Bramall has argued, the CPC eventually adopted the same priorities as the Soviets in allocating resources to education:

> [T]he emphasis on high-quality provision that was an integral part of the Soviet tradition led to the relative neglect of primary education in the rural areas... The Yan'an-inspired goal of a minban school in every village was dropped and neither the total number of primary school children nor the number of primary schools showed much of an increase between 1952 and 1957... secondary schooling in rural areas was largely ignored.
>
> (2000: 156)

The Maoist interest in a more egalitarian educational system was based on a class objective: creating the conditions for the existence of communal appropriation and distribution of SV (creating a new socialist human being). The modernists' conception of transition placed a lower priority on the transformation in human beings and a higher priority on the acquisition and innovation of material technology, particularly urban industrialization. Why expend energy on the education of rural children who were destined to perform low skilled labor in the service of this process of urban industrialization?

But if the rural population was viewed merely as instruments for generating SV for industrialization or cheaper consumer goods for urban workers, then what was to differentiate them from colonial subjects of urban China? What happened to the notion that the peasantry (along with the proletariat) had been "liberated" by the 1949 revolution?

The Soviet model had grown out of Stalinist modernism: another version of modernist Marxism that celebrated the rise of heavy industry, the adoption of more complex forms of technology (and the training of technicians who can deploy such technology), urbanization (and urban infrastructure), and an elitist educational system focused on identifying a subset of young people who could be developed into highly skilled experimental and theoretical scientists and mathematicians. This version of Marxism produced an understanding of economic transition as deterministically related to the acquisition and innovation of certain material technologies and accepted the soft technologies of the capitalist nations (including capitalist wage labor relationships and industrial political processes of hierarchical management, capital budgeting, command, and control) as benign, if not necessary to the use of these material technologies. The technological determinism of modernist (including Stalinist) Marxism reinforced an elitist view of education: the industrial hierarchy was paralleled by a hierarchical educational system geared toward producing different types of human beings to serve in different industrial capacities. Higher level managers would be better educated than lower level managers. Managers would be better educated than workers. And industrial workers would be better educated than rural direct producers. Mao ultimately challenged the assumptions underlying Stalinist modernism and triggered a violent response against this way of thinking (including an attack on academia, which was viewed as an institutional manifestation of this way of thinking) during the GPCR. During the Cultural Revolution the Maoists forced the closure of educational institutions in the cities and the expulsion of privileged students from the urban centers into the rural hinterlands. The effects of this "cultural revolution" reverberated throughout Chinese society, but one consequence was that after the Cultural Revolution the party-state changed the educational system, reemphasizing the need to educate the rural population. In an internal compromise between the Maoists and the modernists, education in the rural areas increased, especially secondary education:

> This expansion was a result of the rejection after 1966 of the views of educational professionals that had prevailed during the 1950s – according to which secondary education was unnecessary for the rural population. When this elitist model of the early 1960s – which focused on channeling a small number of predominantly urban children into "key-point" middle schools – was jettisoned, the "staying-on" rate rose to reach over 94 per cent by 1976... In part, this expansion of the secondary sector was financed by the state. However, the bulk of resources were raised by the communes themselves, either from the collective accumulation fund or by charging tuition fees; these amounted to around 4 yuan per annum in relatively prosperous areas like Chengdu plain... By the 1970s, then, near-universal secondary education existed in the rural areas for the first time.
>
> (Bramall 2000: 159)

The Maoist approach to healthcare was similarly egalitarian and, in conjunction with egalitarian education, was understood as yet another condition supporting the evolution of the "socialist" human being, a subjectivity motivated to engage in communal production, appropriation, and distribution. Given the relatively meager human and material resources that could be devoted to healthcare, the best way to provide basic care to all citizens was to focus on preventative care and readily available medical care technologies. As Knight and Song note:

> In 1949 rural China lacked an effective health-care system... The new government gave priority to preventive over curative care, and organized campaigns against particular diseases including immunizations against half a dozen common diseases. With the formation of the communes, the number of commune (township) health centres increased rapidly.
>
> (1999: 158)

The complexity of Chinese Marxism, and in particular the struggles between modernists and Maoists, is reflected in the way the communes were structured simultaneously to provide more egalitarian access to healthcare and education and as sites of feudal exploitation. Nevertheless, even in terms of egalitarian distribution of social services, the communes did not unambiguously serve the Maoist vision of breaking down the barriers between urban and rural. For example, the aforementioned commune healthcare clinics were often understaffed unlike the hospitals and clinics in the urban areas, and new allopathic medicines were largely unavailable to rural direct producers. Thus, although the Maoists were successful in including healthcare provision in the social contract with rural citizens, the value of that care was considerably less than was the case for urban citizens. In other words, the desire for a more egalitarian healthcare system was only partially successful. Recognizing this disparity, Mao called for a reexamination of healthcare reform in the rural areas:

> Tell the Ministry of Public Health that it only works for fifteen per cent of the total population of the country and that this fifteen per cent is mainly composed of gentlemen, while the broad masses of the peasants do not get any medical treatment. First they don't have any doctors; second they don't have any medicine... The methods of medical examination and treatment used by hospitals nowadays are not at all appropriate for the countryside, and the way doctors are trained is only for the benefit of the cities. And yet in China over 500 million of our population are peasants. They work divorced from the masses, using a great deal of manpower and materials in the study of rare, profound and difficult diseases at the so-called pinnacle of science, yet they either ignore or make little effort to study how to prevent and improve the treatment of commonly seen, frequently occurring and widespread diseases. I am not saying that we should ignore the advanced problems, but only a small quantity of manpower and material should be expended on them, while a great deal of manpower and material should be spent on the problems to which the masses most need solutions.
>
> (Schram 1974: 232–233)

Following this reexamination, the CPC instituted the "barefoot doctors" approach: a large-scale experiment in "low-tech" and preventative medical care technology that could be widely and relatively democratically distributed. The barefoot doctor program trained some rural residents in allopathic medical techniques and diagnosis in order to serve the rural villages. These measures improved life expectancy and overall quality of life for rural people. The internal disagreements and compromises within the CPC, and particularly the influence of the Maoist push to transform human beings, resulting in the allocation of resources to mass education and healthcare, has served as a model for rural development programs and has even influenced public education and health policy in the more industrialized nations. Thus, although the Maoists were unsuccessful in reducing the role of exploitation in the Chinese economy, the struggle to do so may have had very positive effects on the lives of Chinese citizens, rural and urban.

The Maoist break with the modernist vision (particularly, the technological determinism and racist conception of the peasantry) and the internecine struggles between the Maoists and modernists gave Chinese transition a radically different dynamic than was present in other social formations governed by communist parties (particularly the Soviet Union). These struggles influenced the terms of all of the social contracts after the revolution of 1949, including the feudal social contract that arose in the late 1950s, creating the possibility for dramatic change in the content and provision of social services and, therefore, in the composition of that bundle of goods and services making up subsistence for rural and urban direct producers.

However, despite Mao's influence the rural–urban divide has persisted, reproduced in part by public policies:

> The divisions between state and collective and between city and countryside, as well as the choice of state investment and welfare priorities, produced or enlarged wide inter- and intrasectoral cleavages. The rural poor, who were primary beneficiaries of the redistributive land reform and whose interests were protected in the initial phases of mutual aid and cooperation, were among the victims of the extreme collectivist, antimarket, grain-first, and class struggle policies proclaimed in their name in the era of mobilizational collectivism and carried to their destructive limits during the Great Leap Forward and Cultural Revolution... The population registration and control system is the central institutional mechanism defining sectoral differentiation and restricting inter- and intrasectoral mobility... The registration system and associated state controls on jobs, housing, rations, and travel made possible the widening urban–rural and intrarural spatial inequalities of income and opportunity.
>
> (Selden 1988: 165–167)

Selden, like many other analysts, lumps together the modernist and Maoist aspects of the postrevolutionary policies: the tendencies toward exploiting direct producers as an economic growth expedient is fused with the Maoist efforts to break the control that the bureaucracy held over direct producers (mobilizing workers under feudal exploitation is not the same as the democratic collectivism envisioned in communist appropriation and distribution, nor is the household registration system and bureaucratic control over employment part of the same political movement as the Maoist cultural revolution that was designed, in part, to undermine, if not destroy, the bureaucracy). The modernist success at building up bureaucratic power was both a catalyst for the Maoist attempt at a second revolution (the Cultural Revolution) and a condition for the existence of feudal exploitation, as well as of the rise of capitalism in more recent times. Indeed, Selden misses the key point that it is precisely the Maoist "class struggle" that forces the party-state to compromise and institute policies that would ultimately improve the quality of life for many Chinese citizens, as well as reduce the magnitude of the rural–urban divide. Nevertheless, the diminished importance of the Maoist faction, modernist control over all the key leadership positions within the party-state, and the rise of capitalism have produced a sustained attack upon the entire matrix of processes that had produced the aforementioned egalitarian healthcare and education policies.

The early stage of the economic reforms was clearly positive for many rural families, as the legalization of ancientism (productive self-employment) led to rising living standards. Nevertheless, the ancient period of the reforms seems to have been rather short-lived, having been superseded by the current capitalist period, during which time the relative incomes of rural households have not kept pace with urban households, and the social cohesiveness of rural villages has been threatened by wide-scale migration from the countryside to the cities in search of the new wage labor jobs that capitalism has generated.

John Knight and Lina Song acknowledge the role of political processes in shaping China's rural–urban relationships but argue that it is economic processes that have been the primary determinants of the differentiation in subsistence between rural and urban communities. They utilize three theoretical frameworks in order to analyze this disparity: the now traditional Arthur Lewis model of economic growth generated through the absorption (into capitalist industry) of surplus rural labor, the price-scissors model, and the "urban bias" model. In their final analysis, the rural–urban divide is a result of institutional economic relationships and conscious public policies that privilege the urban population over the rural and which have been in place since the 1949 revolution. They do not perceive a shift having occurred as a result of the transition to capitalism. Indeed, they seem to imply that one should have expected the rural–urban divide to diminish as a result of such a transition:

> the land shortage and labour surplus inherited by the communist government, the institutions which it established, and its objective of rapid capital accumulation and industrialization made possible, logical, and acceptable the subordination of the peasants to State interests. The government implicitly accepted the Lewis model of economic development with surplus labour and intervened by means of price-scissors to promote the process. However, the institutional divide that was erected and the latent power of workers relative to peasants produced an outcome which greatly favoured urban-dwellers. The policy bias in favour of urban people is deep-seated and has survived even the rural economic reforms and the marketization of the economy.
>
> (Knight and Song 1999: 21)

"Urban bias" has served for many as *the* explanation for the differences in the state's social contracts with rural and urban citizens. As with other deterministic explanations of the origins of the rural–urban divide, this point of view ignores the complexity of policy formation (and cultural reproduction) over the history of the PRC, and particularly dismisses the differences between modernist and Maoist Marxism. The internal differences within Chinese Marxism (where the Maoist and modernist point of view did not share a common conception of the peasantry) and the complexly determined public policy produced from struggles between these contending viewpoints disappear within cultural determinist theories of the rural–urban divide. For example, Arianne Gaetano and Tamara Jacka (2004) argue in their work, *On the Move*, the rural/urban distinction is the outcome of a cultural process that, by stereotyping individuals based on where they are born (as well as their sex), shapes the lives and opportunities available to rural laborers, especially women migrant laborers:

> This rural/urban distinction "on the ground," as it were, was accompanied by new discourses in which the countryside and its "peasants" were marked as essentially different from and inferior to urbanites . . . this new judgment was essentially the result of a process of "internal orientalism" on the part of a Chinese intelligentsia striving for modernity. In the nineteenth century, as a result of defeat at the hands of colonial powers, the question, What is wrong with China? became of paramount concern, and a central plank in Chinese intellectuals' efforts to answer this question became the notion that the Chinese people, and the peasantry above all, were backward and in need of improvement and modernization. These views mirrored western colonialist views of the Chinese people as a whole, which were likewise a mapping of a rural/urban divide onto an "other" nation, which like "the rural" was alternately abhorred and idealized . . . Thus, Chinese intellectuals adopted the western image of China as backward, but then deflected this inferiority onto an internal "other": rural "peasants." . . . rural inhabitants and rural migrants have been portrayed overwhelmingly as inferior "others" in the media of the reform period. At times they are depicted as criminal, barbaric, or, especially in the case of women, immoral; at other times, they are portrayed as naïve and helpless. These representations of peasants and rural migrants serve as a contrast against which the civilization and modernity of the urban population (and of the nation) is constructed.
>
> (Gaetano and Jacka 2004: 14–16)

Gaetano and Jacka have made an important contribution in understanding the Chinese social formation, describing the "racialization" of the rural population: the reductionist notion that rural people are naturally and fundamentally different from (and, indeed, inferior to) urban people. The modernist vision of urban as modern produces its opposite in the form of rural as primitive. In China, the rural peasantry has served this purpose and the duality of urban as modern/rural as primitive has aided in solidifying the rural–urban divide and inculcated a sense of superiority on the part of urban-dwellers, despite changes in class processes which at times (during the ancient period, for instance) have benefited rural direct producers. However, this approach oversimplifies. The Maoists struggled against the racialization of the rural population, reconceptualizing the modern as a class struggle within which rural and urban direct producers are comrades in modernity (both are potential "socialist" human beings, the bearers of the communal future) and their exploiters represent the primitive. The struggle between the modernist vision and the Maoist vision resulted in various compromises that had concrete effects on not only the quality of life for both rural and urban citizens but also on popular conceptions of modern and primitive.

What is evident is that there are many social and environmental processes that have shaped postrevolutionary social contracts. Gaetano and Jacka are correct that among these determinants is a process of racializing the peasantry and gendering individuals within the peasantry. A rural person faces a different social contract than an urban person. A rural woman faces a different social contract than a rural man. But these identities are not Platonic ideal forms. They are subject to the constant impact of changing social processes, including the internecine struggles within the CPC. The various social contracts, that are shaped, in part, by these processes of identity formation and reformation, are in constant flux. The state feudal social contracts that arose from the late 1950s to the reform era must be understood as an object of continual struggle and change. Similarly, the capitalist social contracts of the present period are complexly overdetermined by political, cultural, economic, and environmental processes, including changes occurring within the CPC, political restructuring outside of the party-state, influences from writers, film makers, musicians (both domestic and foreign), World Trade Organization (WTO), marketization, the rise of capitalism, the physical reconfiguration of the Chinese landscape (rural and urban), protests etc.

At any given moment in a social formation there are multiple social contracts, each of which is shaped by an incalculable number of determinants and in constant flux. The struggles to change the social contract(s) are an aspect of the complexity and contradictions of the social formation, including the identities imposed upon human beings, the type and magnitude of surplus labor performed, and notions of progress. The social contract(s) of the state feudal period were under attack for a number of reasons, not the least of which was the perception of some modernist elements within the CPC that existing contracts provided too much social welfare protection for rural direct producers (in the form of guarantees about food, healthcare, housing, and so on) and too little incentive for them to perform surplus labor. The focus upon social contracts displaced any debate on the class implications of proposed reforms. This was reinforced when the Gang of Four was placed on trial and the modernists took control of key party positions within two years of Mao's death. These developments made it easier for the modernists to mobilize against the continuation of the communes (rather than be forced into a debate over transforming the class nature of those communes, perhaps even shifting from feudal to communist appropriation) and push forward the reforms of the late 1970s and the current transition to capitalism.

In particular, the CPC leadership began to communicate a coherent and unambiguous message that the social cost of maintaining the pre-reform social contract(s) was lost opportunities to modernize the country (because the feudal social contracts – lifetime employment and guaranteed social benefits in exchange for loyalty to the feudal state – were perceived as eating into the potential surplus value that might be otherwise captured for use in modernization). The solution: get rid of the existing social contracts and transition to a new set of social contracts that would be compatible with the requirements of modernization. This translated into a revolutionary transition from state feudalism to capitalism (both state and private) orchestrated by a communist party.

Decentralization: forging a new contract

The long existing tension between the Maoist goal of creating the new "socialist" human being and the modernist goal of rapid technological transformation ("development of the productive forces"), embodied in the term *Four Modernizations*, was resolved in favor of the latter. Indeed, in the modernist worldview efficient innovation of "advanced" technology, rather than transformation in class processes/relations, became the primary characteristic of socialism:

> the fundamental task for the socialist stage is to develop the productive forces. The superiority of the socialist system is demonstrated by its faster and greater development of the productive forces than that of the capitalist system. Speaking of our shortcomings since the founding of the People's Republic, one was negligence in developing the productive forces.
>
> (Central Committee 1991: 2, cited in Bramall 2000)

Once the modernists had control of policy making, they shifted budget priorities and implemented a strategy for more rapid acquisition of new technologies, including the importation of industrial equipment and, at times, whole industrial manufacturing plants (Shi 1998; Gu 1999). However, trade deficits resulted and it became clear that the existing economic structure could not generate sufficient hard currency to fund continued imports. The *Four Modernizations* would require more fundamental change in the economic relationships. In particular, the modernists sought a new social contract(s) that would free more SV for their modernization project:

> Carrying out the *Four Modernizations* requires great growth in the productive forces, which in turn requires diverse changes in those aspects of the relations of production and the superstructure not in harmony with the growth of the productive forces, and requires changes in all methods of management, actions and thinking which stand in the way of such growth. Socialist modernization is therefore a profound and extensive revolution.
>
> (December 1978, Third Plenum of the Eleventh Central Committee of the CCP, cited in Spence 1999: 621–622)

The prevalent system of feudal relations and the iron rice bowl (an element in feudal subsistence) was not "in harmony with the growth of the productive forces." One possibility was to foster a social contract within which the state granted direct producers the right of productive self-employment in exchange for each producer taking personal responsibility for his own livelihood. The ancient class process would not necessarily require much social welfare, much less the elaborate set of public goods provided under the iron rice bowl arrangement.

However, the ancient class process had other problems. It would prove difficult collecting taxes from ancient farmers, for example, resulting in revenue problems for the government. And productive self-employment was never considered an option for industrial production. Thus, the ultimate solution to reducing the obligations of the state to provide for the needs of the citizenry, while fostering a higher total magnitude of surplus value, would come from a shift to capitalism: a system within which the iron rice bowl would be superseded by commodity exchange as the means for meeting the subsistence needs of the Chinese citizenry.

The path toward capitalism was not, however, a straight one. In the rural areas, the reforms initially favored ancients in that rural households were gradually freed from feudal dependency and exploitation, allowed to self-appropriate and distribute the fruits of individual surplus labor. Of course, the party-state was also "freed" from feudal obligations, as the feudal social contracts gradually disappeared. The party-state ceased taking responsibility for providing the iron rice bowl. To the extent any of these social services survived, they became the responsibility of either the local governments (who needed to raise the funds to pay for such services from taxes and fees on rural residents, especially the ancient farmers) or of the citizens themselves. This has resulted, as Jean Oi argues, in an increased burden on ancients in the countryside:

> It is widely known that decollectivization changed the organization of production and increased the incentives under the Household Responsibility System. What is less often noted is that decollectivization also opened the door to increasing "peasant burdens" when it deprived village officials of the rights to use the income from the harvest for village administrative expenses. If a village has no sources of collective income, such as village enterprises, it is dependent on the "village retained fees" (*tiliu*) for the entirety of the village operating budget. Because villages are not considered an official level of government, they receive no budget allocation from the upper levels, unlike the township level and above. The only right village officials have to household income is the *tiliu* assessment, which the village levies above and beyond the national agricultural tax on each household based on income. The central government legislated rules that forbid these fees to exceed 5 percent of peasant income. The problem is that this limit is routinely exceeded as local cadres raise these levies to meet local needs. The poorer the village, the more likely peasants will be pressed for more fees.
>
> (2003: 453)

Pat Howard also provides evidence that the transition from feudal to ancient farming did not mean a lessened burden on rural direct producers. Ancient farmers were subject to a wide array of governmental claims on their self-appropriated surplus and, under the new ancient social contract, their families had to pay for many elements of subsistence, such as health and education, that had previously been an obligation of the state (albeit one that was financed through feudal exactions):

> peasants who have contracted land have been subject to an array of taxes, fees, and levies for such things as cadres' salaries and expenses, health and education facilities and staff wages, subsidies for the militia, and per capita payments into collective welfare and accumulation funds. Recent reforms that commoditize many formerly "free" services, such as healthcare, veterinary service, water and electricity, and film showings and performances, have focused the burden of costs on users and forced many providers of services to pay more attention to cost efficiency.
>
> (Howard 1988: 155)

Despite the problems that feudal exploitation and related social conditions caused, the termination of the old social contract(s) and commoditization of previously free or relatively free elements of rural subsistence negatively impacted the quality of life for many rural laborers and their families. Take the case of education. As Chris Bramall notes the reform process has been detrimental to the quality and quantity of education supplied to the rural populace:

> the Chinese government pursued a policy of cutting back on secondary education (especially in rural areas) after 1977. In essence, the aim of educational restructuring of 1977–82 was a return to the "golden age" of the early 1960s on the grounds that secondary education was wasted on the bulk of the rural population and that the money could be better spent on improving the quality of upper-level secondary schools and higher education... The new approach of the 1980s therefore amounted to recreating high quality "keypoint" schools, reducing the number of general secondary schools (especially in rural areas), and placing greater emphasis on vocational education for the rural population. In other words, the aim was to replace the mass educational system of late Maoism with an elitist system.
>
> [In response,] It was this that accelerated the transition towards tuition fees and self-funding that became increasingly the norm in the mid-1990s as schools were forced to operate like enterprises... Although the government (rightly) claimed that about 91 per cent of primary-school graduates continued their education in 1995, the fact remained that the legacy of the cutbacks of the 1980s was still being felt in terms of total enrolment numbers. The problem was especially acute in poor rural areas, where local government was simply unable to raise the funds required to fund even a minimal level of provision.
>
> (2000: 412–414)

Commoditization of subsistence, along with other social processes and environmental processes, such as summer floods which ruin agricultural land and crops, has been a catalyst in expanding capitalist labor power markets. Large numbers of rural laborers have been transformed into capitalist wage laborers, selling their labor power to TVEs and other state or non-state capitalist enterprises:

> In addition, they recruit their workers from rural residents for whom TVEs have no obligation to provide lifetime jobs or welfare benefits as the housing and various subsidies that most urban workers have... FDI firms do not guarantee lifetime jobs, nor do they provide such welfare benefits as housing and various subsidies.
>
> (Shi 1998: 41)

As in the case of social contracts, perhaps it is more fitting to speak of the creation of labor power markets, rather than to speak as if a singular capitalist labor power market resulted from these social processes. Laborers do not compete in the same labor power markets. In particular, rural laborers face a different labor power market than urban laborers. The possession of an agricultural hukou can mean being denied certain social benefits that accrue to holders of nonagricultural hukou. Rural laborers who migrate to the cities to work as contract labor for conglomerates or non-conglomerates, as Gaetano and Jacka have argued, are often denied social security despite moving to urban areas where social security programs for workers are an element of the social contract:

> Lack of urban registration makes it extremely difficult for them to become integrated into the urban community and limits their opportunities for social mobility. Without local urban registration, even those "rural" people who have lived in a city for many years face numerous obstacles: they are prevented from entering certain occupations and trades; they are denied work-related entitlements to housing, medical care, pensions, and social security; they are often forbidden to buy or build property and are thus relegated to "shantytowns" that have sprung up on the margins of large cities; they and their offspring are excluded from, or charged exorbitantly to attend, local institutions of higher education and elite local schools; and they are excluded from community- and work-based political, social, and recreational activities. In short, they are treated as outsiders to the urban community.
>
> (2004: 20)

Workers in urban conglomerates may be relatively privileged *vis-à-vis* rural wage laborers, but they have, nevertheless, experienced profound changes in the nature of their subsistence, the social services allotted to them, and their job security. In other words, the transition from feudal to capitalist relations has meant a profound change in the nature of the social contract between urban wage laborers and the state. In 1986, the government moved to end the lifetime employment benefit by stipulating that all new workers would have limited work contracts in the state sector, usually ranging from 3 to 5 years. This is in stark contrast to the labor agreement under state feudalism:

> In the 80 percent of urban jobs that were in the public sector, lifetime job security was the rule. Once one got a state job, it became an "iron rice bowl" (*tie fanwan*): No one could be laid off. Though an employee's malfeasance was disciplined within the work unit, the employee could not be fired. Even if one committed a minor crime and served a sentence in prison, one was in theory entitled to come back when the prison term was over. Job security not only applied to each employee, but at certain times could also be inherited by a single child entering the state work unit the parent had abandoned...
>
> (Tang and Parish 2000: 35)

With the breaking of the feudal social contract and the forging of a capitalist social contract, a variety of markets in labor power have been firmly established, with wage income the key to obtaining many of the necessities that had previously been distributed by the state. The party-state has been freed of its feudal obligation to provide lifetime employment and a wide range of social services. Workers in the urban state enterprise sector now have the freedom and the right to leave the state-enterprises and seek employment in TVEs and non-conglomerates. However, as Yizheng Shi notes, enterprises such as TVEs and foreign direct investment (FDI) firms are in a position to take market share from the conglomerates in markets for labor intensive products because the latter continue to expend more on wages and benefits as a legacy of the feudal period. TVEs and FDI firms, on the other hand, generally have no obligation to provide job security or benefits such as those still accorded to workers in the conglomerates. As Mingkwan Lee notes in his work, *Chinese Occupational Welfare in Market Transition*, urban families "strategically involve their members in both [state sector and non-state sector employment] to minimize risks and maximize opportunities and advantages" (2000: 82). However, as he argues further, although the transition to a "mixed economy" has resulted in new employment opportunities and alternatives to the subsistence arrangements of the feudal period:

> Layoffs and bankruptcy, hitherto unimaginable, are now real possibilities. *Danwei* benefits are no longer free, as readily available or as cheap as before... The "iron rice bowl" and the practice of "eating from the common pot" are becoming things of the past. In addition to these is the hard fact of a persistent two-double-figure inflation which reduces their real income and quality of life. The widening gap between their incomes and the much higher incomes earned by workers in the non-state sector has furthermore accentuated a sense of frustration, inequity and relative deprivation.
>
> (Lee 2000: 83)

Thus, as a result of transition to capitalist class processes, the value of urban labor power (wages plus company provided benefits) has been under pressure as the social benefits that had been part of the danwei system disappear. In addition to losing material benefits from the danwei system, workers have also experienced a change in other social and environmental processes, including physical and mental health. The pressures of the labor power market, commoditization of more and more of the workers' life, rapid social transformation, and other factors have conspired to generate a sharp increase in the number of depressed and suicidal people, as well as more general mental health problems: "The demand for psychiatric services in China is soaring and that is why we want to accelerate the process of formulating a national law to protect people diagnosed with mental health problems and improve mental health services" (*China Daily*, March 8, 2005). Ming-kwan Lee also argues that the transition has resulted in a change in cultural processes and other noneconomic relationships between people:

> The *danwei* community is also becoming divided from within by new values that compete with what used to characterize the *gemeinschaftlich* community in the past. The rise of an ethos characteristic of the market, with values placed on profit, individual interest and competition instead of egalitarianism, solidarity and altruism, upsets preexisting values, reduces members' taken-for-granted commitment to their community and induces conflict. (2000: 83)

Thus, Ming-kwan Lee, in summation, writes that despite "new opportunities and options, these changes have also exposed workers to new risks and problems and increased the financial burden on the family of sickness, disability and other misfortunes in life" (2000: 83). Much of the subsistence package for feudal urban laborers, now transformed into "modern" capitalist workers, has undergone a process of commoditization.

Education, for example, was previously supplied to families of urban laborers free of charge. It was part of the nature of the social contract that all those who worked in the system could expect to have their children provided with a relatively standardized education and the opportunity to take university entrance exams or be assigned to danwei. The identity of the urban worker was very much shaped by this social contract. However, many of the educational institutions in the urban areas have been removed from the state bureaucracy and must now rely on fees to sustain their operations. As Jasper Becker's anecdotal history of China reveals, this process of detaching educational institutions from the bureaucracy and granting them autonomy has pushed school administrators to diversify beyond their educational mission and to establish their own capitalist enterprises as funding sources:

> An increasingly large amount now comes from commercial activities. The Xiantao Teachers' College in Hubei province runs a foam packaging plant, makes surge power generators and operates two soft drinks factories and a printing plant. The same college also runs a shop, a kindergarten and a night

> school, and it charges its students tuition fees. Well-connected universities such as Beijing have set up highly successful companies, like the computer giant Legend, and talk of creating science parks. Between 1991 and 1995 alone school enterprises expanded annually by 33 per cent and brought in 300 billion yuan (US$36 billion) in profits.
>
> (Becker 2000: 215)

The school administrators became appropriators of capitalist SV in order to secure the revenues necessary to keep the schools operating. Thus, the reforms have not only contributed to the growth of capitalist enterprises in traditional settings but have even contributed to the growth of capitalist exploitation in some very nontraditional settings, such as within schools.

Becker (2000: 215) also notes that the government has raised money from large domestic and foreign capitalists to fund charity projects that target specific groups deprived of educational opportunities. Thus, in an effort to mitigate some of the potential problems caused by changes to the provision of educational services (such as placing poor, rural students at an even greater disadvantage than might have been the case previously), government officials and school administrators have come to occupy new positions of receipt of distributions of surplus from capitalist corporations, creating closer links between the institutions and, perhaps, influencing curricula and other policies. And in addition:

> A third means of relieving the shortfall in state education funds has been the toleration of private fee-paying schools. The first were set up in the late 1980s and by the end of the 1990s there were 50,000...Known as "aristocracy schools," many of them were boarding schools which required downpayments of up to 200,000 or even 500,000 yuan, as well as hefty fees.
>
> (Becker 2000: 217)

As Becker duly notes, this reform of the educational system to a fee-paying system has increased the burden on not only urban laborers, but rural direct producers as well, who now must secure sufficient income to make payments to meet a basic need that had been provided by the state. As Becker argues, this has negatively impacted the quality of education and of life opportunities for all laborers:

> In particular, the privatization of education means that children from rural China will have less chance of gaining a university place than ever before. Even urban families have difficulty in affording annual university fees of 10,000 yuan. While the state is proposing to establish bursaries for students from poor families as well as a system of student loans, for rural children these represent further obstacles along an already difficult path. The demographics of China, whereby most rural families have two or three children and urban families just one, make it inevitable that higher education will be restricted to less than 2 per cent of the population for decades to come.
>
> (2000: 224)

Decentralization and commoditization of social services have resulted in an increased burden on rural and urban laborers to earn incomes from wage labor, forcing them to increase their participation in labor power markets in order to maintain certain components of their traditional consumption bundle. The fact that employment is not guaranteed has, therefore, meant that this new context for buying social services increases the risk that workers' families will not secure all of the services that had previously been part of the social contract, such as education or healthcare. This increases tensions in the social formation to the extent workers' expectations have not fully adjusted to this new reality. This has been evident in rural and urban protests against the economic reforms. To counter this social instability, as Jean Oi notes, the CPC has begun construction and implementation of various social security schemes:

> As yet, China lacks a fully developed welfare program that would provide guaranteed support for laid-off workers. In the meantime, the state has instituted a three-part program intended as a safety net for workers displaced by the reforms. Laid-off workers are supposed to have access to a reemployment service center, unemployment insurance, and a basic insurance system. But this package is far from fully institutionalized. The provisions are only half-measures in the sense that the center cannot fully fund these programs, putting the burden on the enterprises and the localities. Moreover, the program seems to contain a "catch 22" clause: laid-off workers who decide to participate in the short-term relief and retraining programs will be cut off forever from their state factory. This has become a major stumbling block for many workers who choose not to participate in the state's programs because it would mean that their factory, their *danwei*, would no longer be responsible for their welfare and would no longer be responsible for reemploying them. After the safety period, workers would have to go it alone.
>
> (2003: 460)

Dreams of modernity

The CPC has adopted a vision of modernity, comprised largely of technological imagery from the Organization for Economic Corporation and Development (OECD) nations, and idealized it in the concept of the "Well Off Society." To realize this dream of modernity, or what some believe to be "advancedness," the CPC has adopted the essentialism of "the market" and abandoned any pretense of attempting to create a new "socialist" human being. This has meant also abandoning any notion that the social contract between the state and the citizenry should include guarantees of healthcare, education, income, or other necessaries of life. It is now up to the people to find a means of securing the income required to purchase such necessaries in the marketplace. This means, for the most part, throwing them into the labor power market, making their labor powers a commodity. For it is the "modern" role of the government to be "regulator" of the market, not provider of social services. It is the "modern" role of the Chinese laborer to assume individual responsibility for social services which are provided in "the market." This has led to the deprivation of social services for large segments of the population, but is not seen as a function of transitioning to the capitalist class process by neoliberal theorists as so much a function of an undemocratic political process:

> Due to the incomplete nature of China's economic reform as it progresses toward a market system, the supply of many public goods and social services has lagged. For instance, the investment in agricultural research has dwindled, with notable drops, in particular, during periods of budgetary difficulty. Conditions in many rural schools have deteriorated due to organizational changes, and social security programs are almost entirely absent in the countryside. The collapse of the system of "barefoot doctors" has severely curtailed even rudimentary health services in poor rural areas. And China needs a reliable system of property registration and more transparent laws and regulations establishing property rights, especially, for example, in developing an efficient housing market.
>
> In a market system with democracy, publicly elected officials would represent the voters of their own constituencies and facilitate the provision of such public goods as investments in health services and education.
>
> (Hope *et al.* 2003: 480)

However, this is an essentialist fallacy, as the "market system" or capitalist class process exists in so-called democratic social formations such as the United States and Great Britain, yet many workers in those societies (especially the United States) are not covered by healthcare and other social services even though many citizens want these services.

The CPC leadership's zeal for the adoption of technology, market processes, and all that is "modern" (as represented in the advanced industrial nations) has resulted in reproduction and expansion in exploitative relationships and a fundamental reconstitution of social contracts. In pursuit of modernist dreams, transformation of people, the environment, culture, all the processes that overdetermine the social formation, became subject to the discipline of "the market" and the process of commoditization. Thus, subsistence that was once provided by the party-state in its role as feudal lord is now, in the pursuit of modernity, commodities to be bought and sold. For in the vision of the modern, the party-state becomes the provider of social services as a last resort. Nevertheless, the CPC must find an acceptable solution to the problem of reducing that portion of surplus value that goes to meeting social service needs so as to satisfy desired levels of productive investment, military expenditures, management compensation, various rents, payments to financial enterprises and other claimants to the SV generated within the growing capitalist sector without triggering protests and a full blown social crisis.

3 Working for capitalism

Labor market reform

A fundamental requirement of the transition from feudalism to capitalism is the liberation of labor from feudal obligations to a specific employer qua lord and the creation of a free market in labor power. The focus of this chapter is an examination of the economic, political, and cultural factors shaping the creation and expansion of capitalist labor power markets in China. The dismantling of the communes and erosion of the danwei system brought an end to the feudal bonds between direct producers and the state bureaucracy, creating a large pool of free wage laborers. Economic growth in China has been dependent, in part, upon these processes wherein a sizeable pool of direct producers found themselves at the mercy of "market conditions" and sometimes unemployed. The result has been a widely recognized labor power surplus. Workers who had only a short time before being attached to communes made up a low wage, relatively hard-working labor pool that would fuel an economic boom within TVEs and pour into the cities as rural migrant workers. A similar process in the cities saw these rural migrants competing with "redundant" workers who had been "permanent" employees of state-owned urban industrial enterprises until the flexibility of capitalist labor power markets was instituted. And workers in all the social sites in China faced the insecurity that came as an inevitable side effect of the transition from a social system where they (and their families) were "guaranteed" not only work but all the basic necessities of life to a system where seemingly everything was up for grabs. Uncertainty of employment, of compensation, even of identity is the new order in the reform era.

Adding to the relative insecurity of Chinese workers is the absence of substantive worker rights. In particular, workers have no right to organize labor unions independent of the state bureaucracy. CPC ideology claims that the party represents the interests of the working people. Unfortunately for those who must depend on wage labor employment for their livelihood, there is no mechanism by which to change representatives. The combination of factors working against the bargaining position of workers in this new capitalist labor power market is such that it is epitomized by relatively low wage rates and relatively high rates of exploitation. The surplus value generated by these conditions provides an important basis for recovery (from negative cash flow conditions) in the urban industrial enterprise sector, astounding rates of revenue (and surplus value) growth among the TVEs, and profitable opportunities for capitalist firms, in general. However, these favorable conditions for growth in capitalist production have generated problems. The most rapidly growing areas have exhibited bottlenecks in input markets, including in labor power. In such locales, where exports have been a major source of economic growth, the competition for labor power between urban industrial enterprises, rural-based TVEs, joint venture operations, and other capitalist firms, including foreign-based firms, has intensified. In these areas, there is upward pressure on the value of labor power, embodied in wage and benefit offers from firms to unattached or footloose workers. Some have even argued that these conditions and political pressure (from both domestic and foreign sources) may push the CPC to liberalize laws related to the conditions of laborers, including making independent unions legal. These pressures may intensify as the economy grows more prosperous. Alternatively, the rapid growth of capitalist enterprises may be generating cultural and political trends that could run counter to this liberalization of labor power market conditions. Antiunion rhetoric, homegrown and/or imported from the OECD universe, may dominate arguments in favor of independent labor unions. Those whose income is linked to the growth of capitalist SV, elements in what Jiang Zemin called the "new social strata" may coalesce to form a resistance to liberal public policies. And there is no guarantee that working people will support such liberalization, either. They may be drawn under the spell of the same antiunion rhetoric or be convinced, through various mechanisms, including perhaps partial ownership of the very firms within which they are exploited, that their best interests lie in conditions that increase the general level of exploitation.

Feudal labor power

Under the feudal system, Chinese workers were bound by ties of fealty to the state bureaucracy and, more specifically, to a particular danwei or commune:

> Before 1978, there was strict administrative control over job assignment; wages and benefits were centrally regulated; salary increases were determined by state budgets; career promotions followed ranking systems imposed by central planners; employers were not allowed to lay off workers; and employment was virtually for life. There were neither external nor internal labour markets. It was only during the economic reforms of the 1980s that some limited labour markets began gradually to come into existence.
>
> (Lee 2000: 5)

The ties of feudal bondage formed the basis for the performance and appropriation of feudal surplus labor, but also constrained the size of that surplus as feudal reciprocity required the state bureaucracy to provide not only lifetime employment for the worker but also for the welfare of the worker and his/her family, providing healthcare, education for children, subsidized food, housing, and so on. In particular, the feudal commune and danwei systems dampened worker motivation to perform surplus labor or, at least, this is the standard assumption (Meng 2000: 10–11, 17). Thus, not only was the performance of surplus labor constrained by the motivational problems associated with feudal dependency and reciprocity, but also the amount of total labor/product that was surplus was constrained by a heavy commitment by the bureaucracy to provide a substantial portion of workers' subsistence in the form of collective consumption ("the iron rice bowl"). In return for being taken care of, direct producers were bound to the service of the state within these enterprises, unable to transfer to a different commune or danwei without bureaucratic approval. The children of commune members or of urban industrial workers went to school inside the confines of the enterprise and typically grew up to work inside that same enterprise. In most cases, the only route of escaping this bondage was within that same bureaucratic structure that controlled the boundaries of these feudal domains: pass university exams and ride the meritocracy to some other site within the bureaucracy or be accepted into the People's Liberation Army (PLA).

This system produced one of the most egalitarian distributions of income on the planet. The lords at the top of the hierarchy, living in Zhongnanhai, were relatively few. The vast majority of the bureaucracy lived on relatively equal terms. And the system produced social stability. However, it did not yield sufficient levels of SV to meet all the obligations of the vast bureaucracy and fund the modernization projects envisioned by many of those in the Chinese leadership. This was no minor matter. PLA leaders fretted about the ability of the Chinese army to resist foreign invaders (or, at the minimum, to match the sophisticated weaponry that the United States supplied to Taiwan). Modernists within the State Council were concerned that the slow pace of investment and the backwardness of technologies deployed in industry and in the infrastructure was causing China to lag behind other, more "modern," Asian economies.

It would not be easy to change these conditions. The idiosyncrasies of the state feudal system shaped economic, political, and cultural processes in both pre- and post-reform China. This system may have been feudal at its core (in terms of the fundamental class process that generated the surplus products that made the system possible) but it was also understood, in ideological terms, as socialism. Feudal dependency had become, for many within the party and the larger society, the signifier of socialism. And feudal dependency extended beyond mere employment:

> Worker dependency reached its zenith in China in the 1960s. Increasingly, urban housing and rationed goods were distributed through work units, combined with new limitations on free movement among firms... Individuals dared not offend their superiors, lest housing, promotions, and other rewards be withheld. Those willing to toe the party line, as defined by superiors, received more in-kind benefits.
>
> (Tang and Parish 2000: 129)

This was a system based on loyalty and reciprocity, bonds of feudal fealty and dependence, and the subsumption of the individual worker to the discipline of a hierarchically organized form of exploitation grounded in an ideology of socialism and egalitarianism:

> This culture consists of, first of all, the value of obedient compliance with the direction and wishes of cadres and leaders; secondly, of passivity, of, indeed, expecting and looking to *danwei* leaders to make all possible decisions; thirdly, the attitude which takes it for granted that workers will be cared for by the *danwei* and which regards it as the *danwei's* obligation and responsibility to cater to the many needs of its members; and fourthly, the expectation that, in the provision and distribution of welfare, no one should be left out and everyone should have an equal share; the value, in other words, of 'egalitarianism' (*pingjun zhuyi*).
>
> (Lee 2000: 13–14)

> The *danwei* is therefore more than just a workplace. It brings the state and its state-sector urban citizens together and articulates a relationship of entitlements and obligations between them . . . the *danwei* has become the principle organizational framework through which the . . . state allocates resources and redistributes income. *Danwei* membership is an important status because it entitles a worker to the goods and incomes "redistributed" by the state to its urban population.
>
> (Lee 2000: 7–8)

How could the modernists reform a system that had insinuated itself into every aspect of social life and become woven into the concept of socialism, which was ultimately the legitimizing ideology for CPC rule? The total immersion of the worker in the feudal structure was reminiscent of other manifestations of state feudal social formations, such as the feudal domains of the Catholic Church during Europe's feudal period. This social structure was one that some social scientists might call a "total institution," where political, cultural, and economic relationships were intimately intertwined inside a singular sphere of work, recreation, and home life. All forms of feudalism, state or private, involved customary (or, more rarely, formal contractual) bonds tying workers to the feudal structure and some form of ideology/cultural processes supportive of reproducing these bonds. A particular notion of socialism served this ideological/cultural role in the state feudal period in China. The modernist Marxists had to justify terminating the feudal bonds, even as they reproduced the notion of a socialist China. To some extent, Deng Xiaoping Thought became the ideological foundation for justifying the transition from the state feudal social structure, complete with its iron rice bowl and permanent employment, to the world of free wage labor, unemployment, and social insecurity. However, the most pervasive ideological narrative to be used to displace the state feudal notions of reciprocity (discussed in more detail in the Chapter 4) was and is that of modernity. The promise of modernity (and that of modernist Marxism) is that workers will ultimately be rewarded for the sacrifices that come with subsuming their identity and linking their survival to the dynamics of a capitalist labor power market by a better world for themselves and their children. This world has been described with many terms. Jiang Zemin called it the "Well-off Society." Some traditionalists within the modernist fold (as contradictory as that may sound) continue to use the term "communism" to describe this ultimate telos (after the last transition or at the end of history).

Labor power markets

> One thing, however, is clear: nature does not produce on the one hand owners of money or commodities, and on the other hand men possessing nothing but their own labour-power. This relation has no basis in natural history, nor does it have a social basis common to all periods of human history. It is clearly the result of a past historical development, the product of many economic revolutions, of the extinction of a whole series of older formations of social production.
>
> (Marx 1977: 273)

In the Chinese context, labor power markets were the result of conscious social engineering on the part of the modernist leadership of the CPC. However, these markets are also the result of a complex array of changes in cultural, economic, environmental, and political processes that both shape and go beyond the actions of the party-state. The influence of a global media that celebrates capitalist development permeated the Great Wall, even during the period of relative isolation, and the elite in the party-state was never particularly insulated from these sources of enculturation. The cultural forces pushing the leadership and others toward "reform" can hardly be separated from the glossy images of a rich life in the "West" contrasted to the seeming monotony of life in state feudal China. The destruction of the conditions of permanent feudal employment in the communes and danwei was conditioned by social forces both within and beyond the boundaries of the PRC. The dynamic growth in neighboring countries, such as South Korea, Singapore, Thailand, Malaysia, Indonesia, and especially Taiwan acted as a contributing factor in driving the reform process toward the creation of capitalist labor power markets. The stagnation of the Soviet Union and other CMEA (Council for Mutual Economic Assistance) nations was no less an influence and the complete collapse of this "socialist" bloc must have been particularly stimulating to the urge to transform the conditions of the Chinese social formation. The party-state gradually unraveled the feudal structure and set direct producers in rural and urban enterprises free. The price for entering the path to modernity would be the commoditization of the labor power of Chinese workers.

This commoditization would necessarily occur within terrain shaped by the state feudal past. It is a tradition in neoclassical thought and narratives to treat "labor markets" as natural phenomena, rather than, as Marx instructed, the products of history. Nevertheless, mainstream researchers when confronting labor power markets in China are often drawn onto the terrain of the feudal "remnants" within the burgeoning capitalist social formation. In particular, the feudal era segregation of the rural and urban, conditions for the reproduction of feudal bondage in both town and countryside, has led many social analysts to dichotomize China's "labor markets" into "rural and urban labor markets":

> The reason for this division is the fundamental characteristic of the Chinese economy under planning, namely, the formal segregation of the rural (agricultural-centered) and urban (manufacturing-centered) economies and labor forces. These two sectors were treated as separate entities, critically related to each other, for the entire period of central planning, which started in 1949. This segregation is still the major fact underlying Chinese labor-market problems and policies today.
>
> (Fleisher and Yang 2003: 2)

Fleisher and Yang are correct that this dichotomy was a "fundamental characteristic of the Chinese economy." But it was more than that. The persistence of the dichotomy is not so much because of economic principles carried over from the previous period to the present, but because the dichotomy was more than merely an economic aspect of life. Indeed, it bears pointing out that this dichotomy was not a "labor market" phenomenon until recently. During the feudal era, there was no labor power market. The state did not buy and workers did not sell their labor power. The relationship between state and worker was one of feudal allegiance. When wages were paid, they were simply a mechanism for allocating subsistence resources to workers who had no right to sell their labor power.

During the feudal period, the particular manner in which resources were distributed, including the planning mechanisms employed, was integrated into the feudal political economy, and reinforced the aforementioned rural–urban segregation. In other words, it is not that segregation was a component part of planning, but, rather, that both this form of segregation and the particular planning and resource distribution mechanisms were all integrated inside a state feudal system that achieved coherence by the active reshaping of political, economic, cultural, and environmental processes by agents of the state to meet the needs of feudal exploitation, including placing constraints on the mobility of labor, controlling the distribution and circulation of resources and commodities, and monopolizing the setting of political policies related to both agricultural and industrial production.

Fleisher and Yang's (and many other analysts') theorization of the Chinese "rural and urban labor markets" reveals "remnants" of the feudal structure, but it simultaneously obfuscates the growing complexity of the capitalist labor power markets that are rapidly changing the landscape of the Chinese social formation. Capitalism is not producing a dualistic labor power market in China, but is, rather, generating a complexly heterogeneous array of ever-changing labor power markets. For instance, the labor power of a computer programmer and the labor power market in which the computer programmer competes to sell his or her labor power is differentiated from that of a sanitation worker. They sell their labor power in very different labor power markets even if they are both situated in urban areas and labor in the same enterprise. And although these labor power markets are influenced by the duality of rural and urban identities formed within Chinese history, including the state feudal codification of this dichotomy, to reduce these markets to this duality would be to miss a far more interesting story: the story of the rapid transformation in the conditions for the buying and selling of labor power throughout both China and the world.

Erosion of boundaries to the expansion of capitalism has created a global division of labor, which has further differentiated labor power markets over large expanses of geographical space. Chinese workers do not simply compete with each other in domestic labor power markets but are increasingly in competition with workers in other countries. This decentering of production (as well as other aspects of capitalist organization) has created new opportunities for capitalist management to break up production and other processes, to diversify the geographic locations within which products and parts of products are produced and to buy labor power wherever they want in the world. It has simultaneously disadvantaged workers who lack the freedom of mobility accorded to capital and find it increasingly difficult to meet the changing demands of globalized capital. The growth of labor power markets in China, perhaps more than in any other country, highlight a trend in global capitalism for the labor power of specific direct producers, like the use value of other specific instances of commodities, to become disposable. Workers, like Gillette razors, are ultimately to be used and thrown away. This flexibility is part of the power of capitalism and clearly distinguishes it from other class processes.

Transnational firms are moving into China at an increasing pace. China has eclipsed the United States as a magnet for FDI. Cheap labor is an important part of this dynamic, earning China the moniker of global "sweatshop" of the world. In 2003, the Pearl River Delta was attracting $1 billion of investment per month; Shenzhen was producing 70 percent of global production of photocopiers and 80 percent of the world's artificial Christmas trees; and 40 percent of the global production of microwave ovens was coming out of a single factory in the Pearl River region (Roberts and Kynge 2003). The transition to capitalism, conditioned by the rapid growth of free wage labor throughout China, and opening up of these new labor power markets to a globalized system of capitalist exploitation is understood by many to be the key to "modernization" of China.

Get a job!: the first stage of the Chinese capitalist labor power market

Indeed, in transforming China into a capitalist social formation, the party-state bureaucracy had to encourage both the creation and expansion of capitalist labor power markets and the social institutions supportive of those labor power markets. Capitalist exploitation is unique in that it is the only form of exploitation where workers freely sell their labor power to others, while having the choice not to do so. Thus, among other things, feudal bureaucratic labor allocation in China needed to end in order to allow this peculiarity of capitalism to prevail. The central government began to erode the conditions for feudal exploitation in rural China. The first stage was initiated with adoption of the Household Responsibility System (HRS) and the destruction of feudal labor conditions in the countryside was finally realized with the dismantling of the communes:

> In the 1980s, the policy was one of transferring surplus rural labour to rural enterprises. People did not change their place of residence, only their place of work. TVEs grew up around China, predominantly in the wealthier coastal areas. From 1978 to 1984, the initial phase of economic reform, the amount of arable land decreased, and with limited land peasants sought out alternative means of earning a living. The commune system had been abolished and other policy changes enabled them to seek employment in TVEs. The TVEs that emerged in this phase were those with less technology-oriented production and with hard-working rural entrepreneurs. They absorbed large amounts of the labour surplus.
>
> (Iredale 2000: 221–222)

The HRS freed rural direct producers to become ancients, but it also resulted in freeing some rural direct producers to sell their labor power to the new TVEs (which were controlled by newly formed township and village governments) and other capitalist enterprises, especially in the export-oriented centers. In urban enterprises, new limited work contracts replaced the lifetime employment arrangements guaranteed under state feudalism. In addition, extensive social services and benefits would have to be renegotiated by urban enterprise direct producers. These reforms were carried out gradually so as to avoid major disruptions in the flow of SV from enterprises to various levels of the state:

> As in other areas of Chinese economic reform, the government has, to date, avoided the "shock therapy" applied in Eastern Europe to reform labour markets, unfolding new elements of market development only after the assimilation of earlier phases. Thus despite the insistent calls, particularly from agencies abroad, to deregulate the labour market and wage structures more rapidly, the government has moved cautiously in allowing sectors of the population to move away from a state planned and regulated environment.
>
> (O'Leary 2000: 142)

Perhaps partly out of concern that too rapid increases in unemployment or changed working conditions might spark worker unrest, the party-state took apart the feudal labor allocation system and implemented capitalist labor power markets in stages. If the modernist Marxist narrative is to be believed, the objective of the reforms was to move the Chinese social formation forward along a teleological path toward the telos of communism. The role of labor power markets in this progression was to provide new incentives for the creation of SV which could be used to finance modernization, the acquisition of those forces of production that would make China more modern.

The reform process was a complex algorithm involving the interaction of several varying relationships. The CPC could not know how changes in each (such as foreign influence, labor power market reform, expressions of sexuality, and other cultural changes) would effect SV creation *and* distribution. Realizing the unpredictable nature of change, the CPC experimented with gradual reforms to create and expand capitalist labor power markets, hoping to transition in ways that would reproduce the legitimacy of party power, increase SV production, and result in the deployment of this SV to the acquisition of the coveted "modern" technologies. This approach to transition was not dissimilar from the Meiji restoration in Japan. The feudal system was gradually dismantled in favor of a new capitalist order. The samurai and the serfs were gradually weaned from the old system of allegiances and dependency. By the time capitalism was implemented, serfs had transitioned into wage laborers or ancient farmers. Many of the samurai had transitioned into management positions in capitalist enterprises and their traditional swords had become purely ceremonial. In China, a similar process involving former commune workers and cadre has been unfolding since the reforms were first introduced in the countryside in 1978.

In a process reminiscent of Lenin's *The Development of Capitalism in Russia*, the termination of the communes and growth in labor power markets made it possible for more successful ancient farmers to hire wage laborers and expand their production. Given the opportunity to become at least part-time capitalists (and thus raise their level of income), many did so, despite years of anticapitalist rhetoric. Thus, rather than capitalism attracting wage laborers, it was in many instances the presence of a labor power market that stimulated growth in capitalist relations. Similarly, as urban reforms were implemented, some rural direct producers migrated to the urban areas to find work (illegally at first). These movements in wage laborers would also stimulate the growth in private capitalist enterprises taking advantage of the presence of relatively cheap labor power. These developments were just the beginning of the transformation in class relations triggered by labor power market reforms:

> The shift in the composition of the off-farm labor force towards young migrants who specialize in off-farm work contrasts sharply with the situation in 1990, when most off-farm workers continued to work on the farm on a part time or at least seasonal basis. These findings are consistent with the argument that the emergence of specialized modes of production in different villages across China's geographical landscape has been facilitated by the emergence of labor markets...
>
> (Zhang *et al.* 2004: 237)

Nevertheless, the transition to the new social conditions has not always been smooth, particularly among urban workers who had led a relatively privileged existence in their danwei and who did not take well to being "freed" into the vicissitudes of the wage labor market:

> Nearly fifty years of "the iron rice bowl" has produced reluctance on the part of many laid-off workers to settle for the conditions available in the non-state sector. Reports abound of laid-off workers being uninterested in available non-SOE work, with some 72 per cent rating SOEs their first preference for re-employment. The shift to non-state employment is nonetheless taking place at a rapid pace and non-state urban employment, which contributes over three-quarters of the total profit of all industrial enterprises, now accounts for over two-thirds of the workforce.
>
> (O'Leary 2000: 146)

It takes time for workers to adapt to changed social conditions. It is not easy for workers unaccustomed to marketing their labor power to adapt to the conditions of labor power markets. However, it is quite clear from the trajectory of change in China that worker consciousness and other social conditions, many within the control of the party-state, have been shaped so as to make most workers *dependent* upon wage labor employment for their livelihood. The commoditization of use values that had been part of the "iron rice bowl," particularly housing, and the aggressive advertising of new commodities, as well as a wide range of other social changes, has been effective at drawing millions of people out of the countryside at younger and younger ages. This process simultaneously fills the industrial work spaces with relatively low wage laborers and pressures the reproduction of the ancient farming because it becomes increasingly difficult to keep them down on the farm.

The transition to capitalist labor power markets in China has echoed similar transitions in other social formations. It is a process that almost always involves a certain amount of violence and dispossession, in which ancient farmers are all too often victims:

> [R]iot police swept into the village of Sanchawan and arrested 32 people among hundreds of villagers protesting what they termed an illegal land grab by local officials... The Shaanxi dispute erupted when a relocation plan forced some 15,000 peasants off their land to make way for a municipal economic-development zone. Compensation to the peasants was tiny...
>
> An annual report to Congress issued... by a U.S. governmental body, the Congressional-Executive Commission on China, noted that land requisitions and unfair compensation schemes are fueling a wave of protests across China.
>
> "Farmers end up landless and, once they have exhausted their small subsidies, unemployed and without a source of income," the report said. It noted that central government authorities last year tallied "more than 178,000 illegal or irregular land transactions."
>
> (Johnson 2004)

It is not surprising that this description is reminiscent of the enclosure movement in Britain where feudal serfs were exiled from the land that they and their ancestors had farmed, in some cases for generations. In both cases, the transition was to a capitalist labor power market. It is also not uncommon for government agencies to play a role in the dispossession of workers. This was the case in Britain during its transition to capitalism and it is also the case in China today. The irony is that the party-state in China relies upon the aforementioned ideology of socialism, a product of Marxian theory, to justify its policy making hegemony.

This notion of socialism may be one of the cultural influences driving some workers to resist the changing conditions of labor. There have been protests in numerous cities. But some workers simply try to hang onto their relationship with the state bureaucracy in the hope that the reform process will either stop or be reversed. This may be a reflection of the strength of the loyalties formed in the old system or simply insecurity at losing the "iron rice bowl":

> Perhaps the largest of all restraints on the reform of SOEs has been their role as providers of social services such as housing, health, education, retirement benefits and insurance. These benefits are not portable and are very considerable in relation to those from the non-SOE sector, ensuring that labour transfer is minimal despite the *xia hai* ("leap into the sea") phenomenon where the individual concerned voluntarily opts out of the security of the state sector into the turbulence of the private sector. While work in the non-SOE sector may have higher pay, and in some cases much higher pay, surveys regularly show, as indicated above, that there are many who are still reluctant to forego the security of the housing, pension, health care and tenure of SOE employment.
>
> (O'Leary 2000: 146)

The problem for these workers is that the transition from feudal era reciprocity has continued unabated. The reforms have gradually removed the obligation of enterprises to provide in-kind compensation and social services or to keep workers employed. Inertia will simply not save workers from the revolutionary changes taking place in the social formation. Whether they like it or not, the meaning of being a worker in China has changed. Their identities as workers and citizens have been transformed. The condition of relying upon a labor power market for livelihood is just as totalizing as the experience of being bound to service to a feudal bureaucracy.

These changes are self-reinforcing. Reduction in the social value guaranteed to workers as a right of citizenship in the form of social services or social welfare (discussed in more detail in the Chapter 2) impacts every aspect of the individual's identity, including his/her relationship to labor power markets. When a worker's family can gain access to healthcare only by successfully gaining employment for a wage, then the worker's options are limited. Under such conditions, wages and benefits are likely to be lower than under conditions where healthcare or other such necessities of life are provided as citizen rights. Direct producers may be less likely to pursue productive self-employment, rather than simply joining the labor power market. It also shapes the worker's sense of insecurity once they have found wage employment. "The realization that if they do not perform satisfactorily then they are likely to be sacked has given workers a new sense of urgency" (Liu, Yongren 2003: 339). This heightened sense of insecurity is likely to stimulate greater work effort, thus raising productivity. Thus, as the state withdraws support for Chinese workers, the result is likely to be both lower wages and higher levels of productivity. In Marxian terms, the rate of exploitation for many of these workers is likely to increase. And to the extent the level of investment in capitalist production is positively correlated to the rate of exploitation, then public policies that deny citizenship rights that had previously existed may stimulate higher levels of investment and aggregate demand, more realized SV, and economic growth. If such is the case, the modernist leadership is likely to continue in the same public policy direction.

Get a job!: creating the consciousness of a wage laborer

Under the new capitalist order, management set up new processes for communicating the availability of jobs and job requirements to potential employees. At the same time, workers have had to learn the process of job search. This is a complex process of locating possible employment, interfacing with the institution where the job is sought to set up interviews and/or tests, and to reshape personal identity to meet the expectations of potential employers. Enterprises have had to establish processes for filtering through these applicants to find the "right" ones to meet the firm's needs. As Gabriel and Todorova (2003: 34) have argued, the creation and reproduction of an agent capable of selling labor power on a labor market produces a form of dissociation. This dissociation is an adaptation to a cultural requirement of capitalism. The agent must become the person the employer wants to hire in order to get a job and must then be the person the employer wants to keep employed. Direct producers must do all of this in order to gain permission to participate, on a daily basis, in their own exploitation. Thus the consciousness of individual direct producers becomes fragmented between the employee-person enterprise management desires and the other personalities the direct producer must exhibit to successfully participate in other social relationships. Each persona is essentialized and compartmentalized. The one human being has become multiple agents in the social formation. Furthermore:

> Capitalism may produce its own dissociation through the labor market. It is in the interest of those who seek wage labor employment to adjust their consciousness to the demands of that market, to make themselves marketable. The very process of making oneself marketable produces the appropriate essentialized identity and fragmentation of consciousness. In addition, capitalist society may produce multiple processes by which such dissociation occurs.
>
> (Gabriel and Todorova 2003: 35)

A wide array of social processes reproduces and reinforces this change in consciousness. The act of dissociation required to succeed in the capitalist labor power market may be difficult, at first, but the xia gang system of laying off workers (yet keeping them officially on the employment rolls of the firm) provides incentive for workers, both those laid off and those who observe the laying off, to make the transition more rapidly and completely. This xia gang system is a sort of transitional stage in the process of meting out the ultimate discipline of the capitalist labor power market. It is not outright firing, which remains culturally problematic for many workers, but it is nevertheless quite effective as both a tool for streamlining operational costs and as a conditioning mechanism for those workers still employed. Conditions in which managers have the flexibility to remove redundant workers from the workplace act as signaling mechanisms. They communicate the message: "Don't get on the bad side of management or you might end up on the wrong list." In 2003, furloughed workers numbered 18.6 million (US–China Business Council 2003).

Over time, workers have come to understand that this new system really is a breaking of the old obligations (Tang and Parish 2000: 123). Workers who do not satisfy their bosses can be removed and replaced by those more accommodating or desperate. As O'Leary notes:

> In urban areas recent labour market activities have been dominated by the changes to the SOE-operating environment and internal changes, which are responsible for increasing the highly conservative official unemployment figures to 3.1 per cent, or 7.5 per cent (15 million) if those stood down from SOEs are included. The real extent of the "laid-off" worker problem is difficult to gauge. It is not uncommon to encounter functioning SOEs such as the one visited by the author in December 1997 in a Guangdong Special Economic Zone, which had 3260 workers on its payroll, made up of some 1820 retired workers, 1260 laid-off workers and 180 actually working.
>
> (2000: 144)
>
> The distribution of this official and unofficial unemployment is highly uneven. There is less in the flourishing southern littoral areas where workers displaced from SOEs are much more likely to obtain some work in the non-state sector, and worse in the old industrial heartlands such as the north east or areas where state industry was established in the 1950s to compensate for uneven industrial distribution or strategic reasons... The unemployment is also disproportionately female, and females find re-employment more difficult.
>
> (2000: 146)

Another conditioning mechanism, no less powerful than the xia gang threat, is the increasing reliance upon debt. As the "iron rice bowl" fades from view, many families have found that they could meet subsistence needs, especially privatized housing, only by going into debt. This has been an important motivational force not only in pushing workers into the labor power market but encouraging them to behave "properly" so as to earn the income necessary to meet the debt obligations of their household. Many Chinese families find themselves indebted for medical and educational expenses (once part of the subsistence provided by the state), not unlike many American families who find themselves in similar circumstances because the US government and capitalist corporations provide inadequate health insurance and because of the rising cost of private and higher education. As one set of reforms push households to take on more debt, another set has made it possible for Chinese banks to create consumer loan divisions in order to increase avenues of profit.

Furthermore, the creation and expansion of capitalist labor power markets has been conditioned by and generated changes in cultural processes that are directly implicated in changing social and individual consciousness. Instruments of mass media are being employed to change the self-image of Chinese citizens. The old images of the patriotic worker in her "Mao suit" building "socialism" has been displaced by the images of the yuppie in a "Western" suit with the cell phone and new car. The message is unambiguous: the future belongs to those who succeed in capitalist labor power markets. The "modern, cultured" citizen is the one who has the trappings of modernity. Modernity and consumerism are merged in the popular consciousness and the party hopes that the notion of socialism will somehow blend into the mix, as well. Backward people use backward products and live in backward dwellings. Socialism is about modernity and modernity is about consumption. To paraphrase Marx, the message to the Chinese citizen has become: consume, consume, that is Mao and the prophets. If it doesn't work with the masses, then at least this new imagery has found a place in the consciousness of Jiang Zemin's "New Strata":

> While the majority of Chinese workers struggle to make ends meet, a small minority of petit bourgeois and bourgeois Chinese pursue lifestyles similar to upper-income U.S. citizens, complete with Southern California-style suburban upscale housing, luxury automobiles, gourmet cuisine, and high-fashion clothing and jewelry... The Chinese government now uses May Day to pay tribute to the wealthy exploiters, as in 2002, when the All-China Federation of Trade Unions awarded medals "to the heads of four privately owned companies" while another 17 businessmen were declared "model workers" in the northwestern province of Shaanxi, where Mao once made his revolutionary headquarters.
>
> (Hart-Landsberg and Burkett 2004: 59)

The "high culture" of the new elite may be out of the reach of ordinary workers, but this imagery is not lost on them. There are always low culture substitutes that still ring of modernity, such as relatively inexpensive electronic products or knock offs or even packaged foods that carry some of the patina of high technology. After all, if it was advertised on television, then it must be modern. The continuing evolution of the concept of modernity always pushes the workers to work hard and long in order to make the wages to buy the "next new thing" that falls within their income (or debt) capacity.

The Chinese government has, indirectly at least, supported the widespread indoctrination of the people through media, and other cultural mechanisms. This new cultural campaign is being carried out with a fervor no less than that experienced during the height of the so-called Maoist era, albeit with very different objectives. Rather than orchestrating cultural changes from within the bureaucracy, the modernist leadership has created spheres of cultural autonomy, allowing the infiltration of "Western" advertising and mass media such as CNN and Star TV (Tang and Parish 2000: 44).

> After more than two decades of disappearance, marketing made a comeback in the spring of 1979, when the Shanghai TV station aired a commercial for the Swiss watchmaker Rado. Since then advertisements have multiplied and flooded the mass media and other channels of communication.
>
> (Lin 2001: 4)

While enterprises perform the actual cultural production, the government sets the guidelines, or lack of, by which they do so. The changes in popular culture have influenced people's lives in diverse and intimate ways:

> Popular anecdotes emphasize an increasing materialism among youth in courtship. In the reform era, dating has become increasingly popular among Chinese youth, including visits to dance halls and other forms of commercial entertainment. Dating requires expenditure and forefronts the economic considerations in courtship... Marriage rituals reflect an increased emphasis on ostentatious consumption, including traditional Chinese banquets.
>
> (Tang and Parish 2000: 242)

This transition to capitalism is, therefore, an all encompassing process of change in popular consciousness and in a wide array of social processes within the society. Everything is changing. This means all the social interactions between agents in the society are undergoing a revolution, not simply those within the work sites. However, it is important to remember that while these changes are altering all types of social and environmental conditions, they are simultaneously shaped by preexisting conditions. Thus, forms of consciousness and interactions that had existed prior to the reforms exert various types of influence upon the new forms of consciousness and interactions.

The racialized other and capitalist labor power markets

> Rural agricultural regions, and rural peasants by extension, are paradoxically blamed as the causes of China's underdevelopment and seen as the objects to be developed; they are the necessary "other" against which progress and civilization (*wenming*) are defined and measured. In this schema, being from a "poor and backward" (pinkun luohou) region takes on a social and moral taint that stains those least able to successfully accumulate capital and those

> geographically most remote from the urban centers of modern life... The city, promises to expose rural migrants to new forms of knowledge and "raise their quality" (*tigao sushi*).
>
> (Gaetano 2004: 46–47)

The interaction of the old (pre-reform) and the new (post-reform) can be seen with particular clarity when examining the changing conditions in rural China and, in particular, in the creation of a new type of direct producer – the rural migrant laborer – created in the nexus of preexisting deterministic notions of human nature and the requirements of capitalist labor power markets. These rural migrant laborers are formed in the transition from feudalism to capitalism, overdetermined by changing social processes, such as those described earlier, of alienation from the means of production, destruction of the state feudal dependency relationships, and the rise of a new consumer culture. Rural migrant workers enter the labor power markets as subjects already defined in deterministic terms. In China, to be a rural person is to be fundamentally different from an urban person. This fundamental difference is not simply a matter of different enculturation. Many analysts recognize the discrimination and second-class status endured by migrant laborers but the argument here is that rural subjectivity itself, formed in Chinese history and reinforced by the recent feudal era segregation of rural and urban, has been shaped as inferior to urban subjectivity. The bearers of this rural subjectivity are programmed to see themselves as inferior, just as much as the bearers of urban subjectivity have been programmed to see themselves as superior to the rural. This is not a story of geographic segregation alone but also a story of the creation of distinct "races" of human beings. In other words, the rural being may "raise their quality" by contact with superior urban beings, but the former can never become the latter. Nevertheless, rural migrants will go to extraordinary lengths to try and hide their origins:

> In addition to purchases of clothes and shoes to send to their family members or to present as New Year gifts upon their return home, young women also spend money on their own adornment, in efforts to appear less "rustic" (*tu*). Young women upgrade wardrobes with fashionable clothing and footwear, and purchase moisturizers and whitening creams in the hope of having softer, whiter skin. Many young migrant women cut or style their hair within months of arrival in Beijing, as long, straight hair is perceived as a marker of the village girl... Participating in shopping or tourism alongside urban residents, migrants likewise carve out their rightful place in the urban environment and identify themselves as consummate cosmopolitans.
>
> (Gaetano 2004: 70–71)

A great deal of effort is put into masking rural origins precisely because it is so consequential to every aspect of a person's social life:

> Liu Fanmei is no stranger to public humiliation and discrimination due to her outsider origins. Once while she was browsing in a bookstore, a clerk

> cornered her and demanded proof of identification, as if implying that a migrant worker (apparently identifiable from her less-than-fashionable dress or from her accent) would not be buying books, only stealing them.
>
> (Gaetano 2004: 69)

These notions of the fundamental inferiority of the rural person and of the fundamental superiority of the urban person are important to understanding the dynamics of contemporary Chinese labor power markets, as well as the past state feudal structure. This "common sense" notion of the inferiority of the rural persons lowers their value in labor power markets and, to the extent urban workers are in competition with them for certain types of jobs, may serve to lower general wage rates. Thus, looked at in these terms, it might appear to be in the economic interests of urban workers to struggle against these racialized notions of rural and urban persons. On the other hand, the perceived inferiority of rural persons may be an economic advantage to the urban worker who is chosen for a position of authority over rural migrant workers precisely because of his perceived superiority or who recognizes that discriminatory treatment of rural people may protect his/her ability to secure better housing or other commodities that might be more costly or in scarcer supply if rural people were allowed to fully participate in those markets. And there may also be psychological benefits to being perceived as superior:

> Indeed, the presence of a racialized subjectivity may provide psychological benefits in the context of exploitation. For example, a person who must abandon certain favored behavioral attributes in order to sell her labor power may gain compensatory attributes associated with being a member of a transcendental race. Gunnar Myrdal talked about this in terms of "white" workers gaining status as a consequence of racism. To the extent that certain workers gain status within the workplace as a consequence of racism, these workers may be willing to work for less material compensation. This is one way in which racism may reduce the value of labor power. It also may do so by creating self-doubt, self-hatred, and low self-esteem in those excluded from the transcendental race. The "black" woman worker may, for instance, believe herself lucky to have any job and to be worth less than the going wage, such that she not only willingly accepts the wage but, if faced with the prospect of a lower wage, might be quick to acquiesce. The more workers who have such a self-perception, the more difficult it is to raise wages. In this sense, racism may be of benefit to capitalists, in general.
>
> (Gabriel and Todorova 2003: 34–35)

Substitute "urban" for "white" and "rural" for "black" and the quote is an accurate representation of conditions in China today. The racialized interaction of rural and urban may actually serve to make the transition to capitalist labor power markets easier. To the extent that urban workers focus their attention on their superiority to rural migrant workers, who generally take less pleasant jobs at lower pay and few, if any, benefits, there is likely to be less organized resistance to the overall process of commoditization of labor power. Add to this the manner in which these rural migrant workers may be deployed to improve urban residents' access to the accoutrements of modernity (serving as the spider men building new apartment complexes, and as maids and nannies for the urban princes and princesses) and their presence may even provide a not so subtle basis for urban dwellers to support the commoditization of labor power:

> With the acceleration of economic growth, including a huge construction boom, cities rapidly went from labor surplus to labor shortage, particularly in the more menial construction, transport, textile factory, and service jobs that the privileged urban residents disdained. This increased flow of menial laborers and service providers from the countryside was beneficial for residents.
>
> (Tang and Parish 2000: 30)

This benign perception of rural migrant workers may not, however, be the norm. Perhaps more common is the perception that they are the source of problems for urban people:

> Government policies reflect the view that rural immigrant labour supplements rather than competes with urban labour – a view not always shared by urban residents who continue to complain of increased crime rates and other social problems which they consider are exacerbated, if not wholly caused, by the rural influx. Urban employees also frequently consider their difficulties in finding work after being laid off or in entering the labour market for the first time in relation to the rural labour influx.
>
> (O'Leary 2000: 143)

> The rights of urban citizens relative to those from the countryside have been asserted by municipal authorities who, in some instances, have removed rural workers from urban jobs if they were considered suitable for the urban unemployed. In Xian alone, where there are reported to be 180000 unemployed workers, 15000 were employed in positions from which rural workers were "discharged."
>
> (O'Leary 2000: 147)

The racialization of rural people is not a new phenomenon. However, in the state feudal period, rural people were strictly segregated from the urban population. Thus, there is a perception that this form of identity consciousness is a product of the reform era. As Zhou Changzheng argues, before the reforms, employment discrimination occurred based upon the "class background" of an individual direct producer's family:

> [Now] . . . another form of social origin-based discrimination has emerged to take its place, and this type of discrimination appears to have become

> increasingly common and intense. It is based on the individual's household registration or residence permit system (*huzhi*). For example, at a large worker recruitment and hiring convention [held in Beijing]..., the overwhelming majority of recruitment advertisements indicate that job applicants are expected to have a Beijing residence permit. Even more inexplicable is that in 1998, when our Supreme People's Court opened up the recruiting of justices to society at large, they also listed the holding of Beijing residence permit as prerequisite. It is an explicit violation of the citizen's right to equality of occupation and employment.
>
> (2001: 41)

This form of discrimination has left rural migrant workers in a vulnerable position, particularly in negotiating wages and work conditions. However, the impact on rural women has been even worse, given the degree to which gender discrimination has combined with this origins discrimination to place them in a subaltern position in the society:

> Discrimination against migrant women workers as a "social minority" by urban society is a common social phenomenon... Women-farmers-turned-workers are a minority in urban society... Such discrimination was obvious not only in the almost primitive form of exploitation and oppression by factory owners, the employment policies in some localities that discriminate against migrant workers, the support and protection given by local officials to the illegal business practices of overseas businessmen in order to safeguard local interests and the ignoring of the basic rights and interests of migrant workers, but was also reflected in the widespread prejudice and discrimination against farmer-turned-workers by the society as a whole.
>
> (Tang Can 1998: 71)

The racialization of rural migrant workers has isolated them inside the urban locales where they work and live. There are some indications of changing governmental policy toward these rural migrants, legalizing some forms of work and thereby removing one of the instruments by which these workers could be super-exploited (the threat of being turned into authorities as illegals). However, the government continues to identify rural and urban as distinct beings in various government registration and other processes. By separating the urban and rural workers, government policies serve to reproduce societal and cultural disparities and the underlying racial consciousness. In some ways, this may be in the interest of the modernist leadership. It may make it easier to continue on the current path of reform. As already indicated, these divisions within the working population may make it more difficult to organize workers and it may depress wages and benefits. The rate of exploitation may be positively correlated to the presence of these divisions within the labor force and rates of exploitation are undoubtedly positively correlated to the level of investment spending and, therefore, to the pace of technological transformation that is at the core of modernist goals.

And the ultimate benefit may be to reduce the possibility of social unrest of a more general character, as was evidenced in 1989:

> The divisions between different sections of the working class, visible in the late 1980s as one group suspected another of benefiting more and unfairly from the reforms, were temporarily submerged during the 1989 movement in the overriding hostility towards the corrupt and incompetent top leadership, but are evident again now, particularly as laid-off and long-term unemployed former state workers lower their sights and begin to compete directly with migrant labour from the countryside for scarce urban jobs.
>
> (Sheehan 1998: 227)

For a moment in 1989, Chinese workers appeared as Marx might have conceptualized them, not divided by racial or gender notions, but as direct producers constituting a singular "race" – a "race of peculiar commodity-owners" (Marx 1977: 275) that have nothing to sell but their labor power. The consciousness of workers (and others) grounded in an understanding of humanity as shaped not by some kind of fundamentally different origins (whether geographic/genetic or religious or sexual) but by determinate social processes that segregate the population into those who perform surplus labor, those who exploit these performers, and those who share in the spoils of that exploitation would seem to be more compatible with the Marxian conception of social formations than a consciousness based on rural–urban, male–female, and similar such characteristics. However, there is no evidence that the modernist Marxist leadership would prefer to promote the former over the latter. Just the opposite seems to be the case.

The value of labor power and working conditions

Party-state officials continue to exert tremendous influence over economic, environmental, political, and cultural processes inside and outside of the workplace through both direct control over certain enterprises and through legislation which affects not only wage levels but the conditions under which urban and rural direct producers' surplus labor is appropriated. Whereas under the state feudal bureaucratic structure, strict wage scales based on seniority and fealty suppressed incentives for higher levels of productivity and created little incentive for managers within either urban industrial enterprises or the communes from focusing on value creation, rather than on meeting physical output targets (which were determined by a largely political process), under the reforms the entire structure of production and compensation has been restructured in a manner that places a higher premium on generating SV. Capitalist labor power markets are critical to these reforms. Capitalism, as a social technology, produces flexibility at the fundamental level of production by allowing managers to treat human beings in a similar manner to their treatment of other inputs to production. The firm has no longstanding commitment to its labor force. The individual worker has become disposable and, depending on the depth of the labor markets, replaceable. This has placed a greater emphasis on the skills of managers, as it is their charge to act as the interface between the appropriators of capitalist SV and these labor markets, selecting the appropriate direct producers, overseeing their productive efforts, and implementing the overall strategies designed to create and realize SV:

> Management is a necessary process for industrial capitalists because in its absence they might not be able to appropriate surplus value. The reason for this begins with the market for labor power. Industrial capitalists enter that market intent upon buying what productive laborers wish to sell – namely, their labor power. Presuming that the labor power is exchanged at its value, that alone does not guarantee the production of surplus value by the capitalists. Buying labor power means only that the industrial capitalists dispose of, control, and in a sense "consume" labor power by setting it to work with equipment and raw materials. While working, the laborers may produce more or fewer commodities. Having sold their labor power for a wage payment, they may or may not work hard to produce commodities for the industrial capitalists to sell.
>
> If they do, well and good. The industrial capitalists can then focus attention on distributing surplus value elsewhere to survive competitively. However, suppose that workers, for any reason, cannot or perhaps do not wish to work hard. This worries the industrial capitalists, who know that if other industrial capitalists do have hard-working laborers and so obtain more output from them, they will be able to out compete them. Managers may solve the problem by supervising laborers to ensure that they labor at maximum intensity. The process of managing thereby becomes a condition of existence of surplus labor appropriation; it participates in overdetermining the capitalist fundamental class process.
>
> (Wolff and Resnick 1987: 195)

The transition to capitalism in China has been challenging for those individuals who moved from management positions within the state feudal bureaucracy to similar positions within newly capitalist enterprises (whether state or private). Some have risen to the challenge and others have not. The urban industrial enterprises (and conglomerates) that are typically called state-owned enterprises (SOEs) in the literature have had a particularly rough transition to capitalism. Many of these firms have struggled to meet the various claims to enterprise SV under conditions of increasingly hard budget constraints. Nevertheless, the same flexibility that exists for management to replace workers now exists for enterprise directors to replace managers. The pressure is intense for managers in these firms. They now face a market in management skills where their competitors, either from other firms or newly minted by b-schools or other academic programs, domestic and foreign, stand ready to take their place.

Once enterprises were allowed to go bankrupt, managers and directors suddenly had a stake in the production of sufficient SV to meet enterprise obligations. Intensified competition in output and input markets, especially post-WTO, provides additional motivation to managers and directors to respond with more "efficient" utilization of available labor power. Directors and senior management in urban industrial enterprises and in the rural TVEs have moved to dramatically end one of the "remnants" of the state feudal system: compensating workers with a composite of the money wage, W, plus guaranteed benefits that were carried over from the state feudal reciprocity arrangement, B. In Marxian terms, the value of labor power, V, during this transitional stage of the transition to capitalism, was $W+B$. In other words, $V=W+B$. As part of the corporatization of urban industrial enterprises, directors and senior managers were given the authority to restructure benefits provided by the enterprise to workers. This power to alter benefits, coupled with harder budget constraints and a relatively weak bargaining position for workers, has resulted in benefit reductions at virtually all urban industrial enterprises. Many of these firms have eliminated certain benefits altogether. In Marxian terms, B became optional. Over time, the result has been a fall in the value of labor power for industrial workers. Ironically, the money wage, W, may have risen at the same time that the value of labor power, V, declined. Over time, the lost benefits may be compensated for by higher money wages and some of the old benefits may eventually be provided by the state. However, the early transition to capitalist employment has, for many urban workers, resulted in a decline in the value of their labor power.

This decline has been facilitated by the aforementioned rise in rural migrant labor:

> [to] cut costs, China's state and urban collective enterprises have also been laying off workers, and in some cases have been replacing them with migrant workers from the countryside to take up positions that require little skill, performing the same job at less pay, no benefits and no security.
>
> (Chan and Zhu 2003: 3)

The transition to capitalism has also created a pool of unemployed laborers (over 10 million "surplus" employees since the reforms) willing to replace existing workers. The combined effect of unemployment and rural migrant labor power has made it easier for the restructured urban and rural enterprises to suppress wage levels and raise the rate of exploitation (Howe *et al.* 2003: 337). These conditions have been conducive to rapid rates of economic growth and high levels of FDI.

The CPC recognizes the contradiction in having a government that claims to be "socialist" orchestrating conditions that lower the value of labor power. The Labor Law was designed to set a legal minimum value of labor power as a protection for direct producers. However, it is questionable whether this "protection" is effective in halting the erosion of the value of labor power:

> In the absence of a world standard, how do we judge whether Chinese workers have been paid a "fair" wage? Here we can only use China's own legal minimum wage standards, which have been computed for different

> localities and linked to the local cost of living. In recent years the Chinese government has introduced such standards for its urban workforce and has made these minimum wages mandatory in the Labor Law. In 1997, for a forty-hour work week, the minimum standard per month for the Shenzhen Special Economic Zone was set at Y420 (US$54), Y290 (US$36) for Beijing, and Y315 (US$39) for Shanghai, a scale that in real terms is lower overall than the Vietnamese minimum wage set at US$45 in 1997, given that the cost of living in these Chinese cities is much higher than in Vietnam.
>
> (Chan 1998: 892–893)

> it becomes obvious that legal minimum wages are the lowest possible prices these governments have set to sell their workers' labor in the international labor market while maintaining their workers' physical survival. Unfortunately, this often becomes the maximum price international investors are willing to pay, or not pay if they can get away with it.
>
> (Chan 1998: 894)

Conditions for individual workers may be worse than indicated by the minimum standards set in the Labor Law. Urban industrial enterprise senior managers, as well as management in TVEs and private capitalist enterprises, have also exercised the power to lower wages *below* the legal minimum by imposing a so-called *negative efficiency wage* element, W_e. This represents a negative "bonus." The imposition of this negative wage element, W_e, makes it possible for managers in the various capitalist enterprises to lower the wage below the value of labor power, such that $W < V$:

> The wage system is constructed on a rigid system of penalties, deductions and fines. Factories devise their own sets of arbitrary rules and regulations in open breach of China's labor laws. Workers caught in violation of such rules will be fined. Fines are meted out for being late, for not showing up even in the case of illness, or for negligence at work. There can also be penalties for behavior not related to production: fines for talking and laughing at work, for loitering outside work hours, for forgetting to turn off lights, or untidy dormitories. Thus, some of the wages that a worker has earned during the month can, because of a multitude of deductions, be withheld. This system of monetary penalties induces great anxiety and uncertainty among workers. If these factories do not issue itemized payslips, the level of one's payment basically becomes a guessing game. Most factories adopt a so-called "secretive wage system" (mimi gongzi), which makes knowing a fellow worker's wages a violation that involves a penalty. This practice ensures that workers do not have a recourse for grievances or any channels for collective protests.
>
> (Chan 1998: 894)

In this way the negative efficiency wage element creates another possible avenue for raising the rate of exploitation and generating the level of SV necessary to satisfy state officials and other claimants on distributions of SV from enterprises.

Under feudalism, workers were accustomed to eight-hour work days, provision of basic subsistence, and the integration of community and recreation within the workplace sphere. However, the imperative of management in many capitalist enterprises has been to find ways to not only reduce the value of labor power (such as in the case of imposing the so-called negative efficiency wages), but also to extract even more surplus labor from productive laborers by extending the length of the working day without additional compensation – in other words to engage in super-exploitation of direct producers:

> The extremely long hours of work common in all types of Chinese enterprises pose several hazards. Workdays of 10–16 hours, six days a week, are quite common, and workdays of up to 18 hours and seven-day work weeks are frequently reported... In the toy industry, short order-delivery times during the peak season of July to October have even led to work hours of 20 hours a day, seven days a week, for several weeks at a time. Even in FIEs [foreign-invested enterprises] in the sports shoe industry, where international campaigns around "corporate codes of conduct" have been strongest, the shortest work week publicly reported is 55 hours over six days.
>
> (Brown 2003: 329)

Even the insecurities of capitalist labor power markets may be an insufficient threat to keep workers docile under these conditions. In one incident 3,000 workers protested at an electronics factory in Shenzhen over low wages and bad working conditions:

> One protester said: "Our basic salary is only 230 yuan a month. We have to work 14 hours a day, seven days a week. The compensation for overtime is only 2 yuan an hour. We can't eke out a living with such a salary." The minimum wage level in Guangdong is 574 yuan a month. Shenzhen is one of the richest cities on the mainland and the cost of living there is considerably higher than the rest of the country. "A lunchbox costs you about 12 yuan. With the salary we are getting, we can hardly feed ourselves," one worker said. Many... had suffered injuries resulting from their long working hours but had had to continue working without proper treatment as the company refused to pay medical insurance for them. "My leg was broken during an industrial accident," said one worker, showing her injuries. "But I had to carry on with my work or otherwise I would lose my job."
>
> (Chow 2004)

These may not be ideal conditions for workers, but are likely to result in a healthy quantum of SV flowing into the hands of enterprise directors. The various competing claims to enterprise SV, including from the party-state, are more likely to be satisfied under such conditions. If worker unrest can be minimized, these low cost conditions will most certainly come to the attention of transnational corporations, whose directors are more likely to approve investments, direct or indirect, in the Chinese economy under circumstances favorable to the generation of SV. In the world of global capitalist competition, lowering the unit labor costs of production has become something of a mantra, and China is increasingly viewed as the role model not only for other "industrializing" nations but also for many of the "more industrialized" nations, as well.

There is, nevertheless, a downside to this constant push for more SV, even at the expense of the well being of the working people:

> The relationships between long work hours and increased fatality and accident rates, increased work-related illnesses, and declining general health, have been increasingly recognized and studied in other industrial countries... Routine exposures to airborne chemicals, particulates, or noise that last 60–80 hours a week far exceed any regulatory limits or guidelines. Such long exposure times render meaningless the "health protective" purpose of regulatory limits. The lack of adequate "recovery time" for body metabolisms to excrete contaminants, which is the basis for setting permissible exposure levels, as well as the impact of cumulative and synergistic effects, means that adverse health effects from such lengthy exposure times are highly probable.
>
> (Brown 2003: 329)

In addition, many rural migrant laborers must accept factory supplied housing and meals of questionable quality:

> Tens of thousands of tonnes of spoiled, sometimes mouldy, rice is being sold to feed construction workers on the mainland every year. Its low price has made the spoiled rice so popular that in most main grain and oil markets in the capital it is known as "migrant workers' rice." The owner of one rice store at Beijing's Liulitun Bulk Grain and Oil Market said many migrant workers' labour contractors – who act as middlemen between the labourers and construction firms – traveled long distances to buy the stale rice. "It has been sold for years and no complaint has ever been heard," the supplier said.
>
> Migrant workers in Beijing, who are often fed the old grain, said their top priority was satisfying their hunger. Li Jun, 29, from Xingtai in Hebei province, said: "The food here is okay but it tastes far worse than at home. But we are allowed to eat as much as we wish, especially for lunch, so I am not concerned." Mr Li's lunch was a large bowl of yellowish rice along with a small portion of green pepper and tofu. He pays 5 yuan of his 35-yuan daily income to his labour contractor for the food and works a 12-hour day. Nutritionists warn that stale rice, usually mixed with mouldy grain, can cause serious health problems.

> "Aspergillus flavus, a common bacteria strain that can be often found in stale rice, has caused lung and kidney cancers in laboratory mice as quickly as in 24 weeks," said Professor He Jiguo, from China Agriculture University's College of Food Science and Nutritional Engineering. "Other bacteria commonly found in stale grain can cause diarrhoea, vomiting, or even damage to the blood and nervous system. At the very least, stale rice is less nutritious and can lead to malnutrition."
>
> (*South China Morning Post* 2004)

The competitive pressures for urban industrial enterprises and other capitalist enterprises in their pursuit of increasing flows of SV have resulted in the lack of safety precautions for direct producers. This is jeopardizing not only direct producers' abilities to meet subsistence out of a diminishing wage, but also their very existence as a living human being:

> Lack of hazard evaluation, which extends to safety issues such as machine guarding, electrical safety, and fire prevention, has logically resulted in limited efforts to control workplace risks to life and limb. Most such efforts have occurred only after catastrophic accidents resulting in multiple worker deaths and substantial property losses. But even in the mining sector, where as many as 10,000 miners are killed a year, scandal-generated efforts by government mine safety agencies to enforce existing regulations have failed to significantly reduce the well-known causes of explosions, roof falls, and floods.
>
> (Brown 2003: 326)

For many enterprise managers, it makes more sense to pay for individual direct producers' injuries than to pay the cost of installing safeguards throughout the workplace, which would diminish receipts of SV:

> Local authorities have been quoted in the Chinese media as explaining that regulations would not be implemented for fear that foreign and domestic investors would simply relocate their facilities to other sites in China where regulations were known to be unenforced. With the explosive growth of village and township enterprises, local authorities also have a direct financial stake – taxes, fees and illegal bribes – in the enterprises that they are supposed to be regulating.
>
> (Brown 2003: 332)

Thus, as the Chinese variant of capitalism keeps the value of labor power under constant pressure, this system has also produced nightmarish working conditions:

> Equally horrendous is the high incidence of severed limbs at some of the worst factories. In a factory in Ningbo City thirty workers in the space of one year had their fingers, hands, or arms chopped off. The factory had drawn up

a compensation "price" list: for death or both hands chopped off – Y15,000 (US$1600); per thumb – Y3000; one little finger – Y750. In a cutlery factory in Xiamen, Fujian Province, that employs 600 workers, 142 workers were maimed over a period of four years. Such examples make all too convincing the argument that labor rights need to be recognized as an elemental and vital form of human rights.

(Chan 1998: 897)

The suppression of wages and benefits is an outcome of the same social processes as is the suppression of the "human rights" of workers. These are all products of a social structure within which workers have limited or no access to those institutions generating the political, economic, and cultural influences shaping the new capitalist economy. They have no right to collective bargaining, no political control over the party-state, no access to the major media, or any other formal means of altering these conditions. In the meanwhile, there is, at minimum, close cooperation and collusion between public policy makers and SV appropriators. In many instances, these two social positions are held by a single superorganic agency comprised of government officials.

Nevertheless, the forces shaping the suppression of the value of labor power and creating working conditions like those described above generates contradictions. Reproduction of labor power markets is but one of the conditions of existence of capitalism, but it is critical to capitalism's survival. The social processes that have been compatible with relatively low wages and unpleasant working conditions may already be having negative effects on reproducing labor power markets in some areas of China. The shortsightedness of enterprise managers in the pursuit of increased SV realization may be a factor in producing shortages of labor power in certain development zones of southern China which are dominated by the export sector which relies heavily on relatively cheap labor:

> Despite China's army of surplus labor, some manufacturers are struggling to find workers as rural migrants begin to shun low pay and poor working conditions, . . . Foreign companies flooding into China have counted on what was believed to be a nearly inexhaustible pool of young workers from the countryside eager to take low-paying factory jobs that still pay far more than they could earn back home . . . But even poor migrants from the countryside have their limits, and in recent months, some manufacturers have been struggling to keep jobs filled . . . Manufacturers . . . often try to poach workers from competing companies. Some are cutting production or refusing orders they cannot fill . . . The most noticeable shortages are among women aged 18–25, who are often needed to work in toy, shoe, textile and electronics factories . . . Recent government policies aimed at boosting rural incomes and abolishing farm taxes are improving living standards in the countryside have helped, and many workers apparently are no longer desperate enough to accept very low pay or miserable working conditions.
>
> (Kurtenbach 2004)

These processes may be the result of wages falling below the value of labor power. On the other hand, these labor power shortages may be temporary. Capitalism is still new in China and the process of enculturating individuals to seek employment in labor power markets is unevenly developed and, in some areas, still relatively weak. Over time these labor power bottlenecks may disappear, as cultural and other processes change the consciousness of direct producers such that the value of labor power moves into line with these relatively low wages and benefits. This remains to be seen. In any event, these developments may represent a warning to the CPC that the modernization program could be derailed by the conditions of super-exploitation they have fostered. The central authorities are not unmoved by these conditions and have taken actions to rectify the situation:

> The Ministry of Labor and Social Security has announced a string of measures aimed at improving conditions for millions of farmer-workers currently laboring in cities. The measures include asking companies to abolish all limitations and unreasonable fees on these workers seeking employment. Public consultation organizations are also being urged to offer services to farmer-workers free of charge. Local governments should also draw up professional training and education plans for these workers. Around 100 million farmer-workers currently work in cities, mainly in the construction, catering and manufacturing sectors. They have become a major driving force behind China's urban development.
>
> (Xinhuanet 2004)

In the long term, if the party-state, perhaps influenced by its own "socialist" rhetoric, took actions to raise the value of labor power and compel enterprises to improve work environments, then the result could be higher levels of domestic aggregate demand. The Chinese economy may eventually reach the limits of export-led growth, after all. The growth in the domestic economy may be a necessary, if not sufficient, condition for continued economic growth and movements up the technological ladder that is so important to the modernist leadership. Such a development might, ironically, benefit many of the enterprises wherein workers are currently experiencing unhealthy working conditions and low wages and benefits. A wage-led growth public policy approach might stimulate more sales for many of these firms and result in the realization of more SV. Those that have publicly traded stock could see their market value rise, as portfolio investors recognize the long-term benefits of a growing domestic market. Higher market values for Chinese firms and optimism about the Chinese economy could attract even more foreign investment, both portfolio and direct. Thus, minimum wage enforcement and upward pressure on wages, in general, might be just what Chinese capitalism needs. When viewed in this context, even a movement toward independent labor unions could have a positive impact on long-term economic growth, as well as support the reproduction of Chinese capitalism.

The capitalist's burden: labor unrest and unionization

> Our labor relations are going back in time, back to the early days of the industrial revolution in 19th-century Europe. Many of the enterprises set up with investment from Asian companies, along with privately-owned Chinese enterprises, have reduced working conditions to a situation comparable to the initial period of capital accumulation that accompanied the appearance of capitalism. Forcing workers to labor long hours for very low wages and even workers signing "life and death" contracts with employers.
>
> (Han Zhili, director of a citizen's rights center, interviewed by an official newspaper of China's Department of Labor and Social Security in 2001, cited from Brown 2003: 326)

Workers have not been completely passive in the face of traumatic changes to their working and living conditions. The breaking of state feudal bonds and the transition to capitalist class processes has, for the most part, gone rather smoothly. However, there have been protests from direct producers:

> In 1992 there were some five hundred strikes involving hundreds of thousands of workers... In the first half of 1997 labor disputes soared by 59 percent compared to the same period in 1996. In March 1997 some of the "worst labour unrest since the 1949 Communist revolution" took place in the city of Nanchong in Sichuan Province. More than 20,000 workers from a silk factory marched through the streets to protest the fact that they hadn't been paid in six months. The workers took their manager hostage... then paraded him through the streets in the rain. This happened when they learned that the same manager who had not paid them in six months was preparing to leave on an "official" inspection tour of Thailand at company expense.
>
> (Weston 2000: 260–261)

There has been a long history of worker protests and organizing within China. As Hart-Landsberg and Burkett note:

> Given this history, it should not be surprising that workers have, with increasing energy and determination, protested against the negative social consequences of capitalist restoration. A case in point: beginning in 1979, workers sought to use the openings created by the Democracy Wall Movement (1978–81) to express their opposition to Deng's reform process.
>
> (2004: 70)

The Democracy Wall Movement was an expression of concerns and dissatisfaction of workers with the *Four Modernizations* program. It began in Beijing with the posting of big-character posters on a roadside wall near Tiananmen

Square and the circulation of unofficial journals critical of Deng Xiaoping's administration and reforms:

> Unfavourable comparisons of China with the capitalist West were common during Democracy Wall and later in the 1980s, although this did not mean that activists were uncritical of the West either. Doubts clearly existed about the "superiority of socialism" and specifically about workers' position in society, since they were supposed to be "the masters," yet in most cases had a very low standard of living. Questions along these lines required the authorities to demonstrate the advantages workers enjoyed under socialism, especially the right to participate in management and to elect democratically some of the enterprise leadership. These comparisons and criticisms of China therefore helped to increase pressure for real democratization of management, as well as for more obvious remedies such as price stabilization and improved housing and welfare.
>
> (Sheehan 1998: 159)

On the one hand, the general perception that the "West" was further along the teleological path to "advanced" forces of production supported the modernist Marxist contingent within the CPC in its contest with the Maoists over future public policy. If China was to "advance" then something needed to change. On the other hand, the same cultural processes used to communicate Chinese "backwardness" were deployed to expose the contradiction of "socialism" – understood as a system fostering the rise of worker hegemony within the workplace – in a context where Chinese workers were being exploited. The latter contradiction presented a problem for the modernists. Deng and other modernist reformers, while initially supporting the Democracy Wall Movement as a means of criticizing the Cultural Revolution and the Gang of Four, soon realized that the movement was being used to criticize their policies. A gradual process of suppression and intimidation followed to suppress public protest over the reform program. However, the movement did not die, but helped to shape the "Democracy Movement" that was exposed to the whole world in 1989 when workers not only allied with students in protest over corruption, pro-capitalist reforms, and the absence of genuine democratic processes, but also formed independent trade unions called Autonomous Worker Federations (Hart-Landsberg and Burkett 2004: 71). However, this attempt to create independent labor unions was outlawed following the Tiananmen Square incident and the modernist Marxian leadership has repeatedly arrested independent labor union organizers and passed laws to prohibit the formation of independent unions.

The current leadership has repeatedly demonstrated that "modernization" is the overriding priority for the party-state and neither democracy nor worker rights is understood as elements in this modernization. The modernist Marxists in the leadership are steadfast in their technological determinism: modernization is narrowly defined as the diffusion of "advanced" technology and, although some forms of soft technology (the blueprint for social relationships) are included in this determinism, the choices of which technologies are "advanced" appears to be quite opportunistic. Forms of social organization, such as independent labor unions or processes by which the top leadership in government might be replaced by popular voting, that represent a potential threat to CPC hegemony over politics are excluded from the set of desired technologies.

Perhaps this is the leadership's way of resolving several contradictions: the perception that more worker democracy is incompatible with rapid economic growth and technological transformation, the belief that the CPC is uniquely positioned to move the Chinese social formation forward along the technologically defined teleological path, and the orthodox Marxian belief that capitalism is a necessary stage in this teleological path. The contradiction in this last condition is that it becomes necessary for a communist party to create capitalism in order to move the Chinese social formation closer to communism. Since all of these contradictions can be drawn out of orthodox Marxian thought, the current process of transforming the technological base of the Chinese social formation, including the diffusion of capitalist exploitation, to more closely match the hard and soft technologies deployed within the OECD nations is well within the intellectual universe of pro-Marxian public policies. In other words, the CPC did not need to abandon, nor has it abandoned, the primacy of Marxian theory as ideological foundation for the party-state's actions.

The advance of capitalism and the technological determinism (the forces of production drive the movement along the teleological path to communism) at the core of modernist Marxist public policy has generated a very fundamental contradiction. The labor power market presents wage laborers with the problem of bargaining with more powerful institutional structures. Absent an antiunion enculturation, it would seem quite obvious to many wage laborers that their inferior bargaining position would be strengthened through some form of collective representation. The party-state, on the other hand, does not want to relinquish its current hegemonic control over the "representation" of workers. This is perceived as a critical component in generating the increasing amounts of SV required to purchase and innovate the desired technologies. Given that much of the desired technology is only available as imports from the "West," then a substantial percentage of this SV must be realized in hard currency. The modernist leadership appears only mildly concerned that their priorities and the approach taken to achieve them have led to negative consequences for working people. The perception by working people that they are unrepresented is, however, a problem for the CPC. It is a delegitimizing force in the social formation. Worker protests can only exacerbate this problem, communicating to a wider population that, despite the rhetoric of being a "vanguard party of the working classes," the CPC has become an elite holding onto a monopoly in political power and supported by other elites, both domestic and foreign.

It may eventually become necessary for the CPC to support independent labor unions to reduce the level of tensions created by the transition to capitalism and the growing perception of a general alienation of the party from the people it is supposed to serve. That being said, it should be noted that the formation of independent labor unions does not necessarily guarantee struggle against conditions under which direct producers' surplus labor is extracted or even that the level of exploitation will be moderated. It is even possible that independent unions might be approved under conditions that make them only mildly less accommodationist than the All-China Federation of Trade Unions (ACFTU), which is, for all intents and purposes, a subsidiary operation of the state bureaucracy:

> There was no autonomous occupational power, and trade unions were under the leadership of the ruling Communist Party, co-operating with the government and workplace management to control rather than serve workers... Attempts by early leaders of All-China Federation of Trade Unions (ACFTU) to define for the trade union a more independent and pro-worker role were attacked... Trade unions were disbanded in 1967 and not formally reconstituted until 1974.
>
> (Lee 2000: 6)

It is interesting to note that the resurrection of the ACFTU in 1974 came as a consequence of worker protests. However, bringing back a disciplined ACFTU was only a cosmetic way of addressing worker concerns. Direct producers' often complain that the "union" does not act on their behalf:

> Workers described their official representatives as "sign-board unions"... unions in name only, who did nothing for them, did not represent their views (or even know what their views were), did not stand up to the party committee or management on their behalf, and did not hold regular meetings in some cases...
>
> (Sheehan 1998: 165)

As it exists today, the ACFTU remains a government union – it is an intermediary between central government and enterprises, rather than a representative of workers. The ACFTU is an example of a collaborationist trade union. And while direct producers are only allowed this one choice of "representation," capitalists are allowed the freedom of forming many representative assemblies:

> Furthermore, it should be noted that as China's employers set up their organizations – including, for instance, nationwide employers' organizations, and associations such as the Association of Foreign Investment Enterprises, the Association of Privately Owned Enterprises, the Chinese Association of Entrepreneurs, and so on – they were not organized along the lines of a principle of uniformity or even unity; instead, these associations were organized in a very pluralistic and diversified way. From the point of view of the law, the contrast between the pluralism and diversity in employers' organizations and the unity, uniformity, and integration of China's labor union organization constitutes a kind of inequality of rights in China's labor–capital relations.
>
> (Chang 2001: 76)

Capitalist enterprises have interventionist representation to work for changes in the political economy that will enhance their ability to expand production and SV extraction, as well as elaborate links to political, economic, and cultural institutions via distributive flows of SV, and to gain even greater leverage in labor power market negotiations with workers. Direct producers have no such channels of influence.

At present, the modernist leadership opposes independent unions, perhaps under the assumption that such institutions would drive up the value of labor power and force costly improvements in working conditions, threatening the current level of economic growth and the "modernization" plans this growth is financing:

> China's entrance into the World Trade Organization (WTO) signifies that China is making direct connections with the international market economy, . . . To enter into this market, one must obey the rules of the game that were formed and ratified over hundreds of years by the capitalist nations. This is what is meant by "making direct connection with" the market economy . . . The WTO has had an undeniably positive impact on the realization of the market economy and free trade on a global scale. Such a drive has as its goal and means the expansion of capitalism, however, and, lest we forget, the direct demands of the expansion of capitalism are suppression and exploitation of labor.
>
> (Chang 2001: 57–59)

If the modernist leadership is not successful at suppressing direct producers and raising the rate of exploitation, global capital may decide to reallocate production and technology transfer to other sites where the value of labor power is lower. This is no minor matter as

> among the foreign capitalists investing in China, the ratio represented by multinational corporations and international financial groups has been rising and is continuing to increase. To date, more than half of the 500 major corporations around the world (the global Fortune 500) have already set up subsidiary enterprises or branch offices in China.
>
> (Chang 2001: 62)

The modernist leadership of the CPC depends on FDI from these global capitalist enterprises as one of the sources of hard currency for purchasing hard and soft technology, for providing "political currency" in negotiations with other countries in accessing this technology and capital, and to provide shares of SV to all levels of the state, to the "new social strata," and to a wide range of private firms that are becoming increasingly important employers. To a significant extent, the genie is out of the bottle and the Chinese government has become, like so many other social formations, dependent on the global capitalist system:

> out of a need to make economic development and growth the primary goal of their political agenda and governmental programs, governments around the world have, very naturally and almost as a matter of logical consequence, cozied up to capitalism and have supported and nurtured its growth. As a result, these governments have sacrificed their status as impartial and just arbiters – "honest brokers" – in labor–capital relations. Instead, the phenomena of "governments joined with merchants," "government officials in bed with capitalists," and even "a unity of government and business interests" have appeared in many countries and regions of the world. The pursuit of developing the economy by sacrificing the interests of the working class has implicitly become a starting point for many government policies. One of the primary means by which governments implement such a policy is the formulation or revision of labor legislation to limit the rights of labor unions and workers.
>
> (Chang 2001: 60)

Unfavorable labor laws, including those against labor demonstrations and media coverage of such events, have made unionization and other attempts to organize labor difficult. However, more recently, domestic and international pressure has contributed to the passage of minimum wage laws and workplace regulations such as the ratification of Articles 33, 34, and 35 of the Labour Law which, while placing "limitations on collective bargaining as practised in industrialized countries, confirmed government policy on collective bargaining" (You 1998: 147). In other words, under current labor laws workers have the right to collective bargaining.

However, in addition to not having independent labor unions to represent them in collective bargaining, Zhou Changzheng argues the Labor Law regarding collective bargaining is vague and

> lacks operational significance and practicality . . . Notably, the Labor Law merely stipulates that workers "may" sign collective contracts with the enterprises in which they are employed. The language here implies ability or possibility, not "right." In terms of legal interpretation, "may" would connote a certain arbitrary right. In other words, the party involved "can" act in a certain way or adopt a certain form of behavior, but, equally, may not. Does this then imply that the workers have the option whether to sign a collective contract or not? Or, conversely, does the enterprise also have the option of whether to accept the workers' demand for signing a collective contract, or to reject the demand? Our Labor Law does not have any clear, firm provision in regard to this question.
>
> (2001: 39)

The struggle over the rules of the capitalist labor market are reflected, in part, in the content, including the specific language, of laws, such as Labor Law, in the mode of enforcement of these laws, and in popular understanding of the meaning of these laws. At the end of the day, the qualitative nature of the impact of specific laws on practices that constitute capitalist labor power markets, including the nature of worker representation in collective bargaining, is not an objective phenomenon. Once created, labor power markets – the site where wage laborers engage the management of capitalist firms in a social dance that shapes the quality of their and their families' lives – are the locus not only of laws but of the cultural processes that shape interpretations of these laws. Capitalism, like all social systems, reshapes the meaning of everything, including those laws which arise out of its structural dynamics.

Class consciousness: creating a good capitalist wage laborer

Although incidences of worker protests have risen and there is a grassroots movement in favor of independent labor unions, the participants in these movements represent a small minority of the hundreds of millions of workers who participate every day in their own exploitation. The transition to capitalism has been relatively smooth in China, precisely because worker resistance to selling their labor power in the market has been relatively minimal. This seems to be the case even in rural China, where many direct producers in the countryside had turned to the ancient class process (productive self-employment) when given the opportunity under the early reforms. Productive self-employment was a mode of work and life that had long been an aspiration of rural workers, even before the 1949 revolution. The consciousness of an ancient farmer or artisan is not entirely compatible with either feudal or capitalist exploitation. One could expect the transition to capitalism to be relatively difficult for those with such a consciousness. This may even be the case. China's rural population makes up a sizable percentage of the world's population, so it does not take a massive surge into the labor power markets to create large numbers of available wage laborers. On the other hand, the consciousness that is compatible with feudal exploitation may be more compatible with capitalism. The communes taught direct producers to subsume individual creativity and plans to the demands of a larger institution. It taught obedience. These are traits that are desirable in capitalism. However, perhaps the state feudal period in China did not last long enough to leave a deep cultural imprint upon the consciousness of direct producers. Or perhaps the reciprocity aspects of feudal enculturation may produce worker reaction against the norm in capitalism wherein workers in relatively weak bargaining position are unlikely to receive much, if any, non-wage benefits from employment and the wage itself is likely to be relatively low. The interaction of these influences upon Chinese workers with the conditions of capitalist labor power markets and the capitalist workplace are the initial conditions of the new capitalist social formation that has emerged out of the transition. It will take time for capitalist enculturation to become dominant within the consciousness of the vast majority of workers. This is one of the conditions of the transition, part of its unevenness. Nevertheless, the transition to capitalist enculturation is being carried out (again, in an uneven manner) throughout the cultural institutions in China, such as within schools, the mass media, and popular discourse.

The orthodox Marxian argument that "class consciousness" would be produced within workers as they toiled alongside each other within capitalist worksites may, in fact, be correct, but only in an ironic sense. Workers do not necessarily develop a sense of solidarity with other workers and a notion that the collective of workers could produce more social value if freed from the constraints of serving external masters, in the form of capitalist appropriators and their various agents. This traditional notion of class consciousness does not seem typical of capitalist social formations. Capitalist wage laborers do not seem more prone to revolt the older the capitalist structure within which they work. Social formations that are dominated by capitalist exploitation appear, over time, more likely to develop ideologies and social processes compatible with the underlying prevalent class process. This overdetermines enculturation. Over time, in capitalist social formations, workers have seemed less and less conscious of their exploitation. The real test of Chinese capitalism may be the degree to which a social formation dominated by Marxian theory can generate a reaction where, as Wolff and Resnick (1987: 171) put it, "workers may simply accept doing more unpaid labor. They may even accept ideas and arguments that disguise their growing exploitation."

This takes us back to an earlier point about enculturation. The very process by which workers are changed into consumers, where personal identity becomes intertwined with the specific bundle of commodities possessed, where work is seen only as means to acquisition of such commodities (as it is within the neo-classical parables), is one in which consciousness of class is obliterated and exploitation normalized.

The capitalist class process shapes identity of Chinese direct producers in many ways – such as urban worker versus rural migrant laborer, female worker versus male worker. It also shapes the direct producer's analysis of her abilities and capabilities as an aspect of her identity in the capitalist class process:

> Workers knowledge of technology and the complete production process is limited so that they can not fully replicate the whole of the production process of a specific use value . . . In this situation it becomes impossible (or rhetorical) to raise the traditional revolutionary question: "What do we need the bosses for anyway?" The capitalist as *parasite* – as mere owner – is now disguised innocently as "management." It is the host of managers, engineers, supervisory personnel, planners, etc. – not the average workers – who now appear necessary and essential to the productive process . . . In this situation the prospect of workers' control – which is *the* socialist project in the workplace – appears faint indeed.
>
> (Ehrenreich, J. and B. 1976: 12)

The institution of disciplinary regimes in enterprises, the racism and sexism which divides direct producers in their social interactions, the depredation of health and safety, the desperate need to eke out a subsistence – all these cultural, political, economic, and environmental influences and more come together to shape a certain passivity on the part of many Chinese direct producers in their struggle to survive:

> to the extent that work has been degraded and de-collectivized, stripped of intellectual and social satisfactions – to the extent the basic contradiction of capitalism, the contradiction between the social nature of work and the private purposes of production, is muted, disguised, and for all practical purposes, liquidated. The "large socialized workplaces" which were supposed to generate the "gravediggers of capitalism" themselves become graveyards for human energy and aspirations.
>
> (Ehrenreich, J. and B. 1976: 14)

Capitalism... the end of history?

The neoclassical theoretical framework begins with the humanist notion that all history is ultimately the product of individual human beings making free (completely autonomous) choices in an environment of absolute equality (a romantic utopian notion of society). In this context, the buying and selling of labor (not labor power) is as natural as the buying and selling of knickknacks on eBay. The absence, within the neoclassical framework, of any conceptualization of class processes, allows the richness of modes of organizing labor power to collapse into a stark, if romantic, simplicity. Ironically, the technological determinism of the modernist Marxist leadership has led them to adopt many of the theoretical tools of the humanist and romanticist neoclassicalism. Chinese students make the pilgrimage to "Western" economic programs to learn these tools and to transport them back to China in the service of the modernist vision. This is not so surprising when one considers that the neoclassical framework is the ultimate cultural justification for capitalism and the modernists have been unambiguous in their public policy efforts to expand the growth of capitalist labor power markets in China and to connect the burgeoning Chinese capitalism to global capitalism. Capitalism and the growth of labor power markets fit neatly into the modernist teleology. Another irony is that the neoclassical paradigm is no less teleological than the modernist Marxist paradigm. However, within the neoclassical theory, this intermediary stage of labor power markets represents the end of history. Capitalism is the telos. Thus, the paradigm within which capitalism is telos and the paradigm within which capitalism is a way station on the way to telos converge and become compatible in the present moment.

As many analysts such as Li Yongjie argue:

> Labor relations in China are now undergoing an institutional transition from a planned economy to a market economy. This transition is based on the fact that a market economy can coordinate the interests of the subjects of labor relations and realize the optimal allocation of human resources more efficiently and with lower transactional costs and better economic results.
>
> (2000: 29)

These reforms were implemented under the assumption that the flexibility that comes with the capitalist labor allocation system (allocation within labor power markets) must be somehow fundamentally more efficient than the labor allocation system that prevailed under state feudalism. In other words, and in the specific case of China, it has been assumed, all other things being equal, that this revolutionary change in class processes would generate and will continue to generate more surplus for Chinese economic growth and development than would be possible under the old system. A new land of superhighways, airports, and yuppies with cell phones is sufficient evidence for those following the modernist logic: how else could these wonderful developments be possible other than through the structural transformation that has included capitalist social relations? The teleological narrative that economic growth and development follows a particular trajectory has been reinforced, despite the apparent oscillation of Chinese society between private and state feudalisms, punctuated by ancientism and different degrees of private and state capitalism. Ironically, it is the rhetoric of modernist Marxism, with its shift away from class analysis, that has provided an important smokescreen in obfuscating this oscillation and blocking the advance of an argument against the teleology that contributes to a failure to analyze transitions in an unprejudiced (by a rigid presupposed teleological path) analysis. Having said this, the modernist Marxist diversion has also obfuscated the similarities with other transitions from feudalism to capitalism, in particular the Meiji Restoration in Japan, which has striking parallels to the transition in China.

At the end of the day, the question must be asked of whether capitalist labor power markets are the best way to allocate labor power and to motivate labor? In China, as elsewhere, it does appear to have resulted in more rapid economic growth (measured in terms of GDP) but does this imply that capitalism is necessarily the most dynamic system in generating surplus labor? This is a more problematic claim, since one of the characteristics of the state feudal system in China was the elaborate internal channels of surplus distribution. Surplus may not have flowed to the sorts of uses favored by the modernist influenced CPC leaders, but there was a great deal of surplus consumed during the state feudal period, enough to provide for a massive state bureaucracy, full employment, and a social welfare system that virtually eliminated relative poverty. Nevertheless, there is no question that the capitalist labor power market provides incentives to workers to be more productive. But was this sufficient to claim that capitalist labor power markets were the best form of labor power allocation system? It is clear that nonexploitative modes of labor deployment were not given much of test. The only case where such nonexploitative class processes were allowed to flourish – the ancient class process in rural China – proved to be quite effective in generating economic growth, even if not the tax revenues desired by the CPC leadership. In any event, modernist dominance within the CPC has short-circuited debate over the relative merits of capitalist and other exploitative modes of organizing labor versus nonexploitative forms, such as the ancient or the untested communist approach.

4 State capitalism in rural China

The case of the TVEs

This chapter focuses on TVEs and their relationship to community governments (townships and villages). TVEs are sites of SV production within capitalist class structures. These enterprises are capitalist for two reasons. First, the SV produced within these sites is not appropriated by the direct producers. Second, the labor power of these direct producers is purchased under the conditions of a capitalist labor power market.

As was demonstrated in Chapter 3, the creation and expansion of a capitalist labor power market was the consequence of post-1978 economic reforms. In 1985, the feudal commune structure was dismantled. County, township, and village governments replaced the communes as the local manifestation of state power. The industrial enterprises within the communes (former commune and brigade enterprises) became TVEs (also referred to as "collectively owned enterprises"). As part of the decentralization of surplus appropriation, township and village governments (referred to herein as community governments) took control of the assets of the TVEs and were granted the right of appropriation of SV generated within the TVEs under their jurisdiction. Local officials who had been agents subsumed within the feudal hierarchy, ultimately serving the State Council, graduated into these fundamental appropriator positions: "Reassignment of property rights to local jurisdictions . . . increases the financial power of local officials, thus making them look more like 'principals' than 'agents' of public assets as compared to their previous status" (Lin 2001: 15–16). The decision to transfer these assets and powers to the community governments may have been partly shaped by the central government's desire to gain the cooperation of local officials in the continuing reform process: "Rather than be undermined by economic reform, local officials had the option of leading growth in the countryside by directing local government-owned enterprises" (Oi 1999: 74). However, another related and perhaps stronger reason is that party officials at these local levels had strongly supported the rise of the modernists and the downfall of the Maoists, perhaps in part because of the negative effects of the GLF and the GPCR on local communities. In a sense, the rise of the reformers within the CPC was the political equivalent of the Magna Carta in England with the center having been successfully pressured to decentralize authority on a large scale. Thus, in the transition from feudalism to capitalism in the countryside, community government officials emerged as principals in the new capitalist structure, empowered with control over an extensive array of economic assets and direct producers, with the de facto right of appropriation and first distribution of the SV generated within multiple production sites.

To reinforce the connection between the TVEs and their community governments, the TVEs have a codified obligation to support community governments with taxes and other distributions from enterprise SV: "TVEs have to pay various fees, penalties and contributions that go beyond regular taxes and contributions based on the TVE Law and other national regulations" (OECD 2002: 91). On the other hand, the community governments provide a wide range of support for TVE SV generation, including special access to public resources and loans. The mode of interaction between TVEs and other social institutions within the rural community is mediated by the political power of the community governments and the potential for the community governments to intervene on behalf of its affiliated TVEs.

This intertwining of state power with capitalist exploitation has not gone unnoticed by private capitalist enterprises in the rural communities. Since the initial creation of TVEs, some private capitalist firms (that had never been commune and brigade enterprises) have been able to obtain legal classification as TVEs. In return, the community governments received distributive payments (in excess of normal tax obligations) out of the SV of these private capitalist firms amounting to "1–2 percent of the firm's output value or 5–10 percent of its turnover." (Liu, Yingqiu 2003: 4). These firms, described in the literature as "red hat" TVEs, sought this designation to obtain some of the social benefits that come with the TVE designation. Private capitalists, without the TVE designation, have experienced political and economic discrimination: government officials often make it more difficult for them to obtain licenses or to gain access to electricity, telephone service, or other state provided infrastructure (at least at the desired level of service) and tax authorities tend to devote considerably more attention to their financial statements and other documents critical to determining the level of appropriate taxation. TVE status tends to result in better treatment from those same government officials. Given the decentralization of many powers to local authorities in the post-state feudal environment, obtaining TVE status may be a way for private capitalists to formalize the payment of "protection" to community governments. In other words, their "purchase" of TVE status, and ongoing distributive class relationship with the community governments, may not only reduce the level of discriminatory treatment in accessing resources, but may also reduce the possibility of extralegal harassment by various community government agents.

However, most TVEs are not private but instead *state* capitalist enterprises:

> What defines state as opposed to private forms of capitalism is the social location of surplus appropriating enterprises, and the connection of appropriating individuals to the state.... In state capitalism, individuals with a necessary connection to the state – employed and selected by the state – exploit labor in enterprises that occupy locations within the state apparatus.
>
> (Resnick and Wolff 2002: 87)

The relationship between community governments and affiliated (non-"red hat") TVEs within their jurisdiction clearly constitutes a form of state capitalism. Community governments are linked to the surpluses of these TVEs via not only distributive but also fundamental class relationships: "[township and village] governments have residual claimant rights over [the] enterprise profits" of TVEs (Edin 1998: 101). The community government is the location of the appropriation and first distribution of the SV generated within each and every affiliated TVE situated within its jurisdiction. The Marxian concept of the enterprise as the social space(s) within which the entire fundamental class process (production and appropriation of the surplus) occurs leads to the conclusion that the community government and these TVEs constitute a singular state capitalist enterprise (or conglomerate). Thus, TVEs and community governments represent one unified business entity with TVEs as subsidiaries. This state capitalist conglomeration is herein referred to as a rural state capitalist enterprise (RSCE). These RSCEs dominate industrial production in the Chinese countryside. Therefore, industrial production in rural China can be described as state capitalist, in class terms.

The relationship between community governments and TVEs in this RSCE bear certain *similarities* to that between the board of directors and various subsidiaries in a corporate structure. Perhaps this is why some social analysts have described either the community governments or the community government–TVE nexus as corporate entities. Nevertheless, other social analysts find fault with the conception of community government and its TVEs as a corporate entity. Susan Whiting (2001) gives three reasons that the community government relationship with TVEs should not be understood in this way. First, community government officials are "political leaders" pursuing "sociopolitical as well as economic goals." Second, the community government receives payments from the TVEs that are not simply "profit remittances." Whiting points out that the community government "also received an array of legally mandated fees and illegal exactions…" Third, the community government provided protection to the TVEs against bankruptcy – soft budget constraints (Whiting 2001: 121). Jean Oi, on the other hand, described the community government–TVE nexus as "local state corporatism," although for her

> [the] county is at the top of the corporate hierarchy, corresponding to corporate headquarters; the townships are the regional headquarters; and the villages are the companies within the larger corporation. Each level is the approximate equivalent of what is termed a "profit center" in decentralized management schemes used in business firms. Each successive level of government is fiscally independent and is thus expected to maximize its economic performance.
>
> (1999: 102)

And Che and Qian conceive of the entire local community as the corporate entity: "[C]ommunity residents are the major beneficiaries of the firm, the community government serves as both the board of directors and management at the firm's headquarters, and individual TVEs are separate divisions, branches or subsidiaries within the firm" (Che and Qian 1998: 8). This is all somewhat a game of semantics. Technically speaking, any entity is a corporation if it is incorporated as such. In other words, the corporate designation is legally/politically defined, rather than an economic designation. And, as for profit, it is an accounting convention, not an "objective" reality.

However, this is not the point of the debate. The term "corporation" is a proxy for other terms (or concerns). For example, Whiting's three reasons for opposing the corporate designation seem related to the standard neoclassical essentialism about business firms: in this neoclassical conception the firm is a profit maximizing entity within which sociopolitical objectives do not exist and the firm receives no favoritism from governments, banks, or other institutions that might mitigate negative cash flows (absolutely hard budget constraints prevail). In the real world, not only do corporations come in both for profit and not-for-profit flavors, but even the boards of directors of *capitalist* corporations have been known to include sociopolitical goals within their corporate strategies, place gaining market share and other economic objectives above profit maximization, receive cash flow from a wide range of sources, and secure special relationships with governments, banks, and other institutions that soften their budget constraints. Whiting is not the only theorist to essentialize the profit motive as a defining characteristic of business enterprises, in general, or capitalist enterprises, in particular. This is quite common, even among many Marxian theorists. This form of essentialism would seem to indicate that the modal business entity is Ebenezer Scrooge before the three ghosts visited him. After his experience with the ghosts Scrooge's priorities changed. He started to consider other objectives than profit maximization. In Whiting's terms, he ceased to be a corporate/enterprise/business entity. Of course, this is unrealistic, as anyone who has been involved in the corporate or business world can tell you. The Ebenezer Scrooges are quite rare in the business world, whether the underlying business is centered in capitalist exploitation or productive self-employment. Gibson-Graham and O'Neill (2001) make this quite clear in an excellent case study of the steel division of Broken Hill Proprietary (BHP), one of Australia's largest industrial corporations, where the intersection of internal struggles within BHP interacting with external struggles to influence BHP policies resulted in a change in this corporation's business strategy and priorities. The shaping of corporate priorities is not simply a matter of lining up those activities most conducive to profit maximization and then proceeding from there. The lines between business and the processes of national and/or local government have always been a bit fuzzy. In the United States, for many a model of modernity, it is not uncommon for the same individuals who sit on corporate boards of directors to also serve either in advisory capacities to government officials or even to head up commissions charged with developing sociopolitical strategies for the government. Throughout US history there have been prominent corporations whose close ties to the US government are conditions for their boards of directors' ability to appropriate and distribute capitalist SV.

A recent prominent example is Halliburton, whose close ties to top federal government political leaders, including the president and vice president, and related government contracts may have saved the firm from bankruptcy or, at a minimum, reduced the impact of asbestos-related law suits on the firm's bottom line. The formalization of these connections, in the rural Chinese context, where a singular RSCE combines political leaders and TVE employees does not negate the business aspect of this conglomerated enterprise.

As for the capitalist nature of this enterprise, it is defined in terms of class processes that Whiting and others completely ignore. The wage labor relationship that links direct producers to TVEs and generates the output from which SV is realized, then appropriated and distributed by nondirect producers, constitutes the basis for calling these firms capitalist and is a common characteristic linking these enterprises to other capitalist enterprises around the world and throughout history, regardless of whether the appropriators are private individuals or state officials, a superorganic entity or a singular human being. The existence of capitalist exploitation within the RSCE is significant, if widely ignored, and defines that institution, which is a fusion of government and business conglomerate, as capitalist, albeit the state variant form. Indeed, once capitalist exploitation has been identified within an institution, then this definition does not collapse simply because the specific cultural, environmental, political, or nonclass economic processes do not fit some preconceived notion of what a proper capitalist firm should look like. The institution would be defined as a variant form of capitalism, in any event. To the extent that any institution that involves capitalist exploitation can be defined as a business enterprise, then this issue is simultaneously resolved. This does not mean that the unique characteristics of that enterprise are unimportant. Each variant of capitalism will have its own internal dynamics and unique nexus with the external social formation.

Thus, when analysts, such as Che and Qian (1998), conceptualize the position of township officials as analogous to members of a board of directors, playing the role of private capitalist, they are making an important point. It is not that the township is a corporation, but that the position of these government officials is, in a class sense, the same as that of a board of directors in a capitalist corporation (remembering that corporation is simply a legal designation). In capitalist corporations, the board of directors occupies the fundamental class position of surplus appropriator and first distributor of SV. The internal logic of who, when, and how one occupies positions on the board of directors is separate from the social location of the board as appropriator/first distributor of SV. Similarly, in the RSCE structure, government officials occupy the fundamental class position of surplus appropriator and first distributor of the SV generated in constituent TVEs. The political arrangements by which these officials are selected to serve in this capacity are separate from their fundamental class role. Just as the board of directors of a capitalist corporation acts as a superorganic appropriator/first distributor, playing this role independently of the specific individuals comprising it, so it is that governmental bodies act in this capacity within the RSCE.

It should be noted that county governments were excluded from the definition of community government, which acts as the controlling body within the RSCE, because "The county has no property rights over the residual of township and village enterprises. It relies primarily on taxation from these enterprises" (Oi 1999: 89). Thus, the county is a purely governmental unit, existing outside the boundaries of the RSCEs, connected to them, in class terms, only via a distributive class relationship.

To further complicate matters, community governments are made up of officials and agencies (of the townships and villages) who occupy various positions within the RSCE, as well as officials and agencies external to the RSCE. It is not the community government, as a whole, that acts as the appropriator/first distributor of TVE SV. The community government economic commission (or equivalent body) acts as the superorganic appropriator of TVE SV. This superorganic appropriator/first distributor within the RSCE constitutes the "personality" of the state industrial capitalist. By internalizing the appropriation/first distribution functions within the local bureaucracy, the community government strengthens its economic position and can impose arbitrary fees, charges, and off-budget taxes which its internal superorganic appropriating body, such as the economic commission, can be compelled to pay via distributions from RSCE SV.

Control over RSCEs serves as a conduit of political power for community governments. These conglomerations of political, economic, and cultural processes create intimate ties between various individual and superorganic agents operating in and beyond the rural communities, including banks and other financial institutions, ancient farmers and artisans, private capitalist firms, and foreign and joint venture firms. Because RSCEs have enhanced the political and economic influence of local officials, it has served to broaden the base of support for economic reforms:

> The cadres who benefit most from collective ownership of enterprises were those at the township and, particularly, the village levels. Collective enterprises constituted a crucial part of their personal power base . . . The power of cadres was strongest in those villages with successful collectively owned industry, which provided officials with new resources – replacing those lost with decollectivization – to carry out their administrative and economic responsibilities.
>
> (Oi 1999: 76)

Local officials might not have been content with hegemony within the sphere of political processes alone, given their experience of wielding political *and* economic power during the feudal period, even if the hegemony over both of these processes rested ultimately with the State Council. The transition from state feudalism to state capitalism at the local level was, therefore, logical, when viewed in these terms.

Also, from the perspective of community governments, controlling jobs and the provision of public goods gives them a certain degree of leverage over the local citizenry. Thus, it is in the interest of the community governments to struggle against those reforms that might result in their losing control over the TVEs. And unless there are mitigating factors that would compensate local residents for the loss in public goods that is likely to result from a shift in control over TVEs, it may also be in the interest of the broad citizenry in these communities to fight such reforms, as well. By sheltering the local economies from the sort of external influence that would flow from foreign/outsider (or even private and autonomous) control over these rural enterprises, community authorities limit the degree to which such external (or autonomous) bodies can shift capital out of the local communities, as well as block the development of autonomous centers of economic power. If new power centers shaping jobs and local economic prosperity are created, whether the decision makers are foreign or local, then local residents and institutions become less dependent upon the local government. These new centers of economic power would be able to forge closer ties to local residents and institutions (via control over value flows, among other things) and begin to influence local politics and culture, perhaps competing with the local government for the hearts and minds of residents, or even gaining influence over local government.

Keeping local enterprises under the control of local governments also opens up some interesting possibilities, particularly in the context of increasing local level democracy. Democratic processes for determining the composition of local governments opens up the possibility of grassroots movements, influenced by Maoist Marxism or other versions of Marxism that argue in favor of direct transformation of the social relations of production, rather than the technological determinism of the modernists, gaining control over these local governments. If the current local state capitalism prevailed when such a change of local government occurred, then it is conceivable that the new government could dictate a structural transformation in its TVEs. The local government could transfer the authority over surplus appropriation and distribution to the direct producers, thus transforming the state capitalist TVEs into communist TVEs. The central authority has consistently transferred authority over surplus appropriation and first distribution into the control of local governments. There is no reason to assume that such experimentation might not occur at some point in future.

The logic of this transfer of authority over industrial enterprises may also have come out of the central government's desire to make the local governments more self-sufficient in the transition from the feudal arrangements, to cut the value redistribution cord, so to speak, between the center and the various localities. The SV consumed in maintaining bureaucratic processes for redistributing surpluses from center to these localities might have been perceived as a potential source of funds that, if freed up, could go to modernization. The result of the decentralization is that community governments are now dependent upon RSCEs to meet various claims on their government revenues. For example, the central government expects a certain amount of revenue from provincial governments, who expect a certain amount of revenue from county governments, who expect a certain amount of revenue from township and village governments, who are obligated to comply with such requests. SV extracted from the RSCE structure is critical to community government's ability to satisfy these cash flow demands:

> They [TVEs and other small and medium-sized enterprises] provide financial support for agricultural development and the budgets of governments at the county level. At the present time, the rural economy has to depend on small and medium-sized enterprises rather than agriculture for further development. The major sources of income for governments at a county level and below are the taxes and profits paid by such enterprises. For example, in 1994, rural enterprises across the country turned in 159.1 billion yuan to the government, i.e., 31.03% of the annual income derived from taxes of all types.
> (Liu 1999: 6)

Assuming that mitigating factors do not emerge as the reforms continue, the burdens of the central–local government fiscal arrangement would be unrealistic in a context where TVEs, as components in larger RSCEs, could not be used as local cash cows for the community government (OECD 2002: 91). This is not purely a result of the economic growth generated by the TVEs. Income growth has often been quite dramatic in those areas where the ancient class process dominates the landscape. However, local governments in those areas have not done nearly as well as those in local communities with strong TVE-based economic growth, even when the latter have exhibited a lower rate of overall income growth. When the local government does not have access to a major revenue generating RSCE, then public revenues and funded services have suffered. This may be, in part, because ancient farmers and artisans have proven quite adept at tax avoidance (if not outright tax evasion) and there are fewer nontax channels for local governments to extract surplus from ancients. This is part of the reason that the RSCEs remain critical to the economic viability of community governments. Indeed, the relative prosperity of community governments is directly correlated to the economic vibrancy of their RSCEs:

> The cities of Wuxi of Jiangsu province and Wenzhou of Zhejiang province represent two extremes of ownership structure in rural industries. In Wuxi, TVEs are dominant, and private enterprises are extremely rare; in Wenzhou, private enterprises are dominant. As a result, in Wuxi, TVEs are the chief source of revenue for the township and village governments to invest in agricultural machinery, bridges, power stations, field terracing, and other agricultural improvements. In contrast, in Wenzhou, township and village governments are unable to perform their basic administrative functions. In a World Bank study, . . . [in 1983] township governments in Wenzhou were "impotent in performing their administrative functions," and "basic facilities and public works in the townships of Wenzhou Prefecture were rather backward, considering the rate of capital accumulation. Farmers were building three- and four-story houses with kitchens and bathrooms, but their kitchen slops were running in the streets for lack of sewers. Cultural, public health, and other public undertakings were lagging behind other areas."
> (Qian 2001: 306–307)

Community governments without extensive RSCE suffer under private enterprise, even if economic growth is robust, because they do not have direct access to the surplus. RSCEs give the community government direct control over value flows and make it possible to direct SV to targeted community and/or enterprise investments in a manner that would not be possible if forced to rely solely on the tax revenues generated by private firms.

On the other hand, fusion of the spheres of political and economic hegemony within a single entity can generate problems. In particular, community government control over public assets and the allocation of public rights, as well as of TVE SV within the RSCE can lead to corruption, where corruption is defined as the use of public assets or public rights for personal/familial gain:

> local cadres could readily pursue certain personal benefits within the system with relatively little risk to their positions and careers. Nonproductive expenditures such as lavishly appointed government office buildings equipped with heating and air conditioning and staffed by an expanding number of employees with connections to local officials, luxury cars at the disposal of government officials, and large entertainment budgets were commonly justified, for example, in terms of the need to attract foreign investors. Such expenditures were financed by rural enterprises, and the excessive extraction necessary to pursue these types of projects often left insufficient retained earnings for normal enterprise development. Collective firms, in particular, which remitted profits in addition to paying taxes and fees, were left with very few retained earnings, thereby limiting their ability to provide for their own fixed or working capital needs or to repay bank loans.
>
> (Whiting 2001: 117–118)

The personalized nature of economic relationships within state feudalism may be one of the influences upon this type of behavior. Then again, governmental and corporate corruption is not unknown in social formations with a long history of capitalism, including OECD nations. Thus, it may be that there are many possible paths by which a public official, such as those entrusted with community assets within the RSCE, may come to misuse those assets for personal/familial gain. The same cultural processes that are programming individuals to identify self-worth or social status with conspicuous types of consumption may also encourage individuals with effective control over public assets and public rights to use these resources to acquire those commodities necessary to a change in identity or status. These pressures may be particularly difficult to resist during a period of transition, when identities are already in a state of flux. To counteract those forces pushing officials to engage in corruption, the central government has made an example of many local and national officials by prosecuting, jailing, and sometimes executing them. Nevertheless, by all indications the problem continues to grow.

Transition to joint stock cooperatives

The fusion of local governmental power and capitalist exploitation is a potent mix that provides TVEs with certain advantages. However, the competitive environment in China is becoming increasingly intense, particularly in the wake of China's entry into WTO. The ability for TVEs to remain competitive, and in some cases to survive, will require adjusting to this new environment, including making changes to business strategies. Intensified competition among capitalist enterprises is being played out in a variety of activities, including struggles over input and output markets. The instruments deployed in these struggles include both hard and soft technology, as well as political connections, which has been a strong point in favor of the TVEs. The favored technologies are those that have been developed in the context of capitalist exploitation and are, therefore, likely to be compatible with the capitalist social relationships (which, in the context of the technological determinist framework of modernist Marxism, may be viewed as nothing more than another instance of soft technology). There is a perception, whether it is justified by the facts or not, that TVEs operating with "inferior" forms of technology (those that appear incompatible with raising rates of exploitation and making the firm more competitive) will be disadvantaged in a post-WTO world. In keeping with the general thrust of modernist economic policy, the push is for community governments to seek the means to acquire the necessary technology to alter the conditions of exploitation within their RSCE, as a whole, or specific vulnerable TVEs, in particular.

The party-state, at the highest levels, has repeatedly demonstrated a commitment to continue structural transformations in the institutions and relationships that comprise the Chinese economy and to do so in a manner that encourages "modernization" at all levels. Thus, there have been numerous reforms to laws governing enterprises and it is in this context that community governments must develop these new politico-business strategies. In particular, there is a push to adopt corporate structures for business enterprises, including the TVEs. This may ultimately mean the convergence of the legal structure of TVEs, urban industrial enterprises, and private industrial enterprises toward the "Western" corporate model that prevails within the OECD universe: a world where corporate ownership has been largely commoditized. In addition, the central government may encourage private (over state) capitalism, in part, as a way to reduce collusion between community governments and TVEs. Taxes are levied on individual TVEs. However, as has been pointed out, those TVEs that are owned by the community government are actually part of a larger RSCE. The administrative powers of the parent community governments make it possible to shield individual TVEs within this larger state capitalist structure from taxation (or to reduce the effective rate of taxation) by manipulating value flows between the component parts of the RSCE. This behavior can reduce central government revenues. Insofar as the central leadership assumes privatization will sufficiently distance community governments from TVEs, so as to reduce collusion, they are clearly oversimplifying the situation. The central government may be underestimating the ability of the community governments to establish special relationships with privatized TVEs such that the community government gets its distributive class receipts from nontax sources, while the privatized TVEs continue the practice of tax evasion that has been a major concern of the central authorities. Collusion between firms and government institutions (whether local, municipal, provincial, or central) is not reducible to situations in which the government entity owns and/or directly controls those firms.

If the RSCEs are broken up and their constituent TVEs privatized, the result could be negative in terms of rural employment levels and public goods provision. Under the present arrangement, community governments use the RSCEs to maintain acceptable levels of employment in the local community, even if this means that the overall level of productivity is lower than might be the case with a smaller work force. In other words, the community government accepts lower levels of SV in exchange for higher levels of employment and greater social stability. If SV appropriation and first distribution is shifted out of the community government's control into private boards of directors, it is unlikely that the current level of rural employment would be maintained or that the community governments would be able to maintain existing levels of public spending.

Nevertheless, recognizing that the reform process may create pressures to restructure the relationship between government and firms, community governments have had to find the means to retain control over their enterprises, even under conditions of restructuring.

It is in this spirit that the community governments have taken advantage of a provision in Chinese corporate law that allows for the creation of a *joint stock cooperative* (JSC), a corporate form that is structured in such a manner as to allow the community governments to both commoditize ownership and retain control over the appropriation and first distribution of enterprise SV. According to the OECD, 167,910 TVEs had been transformed into JSCs by 1999 (OECD 2002: 90). The JSC does have many of the features common to other corporate forms, including an elected board of directors. However, when TVEs are transformed into JSCs, the board of directors does not typically gain control over SV flows. The local government retains this fundamental class position and remains in control over distributions of SV, including the enterprise's investment portfolio decisions. In other words, the community governments have attempted to satisfy the various pressures to restructure the TVEs without giving up control: "Note that a large number of these JSCs were still controlled by their community governments in one way or another, particularly in those whose majority of the total shares was continuously held by their community governments" (Sun 2001: 2, footnote 4).

On the other hand, the community governments have typically relinquished control over management. In most cases, direct oversight of management has been shifted from the community government to the board of directors of the JSC. Nevertheless, in class terms, the retention by community governments of the fundamental class position of appropriator/first distributor means that the directors in such JSCs are holders of distributive (not fundamental) class positions. Under this typical arrangement, the board of directors receives an allocation of SV from the community government. Senior management also continues to hold distributive class positions, even if their salaries and benefits are determined by the board of directors, rather than the community government, if the community government retains control over management budgets. In other words, even when management salaries become nonclass payments from the secondary SV distributed to the board of directors from the community government, their budget allocations may remain as direct connections to the fundamental appropriators. Thus, senior management and the board of directors would both occupy distributive class positions with respect to the community government. In the struggles over the distribution of SV from the community government, the board and the managers they hire may be in competition. To the extent this is the case, it may actually strengthen the community government's control over enterprise policy and operational activities, as the community government retains direct channels of influence over both the board of directors and management.

One of the advantages of the JSC structure is that it can help the community government address the shortage of available capital for investment. The JSC structure is designed to support raising capital for the acquisition of hard technologies and as a direct innovation of new social relationships (soft technology) that can generate more SV to meet enterprise obligations and finance further investment. The latter aspect of the JSC, the restructured social relationships, is aimed at creating new ownership ties between various social agents and the enterprise, beyond those relationships that had existed under the previous structure. The JSC form allows for both the commoditization of ownership and the extension of ownership beyond the community government to include enterprise employees, community residents, and nongovernmental institutions. Employee ownership is structured as follows:

> There are typically different types of shares. One of them, for example, may be similar to a trust fund for employee pensions, the fund is owned by employees as a whole and benefits from the fund are distributed mainly according to seniority. Shares that confer the greatest ownership rights are those that have been subscribed by employees as individuals, which we call the most active shares. However, because of the smallness of the firms, these most active shares are not freely marketable. This makes these individually subscribed shares much closer to a venture capital investment with a simple profit sharing scheme than to the shares of western public companies. The profit sharing scheme is typically that: a fixed proportion of total profits (after taxes) is earmarked as the shareholding fund for the distribution of dividends.
>
> (Sun 2001: 2)

Employees in this arrangement receive, via the shares, the right to occupy distributive class positions *vis-à-vis* their employing TVE. These ownership shares embody and condition the right of specific persons to occupy these distributive class positions. When these shares are held institutionally, they are illiquid. However, when employees hold individual shares, as is the case with shares held by community members, then the shares are marketable, although still relatively illiquid. There is not much of a market for JSC shares and, when it is possible to find a buyer, the transaction is invariably a local one.

The commoditization of ownership shares and creation of new distributive class positions occupied by direct producers and managers in the TVEs may also serve the purpose of motivating behavior in ways compatible with the expansion of SV. Ironically, direct producers who also occupy distributive class positions as owners may be motivated to raise their own rate of exploitation. Distributive class positions may, in this context, enhance worker productivity by altering the consciousness of the worker. She may come to see herself as an owner whose well-being is linked to the level of SV creation within the enterprise. The ownership relation may also motivate the worker to the extent dividend payments are used to supplement workers' wages. Such dividend payments might provide workers with material evidence of the link between greater enterprise SV and their livelihood.

If worker-owners respond in the way suggested here, then this form of ownership may reinforce the existing form of exploitation. The community government may even be able to maintain control over enterprise SV. However, the shift to majority worker ownership could threaten the existing state capitalist structure. Community governments have been transferring shares, sometimes a majority of shares, to employees and other nongovernmental entities, in all but the so-called backbone TVEs (TVEs considered of such strategic value as to warrant keeping them under close community government ownership and control). If the legal system recognizes the right of owners to determine boards of directors and directors are granted the unambiguous responsibility over SV appropriation, then majority worker ownership could result in a revolutionary shift in the underlying class processes of such firms. Owner-workers may conclude that the ownership shift represents (or ideally should represent) a fundamental change in control over the enterprise, including control over the appropriation and first distribution of SV. To the extent this is the case, owner-workers could take actions to make their perception a reality, perhaps even to attempt to transform the TVE into a communist enterprise by exerting control over the appropriation and distribution of SV. This struggle could take the form of workers attempting to use their collective ownership rights to determine who sits on the board of directors and to then exert the rights of the board (over that of the community government) to the first distribution of enterprise SV. A struggle over control of the enterprise (whether of management or value flows or both) could lead to a disruption in the performance of surplus labor, a fall in rates of exploitation, or even a crisis that threatens the continued survival of the enterprise. Alternatively, a form of democratic capitalist structure could be established whereby the direct producers appoint the surplus appropriating board of directors, receive distributive class payments from it, yet themselves have no direct control over the fruits of their labor. There is no indication that either of these scenarios has yet occurred in the TVE sector, despite the fact that there are JSCs operating under majority employee-ownership. To date, the institutional structure within which most worker shares are held has been conducive to maintaining community government control, with the community government (and local CPC party secretaries or other "grassroots" officials) exerting influence over the body that manages worker shares. However, this could change in future.

Another possibility is that worker-owners could perceive the enterprise as nonexploitative simply because they participate in ownership, whether or not majority employee ownership prevails, absent any change in the mode of surplus appropriation and first distribution. The simple fact that they are owners may be sufficient for these workers to believe that the enterprise has undergone a fundamental change in its nature, to have become nonexploitative. Insofar as this occurs, community governments may not only maintain control over the appropriation and first distribution of enterprise SV but even find it easier to reproduce their fundamental class positions, perhaps even easier to raise the rate of exploitation.

Managers have also been receiving ownership shares in JSCs. Community government leaders anticipate that giving management additional distributive class positions will strengthen their stake in the SV generation process. Indeed, managers may feel motivated to perform their function more effectively when given additional distributive class positions. If TVE managers believe that higher rates of exploitation may result in their receipt of larger distributive class payments, perhaps in salary, dividends, and capital gains under the new corporate structure, then they may be more aggressive in finding new and more effective ways to exploit workers, including putting more time and effort into learning and adopting techniques that have worked well in OECD transnationals. If this results in adoption of OECD type technology in TVE work spaces, then one of the societal objectives of the modernist CPC leadership will have been achieved.

Another motivation for community governments to restructure the TVEs was the need to address a growing TVE debt load. The rapid growth in TVE production operations was largely debt financed and "by the end of the 1990s many of the TVEs had collapsed under a mountain of debt" (Becker 2000: 69). Restructuring of the TVEs into JSCs provided a partial solution to the debt problem by opening an alternative channel for the community government to raise capital that could be invested in the TVEs:

> The adoption of JSCs well meets the urgent need for TVE capitalization. In those provinces such as Zhejiang, Jiangsu, and Anhui, where have been the leading areas for TVE development, this adoption leads to an intermediate reduction of the debt/asset ratio by 10 percentage points at average.
>
> (Sun 2001: 1)

In any event, the TVE sector continues to lead Chinese economic growth, countering the old view that state enterprises (irregardless of the underlying class process) are somehow more inefficient (or less growth generating) than private sector firms (and a cause of economic stagnation). In economic terms, the restructuring of TVEs into JSCs has produced an even more effective generator of SV: JSCs have been an unambiguous success, continuing the dynamic role the TVE sector has played in overall Chinese economic growth:

> While the performance of JSCs may widely differ across individual enterprises, their average performance has been outstanding... it is widely reported that those TVEs having transformed themselves into JSCs have typically shown a significant improvement in performance, exhibited more dynamic features, and played the leading role in maintaining the TVE miracle.
>
> (Sun 2001: 1)

The JSC corporate form may give those who define socialism as some form of public ownership/control over enterprises some hope that China remains a socialist nation. Indeed, the coexistence of community government based appropriation and local level democratization could form the basis for a class revolution toward nonexploitative class processes in the Chinese countryside. On the other hand, and perhaps more likely, given the predilections of the modernist leadership, the JSC form may be a precursor to more liquid shareholding in future, including the complete commoditization of the shares of these rural industrial enterprises. If corporate law continues on its current trajectory, it is reasonable to assume that such will eventually be the case. Under that scenario, local communities are likely to lose control over these enterprises, at least to a significant extent:

> stock ownership arrangement and its accompanied governance structure, such as the board of directors, reallocate the control rights to the TVE's most important contributor. When the local government is not the most important contributor, this will limit if not eliminate its power in interfering [in] the affairs of a TVE.
>
> (Chang *et al.* 2000: 16)

However, the reduction in community government control that Chang *et al.* envision has yet to come to pass, despite increasing corporatization. Indeed, these authors admit that "due to incomplete legal institutions and [the] power of [the] communist party, the local government still had significant power over a TVE even after it changed to stock ownership." Indeed, TVEs transformed into JSCs remained "instrumentalities of local government" (McIntyre 1999).

The complete corporatization/privatization of these rural industrial firms might come about as a result of national policies – the modernist leadership has a predilection for replicating OECD institutional structures – or for any number of other reasons. Some combination of changes in corporate laws, intensified post-WTO competition, community government financial needs, etc. could lead to privatization in future. On the other hand, the TVEs and JSCs, both of which may be components in a larger RSCE, have exhibited rapid economic growth and generated large sums of SV under the control of community governments. Why give up these geese and their golden eggs? Community governments may fight to retain control over the RSCEs and the central government may even remain accommodating with appropriate corporate laws and regulations (within the boundaries of WTO legality, of course). However, the trend toward commoditization of ownership (throughout China) produces its own dynamic. The more extensive and complex the relationships conditioning the existence of the firm and capitalist exploitation within the firm, the more potential sources of problems/contradictions in reproducing those relationships. While the initial purchase of ownership shares may be a source of capital for the firm, and thus provide support for reproducing existing social relationships within the firm, the extension of ownership beyond its original institutional boundaries may ultimately problematize control over the appropriation and first distribution of SV within the firm, particularly if the commoditization of ownership shares allows external agents to shape the composition of the board of directors and corporate law grants the board the right to act as appropriators and first distributors of enterprise SV. Possible ways of avoiding this problem include making it difficult to sell ownership shares outside the local community, selling preferred shares with rights to dividend distributions but no right to vote on the board of directors, and/or making it difficult to alter the composition (or rights and responsibilities) of the board of directors. The problem with these strategies is that they make owning the shares less attractive and, therefore, reduce the ability to raise capital by the issuance of shares. But there is a more positive way of looking at the commoditization of ownership. The commoditization of ownership is another way for enterprises to forge alliances with a wider array of social agents, to build wider and deeper alliances between the capitalist appropriator/distributor (whether situated within agencies of the community government or within the firm's board of directors) and those social agents occupying distributive class positions. The wider the array of alliances, the more these firms may be able to shape the overall sociopolitical environment to satisfy their objectives, including reproducing existing forms of SV appropriation and distribution.

The success of rural state capitalism continues to depend, among other factors, on the ability of community governments (through constituent agencies) to serve as the appropriator/first distributor of RSCE SV, while simultaneously acting as the administrator of local public assets and rights. This dual position of the community governments can both provide advantages to RSCE firms, as well as serve to block or, at least, retard the ability of competing firms to threaten RSCE markets. OECD reports that "the extensive regulatory environment which enterprises face with respect to investment project approval, safety standards, tax compliance, labour and environmental regulations, etc., requires enterprise managers to maintain a good relationship with local government" (2002: 93). The community governments' personality as surplus appropriators and internal agents of state capitalist firms routinely interacts (both in concord and in conflict) with their personality as governing bodies in local society. In other words, governance functions are not performed in a vacuum. In many cases, the actions that the community governments take on behalf of their own firms are outside of the letter of national laws. Thus, central government acquiescence may also be necessary for local-based state capitalism to continue in its current form. It has been clear that TVE performance has been a major factor in achieving the macroeconomic objectives of the modernist leadership:

> In 2003, the actual increase in value of China's township enterprises reached 3,668.6 billion yuan, accounting for 31.4 percent of the country's GDP. Having become a key prop of the national economy, the township enterprises have provided jobs to 136 million surplus rural laborers, or 27.8 percent of the rural workforce.
>
> (CPC White Paper, sec. IV, April 26, 2004)

If central government authorities start scrutinizing the behavior of community governments and TVEs more closely and more rigorously enforce existing laws (including WTO provisions), it is unlikely that community governments will be able to as effectively protect the markets of their TVEs (or even maintain direct control over the appropriation of SV in many of them) and this economic growth machine may not be nearly as effective in meeting the macroeconomic needs of the leadership.

The integration of the Chinese economy with global capitalism may create an environment where the continuation of state capitalism or the possibility of rural state capitalism evolving into some form of nonexploitative social relations of production and distribution is not under the control of either the local or the central government authorities in China. This is certainly not the case at present but it is not out of the question that external transnational enterprises and/or foreign governments may be able to use international agreements, such as WTO, as instruments for changing internal policies, including laws governing corporate forms, within China. These external entities may certainly gain sufficient leverage to pressure local governments to stop providing favorable treatment to TVEs.

On the other hand, such pressures may not be in the interest of the transnational firms. Many of these firms have forged close relationships with TVEs and other domestic Chinese enterprises, particularly subcontracting relationships, and benefit from low unit labor costs and cozy relationships between firms and local governments. Wal-Mart, one of the most aggressive transnational merchanting firms on the planet, has turned China into its primary source of commodities and benefits from the cheap labor and close collaboration between local governments and enterprises making toys, electronics, and other commodities that fuel Wal-Mart's competitive advantages over other retailers and concomitant revenue growth. Thus, these transnational firms may support maintaining the status quo, rather than more radical structural reforms, and may even pressure their home governments to play along. The Chinese government recognizes this, both at the local and central level. Foreign transnationals want cheap commodities more than they want liberalization. Pringle and Frost note the "contradiction between promoting a safe workplace environment and inducing more foreign investment, much of which enters China to minimize costs (one of which is the expense of providing such a workplace)" (Pringle and Frost 2003: 312). If the community government–TVE nexus is broken and TVEs are forced to abide by the laws and regulations, absent mitigating factors, their costs of production will rise. The TVEs engaged in subcontracting and joint-venture arrangements with foreign firms would have to either internalize these additional costs (hence less retained SV), reduce distributive class payments to other social agents, perhaps even to government, pass the increased costs along to their foreign partners, or some combination of the above. TVEs have to be careful in this respect. If they reduce distributive class payments to allied agents, depending upon the varying overdetermined tolerance levels of these agents, it could become more difficult to secure conditions for continued SV production and receipt. If the problems faced by TVEs increase, as a result of these changed conditions, then foreign transnationals may reassess the risk of doing business with them. Fewer subcontracting arrangements (or a reduced monetary value of such arrangements) could negatively impact the ability of TVEs to act as generators of SV.

In the brave new WTO world of Chinese (and globalized) capitalism, the survival of RSCEs (and other instances of state capitalism, whether local or national based) is partially dependent on the ability of these firms to generate levels of SV sufficient to meet the demands of a wide range of social agents, including their parent community governments and other governmental bodies. It will not be easy to reproduce the distributive relationships with these agents in the face of pressures from both within and outside of the Chinese social formation, both competitive attacks on RSCE input and output markets, structural attacks on the legality of the corporate structure of these state capitalist firms, and pressures to take these firms "public," making their ownership shares available for purchase by private entities with little interest in allowing continued community involvement in decisions on the appropriation and distribution of SV. If history is any guide, there will be many battlegrounds in the struggle over the underlying class processes, ownership structures, and management configuration of these firms.

5 State capitalism in urban China

The case of the SREs

Urban localities in China, like all other sites of human activity, are a complex web of social and environmental processes. Existing Chinese law, custom, and a wide range of related social and environmental processes have generated a distinction between urban and rural localities that is reminiscent of the boundaries between two countries, albeit governed by a single party-state bureaucracy. The objective of this chapter is to elaborate a subset of the overdetermined effects shaping changes in the production and appropriation of surplus within these urban localities – showing how these changes simultaneously effect and are effected by the plethora of relationships composing the social formation, including the aforementioned processes shaping the urban and rural as distinct geo-social spaces within the larger Chinese social formation. Elaboration of the dynamic processes of change and the consequent contradictions exposed within the urban sites of production and appropriation of surplus provide another step forward in comprehending the larger transition to capitalism in the Chinese social formation, a transition that may ultimately undermine the boundaries between urban and rural (as well as the boundaries between China and an emerging global capitalist economic space).

The primary objects of analysis in this chapter are the SREs, typically described in the literature as SOEs. From the late 1950s until the reform period, these urban industrial enterprises were part of an elaborate state feudal structure that encompassed both urban and rural enterprises, as well as the entire state bureaucracy. This feudal structure depended critically upon a wide range of political, economic, and cultural overdeterminants, including the aforementioned boundaries between urban and rural, in particular those processes restricting the mobility of rural direct producers into urban spaces. This boundary was itself overdetermined by modernist ideology, which included an essentialist understanding of the urban as a site/center for modernity/progress, while rural was understood as backwards, primitive, and retrograde. During the feudal period, these notions of rural and urban provided a basis for justifying laws designed to block rural migration to the cities, where such migration was understood as the pollution of the modern by the primitive. As with all forms of pollution, there was a perceived need to control it as much as possible. The household registration laws of the late 1950s provided a mechanism for such control, but also for blocking the path of rural direct producers out of that feudal domain created by the establishment of the commune system. This bifurcated world of rural and urban, where direct producers were obligated to serve the state in their respective geocultural spaces, with political constraints on their mobility and other choices, was the ground upon which the reforms would be applied. This chapter focuses specifically on the urban industrial enterprises that came out of the state feudal structure. It argues that the party-state, at various levels, has maintained its position of surplus appropriation, albeit in a capitalist context.

Reshaping corporate behavior: decentralization – modernist motives

The period of 1949–78 was marked by various struggles over the processes comprising Chinese enterprises. During this period, modernist arguments were generally supportive of centralized administrative (bureaucratic) structures, centralized planning of industrial inputs and outputs, and increasing state control over the surpluses generated in industrial enterprises. These same conditions prevailed in the USSR without resulting in feudal exploitation (Resnick and Wolff 2002). However, in the context of political changes that were implemented during the GLF, particularly the imposition of restrictions on the mobility and employment options of direct producers, the bureaucratic control over economic relations became conditions for the reproduction of a state feudal variant in China (a form of state feudalism in which the surplus was ultimately appropriated by either the State Council or local state institutions subservient to the State Council who then redistributed the surplus to satisfy the reproductive needs of the bureaucracy). Under this system, the senior management of SREs had limited powers and was largely subject to the dictates of the party-state, including production quotas, allocations of inputs, and predetermined limits on how much of the enterprise's funds could be expended to pay for wages and other costs of production. Wage scales, personnel decisions, and a wide range of work rules were all shaped within a single bureaucratic maze of firms, state agencies, and the complex relationships within and between them. The end result of these administrative controls and restrictions was that urban workers were bound to the service, directly or indirectly, of the State Council and under the immediate command of state functionaries, who were dependent agents in a feudal hierarchy.

Party members who followed the Maoist line fought periodically to decentralize this administration and to shift the loci of economic decision making and surplus appropriation in the hope of producing nonexploitative class processes. During this feudal period, struggles between the Maoists and the modernists generated a great deal of uncertainty regarding the direction the economy might take. In particular, there was concern that Mao's "permanent revolution," embodied in a constant drive to reconfigure economic processes (ostensibly with the goal of moving China in the direction of communism), was slowing the process of technological transformation (the *deus ex machina* in the modernist narrative of transition) and creating a more insecure political and economic environment.

The modernists in the leadership would eventually conclude that the organizational costs of the state feudal bureaucracy, as well as this continual struggle with the Maoists over the extent of bureaucratic control over the economy, crowded out resources needed to fund development of the productive forces and economic growth.

The deep penetration of the state-bureaucracy into the sites of surplus production, the party-state control over surplus distribution, and the peculiar types of value distributions required to reproduce feudal reciprocity created a series of leakages that drained surplus before it could ever be made available for "modernization." Deng Xiaoping (1992) wrote:

> Modernization does represent a great new revolution. The aim of our revolution is to liberate and expand the productive forces. Without expanding the productive forces, making our country prosperous and powerful, and improving the living standards of the people, our revolution is just empty talk. We oppose the old society and the old system because they oppressed the people and fettered the productive forces. We are clear about this problem now. The Gang of Four said it was better to be poor under socialism than to be rich under capitalism. This is absurd.

This was a very telling statement from the leader of the CPC modernists. It revealed the modernist order of priorities and signaled a willingness to make "pragmatic" policy choices deemed necessary to unfettering the productive forces, including social reforms that might run counter to the explicit Maoist aversion to capitalist exploitation. Nevertheless, as long as the Maoists were in contention for party leadership, placing modernization above class relations in the party's priorities would be problematic and implementing a transition to capitalism out of the question. The Maoists may have been only partially aware of the implications of the bureaucratic structure that came out of the GLF period, not recognizing that the commune and danwei systems were implemented in such a way as to restore feudal exploitation, but they were certainly conscious of conditions that would foster capitalist exploitation and were constantly struggling to keep these conditions in check. The victory of modernist over Maoist Marxism following Mao's death and epitomized by the trial of the Gang of Four liberated the party leadership from these Maoist constraints and allowed the technological determinism of the modernists to shape national priorities. The Maoist "class struggle" line fell out of favor and official party ideology was reshaped in accord with the modernist vision: development of the productive forces, as understood within modernist Marxism, became the key litmus test for national economic policies.

This shift in party philosophy has been an important influence in the transition from state feudalism. The modernist vision has been made concrete in the reshaping of state and non-state institutions and in transformation in a wide range of social and environmental processes, including class processes. In particular, the decentralization of management decisions and control over SV flows (mostly from central to local governmental authorities) has been a critical component of the strategy to modernize the Chinese economy by reducing that portion of SV that went to maintaining the central state bureaucracy and the larger value flows necessary to reproducing feudal reciprocity, transforming the social contract between the party-state and the citizenry such that the value of labor power would contain a smaller quantum of socially provided resources, and both empowering and encouraging enterprise directors and managers to use a portion of the surplus value under their command to modernize their enterprises.

Ironically, the pursuit to "modernize" China through "economic reforms," while de-emphasizing class struggle, has brought about a revolution in class processes. Resnick and Wolff delineate the difference between reform and revolution in the context of the capitalist class process:

> There is a tradition in Marxism that distinguishes between basic changes that are reforms and those that are revolutions. We might interpret that tradition as follows: a reform of the capitalist state is a change in its position as a provider of conditions of existence of the capitalist fundamental class process. A revolution of the capitalist state involves two interdependent parts: its [*sic*] goes beyond reformist change to considerably or entirely eliminate its capitalist distributive class position and at the same time impede or block other sites in society from securing those capitalist conditions no longer provided by the state.
>
> (1987: 267)

The word feudal can just as easily be substituted for the word capitalist in this extract. The post-Mao class revolution would entail the party-state not only eliminating its feudal distributive class position but also its feudal fundamental position as appropriator. These feudal positions would be replaced by the state participating in capitalist exploitation, as a recipient of distributive class payments (from private and state capitalist enterprises) and also as an appropriator within state capitalist enterprises. Therefore, the so-called reforms, or particularly the liberation of direct producers from their obligation to serve the state in exchange for employment security, constituted abolition of feudal bonds of reciprocity and the first stage in the development of capitalist labor power markets, as well as expansion in the realm of productive self-employment (the ancient fundamental class process). These changes constituted not merely reform, but a class revolution – the elimination of feudal class processes accompanied/substituted by the establishment and enforcement (by several actors, the state included) of capitalist and ancient class processes.

Surprising, the CPC leadership may not entirely disagree with the notion that the transformations constituted revolution, although their concept of revolution, like their conception of the teleological path to communism (progress), is grounded in a form of technological determinism: "Revolution means the emancipation of the productive forces, and so does reform" (Deng Xiaoping 1992).[1]

Decentralization – SV flows and conduits of incentive

The modernist leadership's first attempt at decentralizing authority, began in Sichuan Province[2]: "Policies designed to raise productivity were launched in Sichuan in October 1978 with the introduction of a scheme whereby state enterprises were allowed to keep a proportion of their profits instead of handing them over to the state" (Bramall 2000: 390). It was another of the "crossing the river by feeling for stones" experiments that has come to epitomize the post-1978 reforms. The first reforms were designed to give senior enterprise management a portion of SV which they could do as they wished with (within certain limits). This was not yet a revolutionary change, since it did not threaten the feudal nature of exploitation. Instead, by gradually giving management more control over SV and linking individual manager compensation to profit levels, the early reforms were an attempt to refocus management priorities away from simply pleasing higher-level state officials to developing more effective strategies for increasing enterprise SV. In this sense, the CPC leadership's objective was to improve the SV performance of the existing feudal structure, rather than to overturn that structure, by establishing a more direct correlation between enterprise performance and compensation to management (and similarly to the feudal direct producers, in the form of bonus pay).

However, a reformed feudal bureaucratic structure was only a first step. The post-Mao leadership had a vision of modernity that went beyond simple reform. This vision required a restructuring of the soft technology of social relationships, including class processes. The model for these technological transformations was and continues to be the OECD nations, where the soft technology of social relationships included capitalist class processes.

The absence of Maoist "class struggle" as a factor in CPC policy making after 1978 and the dominant position of the modernists have directly overdetermined a restructuring of social relationships in the urban state sector that has been almost as continuous as the transformation in the physical landscape of China's coastal cities. The restructuring of social relationships has eliminated the role of the state's ownership position as a condition of state feudal exploitation: this occurring once the danwei system of obligatory labor and permanent employment gave way to capitalist labor power markets as the primary system for accessing labor power.

Instead, the state's ownership position became a condition of state capitalist exploitation. The state, through its functionaries, served as principal in the new capitalist formation. Boards of directors were formed, but became integrated into the state bureaucracy:

> At present, boards do not have a separate identity in the company; they are rather viewed as a continuation of management. As in many Asian countries, including Japan, board power is very limited... Although in theory boards are supposed to appoint the management of a Chinese company, the latter is usually appointed directly either by the local authorities or by the SOE

> holding that controls the listed company. Few boards have independent directors... In China, parties (or the state holdings that usually control the listed companies) have enormous power... In practice, local authorities and the Party, who are also in control of the holding companies, currently nominate most directors.
>
> (OECD 2002: 445)

Reform measures, such as the Company Law, were publicized as measures that would, in part, separate government and enterprise. However, SREs continue to be instruments of state controlled exploitation, albeit within newly formed capitalist class structures.

Despite corporatization, the State Council has retained ultimate authority over central government owned SREs, and hence their value flows as well.[3] For those SREs under the "control" of local governments, surplus appropriation is assumed to be performed by local government agencies and not the central government. However, it is quite possible that the State Council is the appropriating body in at least some of these SREs.

Many (overlapping) layers of bureaucracy are charged with managing SREs within these state capitalist class structures. The State Council and local government leadership delegates control over SREs to specific agencies, departments, state asset management companies, and party organizations. At various levels along the party ladder, SRE management is directly shaped:

> The Party has exercised its control over the selection and dismissal of SOE managers through its Organization Departments at different levels. For example, the Central Party Organization Department has the authority over appointments of the top managers of very large SOEs (the level of minister or deputy minister), as does the Provincial or Municipality Party Organization Department for most large and medium-sized SOEs (the level of bureau chief or deputy bureau chief). This authority applies to joint-stock companies as long as the state has the majority share, even if they are listed on the stock market or are located in the special economic zones. The appointment and dismissal process represents the most important channel of political influence over enterprises by the Party... Under the Party control personnel system, SOE managers, like mayors, ministers, and Politburo members, are political appointees of the Party.
>
> (Qian 2003)

SRE senior management, once agents of the feudal bureaucracy, continues to be agents of the state. Yet the state is no longer a feudal bureaucracy but has instead become a capitalist bureaucracy. The Chinese party-state is, among other things, a capitalist state. The adjective "capitalist" is appropriate here given the party-state's participation in fundamental class processes of a capitalist nature.

These new class relationships are no less interdependent than those that existed in the feudal period. However, the focal point of the relationships has shifted from reproducing the exploitative capabilities of a feudal bureaucracy to those of a capitalist bureaucracy. From a class theoretical standpoint, the principal–agent relationship between state and SRE has been largely unchanged. As far as surplus appropriation in SREs, the state has, in most cases, continued to act as the principal. Under the new capitalist structure, the receivers of distributed shares of SV, including governmental entities, depend upon reproducing their relationships as principals and agents. Simultaneously, the boards and other management bodies within SREs depend upon the state to secure the conditions by which they receive distributive class payments. Given the differences in the conditions of existence of capitalist versus feudal exploitation, this shift had important implications for changes in public policy orientation, as well as in the behaviors of a wide range of social agents.

Central and local government bodies continue to be governors of value flows. Yet typically, under the OECD variant of capitalism, it is the social function of boards of directors to act as the governors of these value flows, to collectively occupy the role of industrial capitalist:

> The industrial or productive capitalist [or other fundamental appropriator] is the occupant of the fundamental class position of direct receiver of surplus value: "he is the person who at first holds the whole surplus-value in his hands no matter how it may be distributed between himself and other people under the names of rent, industrial profit and interest.
>
> (Resnick and Wolff 1987: 144)

These boards qua industrial capitalists act as superorganic entities receiving capitalist SV who then distribute portions of that SV to occupants of distributive class positions, agents who secure conditions whereby the boards may continue to receive the surplus. If the position of surplus appropriation and distribution was shifted to the boards of directors of the firms currently designated as SREs and these boards became private entities (not directly selected by state officials), this would have important implications for changes in the dynamics of the Chinese economy in and beyond the transition to capitalism.

Indeed, there does exist a significant push toward making SRE boards independent, to align them more fully with the spirit of the new laws. One scenario in which this is likely to happen is if state capitalist exploitation generates insufficient SV to support realization of the modernist vision. If the top leadership in the party-state were to become convinced that private capitalism provided a better fit to their vision, then future reforms could follow the OECD corporate norm more closely than at present – SREs could make the transition to private capitalist corporations. Indeed, many social analysts believe that state capitalism will eventually give way to private capitalism, in any event, since SREs are contributing relatively less to the economy.

If the power to directly shape the binding agreements and SV commitments of the SREs is shifted from the state bureaucracy to autonomous boards of directors, then it becomes possible for these independent directors to influence the actions of a wide range of agents, including state functionaries. By doing so, this would alter the means by which Chinese capitalism is reproduced. Thus, the restructuring of SREs such that directors and management would move from component elements of the state bureaucracy to actors operating outside this bureaucracy would have far reaching implications for the future direction of reform. More specifically, the very fact of the relative autonomy of boards of directors would reshape the economic, political, and cultural configuration of Chinese society in ways that weaken the power of the party-state to alter those initial conditions by which the boards of directors gained their relative autonomy in the first place. In other words, releasing control over surplus flows to independent boards of directors would create a substantial dependence of the party-state (and others) on enterprise directors for revenues (in the form of distributive class payments) and, to the extent communism remains a goal (the end point of the intended teleological path) of the CPC, may serve to undermine the long-term intentions (and certainly the relative autonomy) of the Chinese leadership.

How are the goals and objectives embedded within the institutional structure of the Chinese economy altered by the reforms/class revolution? Western corporate finance theories often start from the essentialist assumption that the primary mission of management within capitalist corporations is value creation: the board of directors and managers are assumed to select those assets and activities that will generate the higher net present value of cash flows generated by the enterprise. In Marxian terms, cash flows are simply an accounting convention that can be understood as a mathematical transformation of SV. Thus, if boards of directors are maximizers of cash flow, then they can also be considered to be maximizers of SV. The assumption that this behavioral characteristic is common to managers, even if simplistic, would likely have an impact on management decisions, to the extent that it is well known and accepted. The modernist leadership in China has encouraged the spread of Western corporate finance and other related intellectual frameworks within the business community. One of the objectives of the modernist leadership was to encourage directors and management within the firms undergoing transition to focus on identifying and implementing operational strategies and specific investment projects that were more likely to result in higher levels of SV (if not the extreme of SV maximization). It was assumed that such a management approach would lead to more rapid modernization (since it was assumed that optimal strategies would embody OECD-type technologies) and therefore contribute to meeting the paramount objective of the modernists.

It is possible that some variant of state feudalism could have produced the type of technological innovation that the modernists had in mind. However, the postrevolutionary experiences of the modernist leadership, particularly the GLF and the GPCR, convinced them that this was not the case. And, besides, the modernist leadership wanted nothing more to do with experimentation with alternative social processes and hard technologies, which was a strategy associated with the Maoists. The modernists concluded that the feudal structure and Maoist-type experimentation were important, if not primary, sources of economic and cultural lag, and particularly detrimental to the development of the urban economy (again, based on their experience with the GLF and GPCR). Instead, the modernists believed the technologies (hard and soft) that would achieve their objectives already existed in the capitalist economies of the OECD and that experimentation should be restricted to the gradual innovation of selected social processes and hard technologies. Therefore, the modernist type of experimentation began cautiously, particularly in the state sector.

In order to then understand the structural transformation in the state sector, it is necessary to start with the initial conditions, given that the modernist leadership wanted to proceed gradually by introducing innovations into these existing social relationships. Prior to the reforms, the state sector was governed by the dictates of a central plan (albeit one which enterprise senior management could directly and indirectly influence). Managers were informed of output quotas and other outcomes expected to be generated by their firm (after a series of negotiations and bureaucratic processes). A number of problems made it difficult for the central planning process to achieve the modernist objectives of increased SV flows to modernization. First, the social contract under state feudalism provided direct producers and managers with permanent employment security and a guaranteed subsistence base. Failure of economic agents to generate higher levels of SV did not directly threaten either job security or subsistence. The primary determinant of success was the ability of economic agents to meet certain political/loyalty requirements of their superiors in the feudal hierarchy. The entire state feudal edifice was ultimately constructed around loyalty and reciprocity. The concept of "guanxi" was integral to the feudal dynamic. A second and interrelated problem was that there was very little transparency about the potential for the component enterprises of the feudal structure to meet any given set of objectives. Planners and high-level state officials necessarily had to rely upon information provided by enterprise management. And even if enterprise management believed it possible to extract significantly larger quantums of surplus labor from enterprise direct producers, it might not have been in their interest to do so. Given the uncertainties that always exist in production, if they used their influence over the formulation of the plan to push up output quotas, for example, then this would have increased the risk that these quotas would not be met. Since they were evaluated on the basis of the firm meeting these quotas, then the enterprise managers would be increasing the risk to their careers from a failure to meet or exceed the quotas. In addition, raising production quotas might have alienated enterprise management from the enterprise direct producers. In a system where loyalty, reciprocity, and maintaining a relatively trouble-free working environment were critical to most interactions, creating such tensions might also have been detrimental to the personal careers of enterprise management. Managers also had very little incentive to influence investment decisions in ways that might increase value in future periods (particularly if this attempt to increase value also increased tensions between management and workers), rather than seeking investments that would aid in the attainment of existing output and employment targets with a minimum of disruption to existing work processes. In other words, so long as managers operated under the conditions of feudal reciprocity, wherein the state qua feudal lord provided the enterprise work force with security in exchange for their fealty, failure to generate higher levels of SV did not pose a serious threat to enterprise survival. Perhaps even more to the point, since managers' performance evaluation was based largely on political factors (particularly assessments of loyalty to higher level officials), then any failure to increase (much less maximize) value did not impede their attainment of personal success.

As integral elements in the feudal bureaucracy, SREs were instruments for satisfying the implicit state feudal reciprocity arrangement (which was overdetermined by struggles over the content of Chinese Marxism). SREs continue to be, in the state capitalist context, a means by which the lingering elements of that reciprocity arrangement are supported. Li describes this context:

> Since enterprises are indispensable to the government not because they earn profits, but because they provide employment, secure certain outputs, and shoulder many social services, the government cannot shut them down simply because they are unprofitable. Instead, in order to keep the money-losing firms operating, the government must take funds from profitable firms to subsidize the unprofitable firms – like a father who forces the well-to-do brother to help out his poorer siblings. The government also orders state banks to give loans to these failing firms, knowing full well that the latter will never be able to repay the loans. As a result, the budget constraints of the state-owned enterprises are soft.
>
> (1999: 55)

During the feudal period, loans were treated largely as grants (which loans had originally replaced) between one part of the bureaucratic structure, the banks, and another part, enterprises. The debt accumulated by SREs during the feudal period were such that, in conjunction with other claims on enterprise SV, it would be difficult to generate sufficient SV to remain solvent without continued subsidies from the state (soft budget constraints). This was consistent with the aforementioned conditions of feudal reciprocity, but contrary to the objective of distancing these enterprises from the state such that enterprise directors and managers could take actions consistent with value maximization. The resolution to the contradiction would ultimately be a class revolution.

Before this class revolution could be successful and SREs transitioned into the world of capitalist labor power markets and harder budget constraints, there had to be a solution to the accumulated nonperforming loans that had been granted on the basis of feudal reciprocity. As long as this debt remained, most SREs would be unable to free enough SV to meet the debt payments due and many of those capable of generating sufficient SV to meet such obligations would only be able to do so by sacrificing new investment. In other words, the debt problem presented a serious obstacle to the modernization plans. The short-term solution to the liquidity problems faced in the transition to capitalism was the establishment in 1998 of a recapitalization program modeled after the US government's rescue of the savings and loan sector in the 1980s. Due to the huge debt burdens of

SREs, or from the other angle the huge burdens of nonperforming loans of state banks, the state set up four asset management companies (AMCs) to shoulder the responsibility of recovering value from these nonprofitable assets. These efforts seem to have had the desired effects: In February 2001, the four major AMCs had already bought back nearly 1,400 billion Renminbi (RMB) worth of debts. That is 1,400 billion RMB in debts recovered out of a total responsibility of 1,500 billion RMB (OECD 2002: 179).

In order to discourage future bad lending while simultaneously creating conditions by which capitalist firms could secure finance capital, the banking sector was restructured to operate outside of the state bureaucracy (as private banks subject to hard budget constraints) and the AMCs were restricted to buying old loans, particularly those especially difficult to recover.[4] If one of the objectives was "creative destruction," to borrow Schumpeter's phrase, then the reforms seem to have worked:

> Thousands of inefficient SMEs in the state and collective sectors were progressively starved of funds. In tandem with a market dominated by demand, it is now more difficult for the local authorities not just to embark on industrial projects where demand is already saturated or dominated by efficient producers in other provinces, but also to sustain local companies... there is no longer a policy, as in the 1980s, of granting loans to loss-making companies for purchases of production equipment or other costly investment projects.
>
> (OECD 2002: 181)

Hard budget constraints provided an incentive for enterprise directors and managers, working with reduced debt, to make decisions conducive with generating the higher-level of SV necessary to meet enterprise obligations, including distributive class payments the state would make to itself. Thus, the State Council anticipated that these reforms would simultaneously improve cash flows from enterprises to the state and reduce cash flows from the state, in the form of subsidies, freeing up more SV to be invested in modernization. Bank officials had an incentive to get with the program and improve their lending practices, providing future loans only to those firms who could demonstrate the capability to generate sufficient cash flow to pay such loans (Jefferson and Singh 1999: 81), providing an additional incentive for enterprise managers to improve their strategic planning and implementation over the long term.

Thus, the elimination of the reciprocity arrangement by which the state guaranteed enterprise survival, including directing policy loans to SREs whose obligations to pay SV exceeded the amount of SV internally generated, has meant that directors and senior management must rely more heavily upon the value generating potential of their work force to meet the expectations of internal and external occupants of distributive class positions. This has created a whole new set of responsibilities (displacing the unique set of feudal responsibilities) for managers. In many, if not most, SREs, hard budget constraints under the capitalist order has motivated senior management to invest in new technology, provide bonuses and benefits (to both workers and management) based on activities that raise SV, and to seek strategies that either raise worker productivity or lower the value of labor power or both. For the vast majority of SREs, there is no longer any expectation of huge subsidies from the central government or easy, sizable loans from state banks and evidence indicates that this has motivated senior managers to take actions to generate more SV within the enterprise and adopt hard and soft technologies in line with the expectations of the modernist leadership. In other words, these managers are implementing operational, investment, management, and personnel strategies and policies that look increasingly like similar strategies and policies of OECD-based capitalist enterprises.

Nevertheless, value maximization is not the only priority of the party-state. Partly for this reason, SREs have remained within the state bureaucracy. The budgets of these firms remain integrated with the state budget (soft budget constraints prevail) and the state retains control over value flows. Although SREs have been corporatized, the directors remain state functionaries who administer the firm budget and enter into contractual obligations subject to constraints determined by higher-level state officials. The firm budget, as well as the composition of the board of directors, is directly shaped in the context of dictates, objectives, and interests of these higher-level state officials. By remaining within the state bureaucracy, SREs have been able to retain some of the privileged relationships with other state entities that prevailed during the feudal period:

> State commercial banks certainly continue to provide loans to unprofitable companies, on the orders of the central authorities... Bank loans are now handed out sparingly in order to reduce the social costs of transition, while waiting for these companies to be privatised, merged, or put in bankruptcy.
>
> (OECD 2002: 181)

The official CPC rhetoric justifies the existence of these state capitalist enterprises as a way of protecting the "socialist" nature of pillar industries, to maintain the "backbone" of the Chinese "socialist" economy, and for military defense. In fact, the decision to retain a direct SV appropriation role for the central government in the burgeoning capitalist economy is based on a desire to block private control over certain markets and assets deemed strategic by party-state planners. It remains to be seen whether the influence of WTO and, more generally, of private capitalist firms will eventually push the State Council to abandon this role and to expand the scope of private capitalism into these protected sectors.

Externalizing welfare and the rate of exploitation

Although the internecine struggle over the direction of social change between modernists and Maoists appears to have ended in a decisive victory for the former, this should not imply an end to struggles over public policy within the CPC, including those policies that relate to the restructuring of the state-run conglomerates and the quantity, quality, and mode of provision of social welfare protections for

Chinese citizens. The modernist Marxist CPC leadership has continued to push for changes in social relationships and to terminate the vestiges of feudal reciprocity, dismantling many of the social welfare protections that were part of that reciprocity arrangement, but there is opposition both within and outside of the party to these changes.

This opposition is likely to grow more acute as the withdrawal of state welfare protections is coupled with reductions in benefits provided at the enterprise level. Given the newly profit-conscious nature of SREs, senior management is in a position where they are now motivated to increase the rate of exploitation within their firms. Such motivation has manifested itself in various forms, including reductions in enterprise benefits, such that the value of labor power, which is a composite of the money wage and the benefit package provided to workers, has come under pressure. Furthermore, pressures to improve the competitiveness of domestic firms in the face of WTO may result in even more intense enterprise level struggles over wages and benefits.

Distributive class payments and internal management

The new state capitalist structure of the economy presented both new problems and more intense versions of old problems for the management of SREs to solve. More intense competition between firms over both inputs and outputs was one of these problems. However, competition was not new. Enterprises had a long history of competing over the setting of prices, inputs to be received, and markets where the commodity values were to be realized, although this competition was more often settled within the political, rather than economic, sphere during the feudal period. Managers with stronger ties to those higher in the feudal hierarchy were in a stronger position to achieve firm objectives than those with less influence. By attacking the feudal bonds of reciprocity and fealty and encouraging independent exchange contracts, the reforms reduced the political competition over prices, inputs, and markets in favor of economic competition over these phenomena. Directors of newly autonomous SREs had to restructure management to meet the challenge of these changed conditions. They did so, in part, by emulating certain aspects of the internal organization of OECD enterprises, creating specialized internal departments to address such issues as capital budgeting, marketing, personnel issues, etc. that had previously been determined at higher levels of the feudal bureaucracy.

The need to build a more complex internal bureaucracy within the urban industrial enterprise resulted in the expansion of internal distributive class occupants/positions:

> By the early 1990s...managers decided most key issues. They needed to co-ordinate input supplies through the market, to evaluate the capability of different suppliers and to bargain about price and delivery. They had to decide the product mix and product price, and to compete for markets. Accountancy and marketing departments grew rapidly. In large SOEs

> producing complex engineering products such as power equipment, product reliability and after-sales service became significant elements in inter-firm competition.
>
> (Nolan and Wang 2000: 23)

The senior managers hired and paid by the SREs to command these departments received distributive class payments for their administrative and other functions, which aided in capitalist exploitation.

In this brave new world of capitalist exploitation, hard budget constraints, and intensified competition among firms, internal managers would need to be motivated to take aggressive steps to raise the SV required to meet radically changed enterprise commitments. Sometimes this meant pushing workers to work harder or with fewer benefits than would have been considered acceptable during the feudal period. Ironically, the push to get more out of workers was partly motivated by the desire of a wide range of recipients of distributive class payments to receive more under the new social order than had been the case under the feudal order. Many of the managers who took up positions within the capitalist firms, as well as many of the other social agents receiving distributive payments from enterprise SV, shared the modernist worldview of the CPC leadership. Their worldview had a personal, as well as enterprise and social, dimension. They wanted to live like managers in the OECD universe, complete with personal computers, motor vehicles, cell phones, the latest systems for video and audio entertainment, and other technological trappings of modernity. The commodity bundles necessary to live the modernist lifestyle would require salaries and benefits far in excess of the compensation common to managers during the feudal period. These salaries, bonuses, and benefits made up an important distributive class nexus uniting the personal interests of managers and directors with the drive to raise the rate of exploitation of workers. The very process of circulating SV created vested interests in the new capitalist structure and in favor of further reforms.

Ownership of means of production

Another potential social nexus between the SRE (and the exploitative processes underlying the SRE) and social agents is ownership of the means of production. In many social structures, the owner of the productive forces utilized within exploitative class processes is but one of several social agents providing conditions for the existence of exploitation within the enterprise. In the typical (for profit) corporate structure, the owners are the shareholders of the enterprise. These shareholders grant use rights to enterprise assets, including the means of production, to the directors in return for either an explicit (dividends) or implicit (capital gains) claim on enterprise SV. In China, the state occupies, along with other social agents, the position of shareowner of the means of production. As owner, the state is in a position to claim a portion of the SV in exchange for providing the means of production. This distributive class payment to the state as owner may often be hidden inside tax payments. As surplus appropriator, the state is in a position where it can easily maximize the value of these payments. Thus, the value of tax payments to the state is conditioned by the state's fundamental class position. Also, from a class standpoint, tax payments may represent a composite of distributive class payments to the state for providing a range of conditions for the existence of (state) capitalist exploitation, including provision of the means of production.

However, as a result of the economic reforms, ownership has broadened beyond the state and other social agents are increasingly occupying this social position. One of the early efforts to replicate OECD-like corporate structures resulted in the transformation of many SREs into joint-stock companies:

> For example, in the province of Guangxi, between 1993 and 1998, 1 205 state SMEs (about 15 per cent of the total number of SMEs in Guangxi) were reformed in various ways: 93 were transformed into joint stock companies in which the state remained the major stakeholder; 222 companies were transformed into joint stock companies and sold to their workforce in the framework of the so-called co-operative shareholding system (gufen hezuo zhi); 29 were sold to a Chinese investor (without it being specified whether it was the director of the company, a local investor, or one from another province); 44 were merged with another company in the region; 469 were leased; 30 went in liquidation; and 318 were reformed using other, unspecified means ...
>
> (OECD 2002: 181)

The corporatization of SREs that had been solely state-owned has produced multiple occupants of the ownership position and diversified the class of owner-claimants to distributive class payments out of enterprise SV. Those SREs that have been transformed into publicly traded corporations have even seen some portion of the ownership shares to enterprise assets turned into commodities. This commoditization of ownership simultaneously expands the number of individuals with an interest in the current corporate form of the SRE, as well as the underlying capitalist exploitation that generates SV for the enterprise, and potentially shifts the power balance between owner agents and directors and senior management of the SRE. To the extent ownership becomes widely diversified, SRE directors and senior management may gain increasing autonomy in their decision making within the enterprise, since no single owner agent may be in a position to exert pressure on the directors and senior management. It is also possible, however, that the commoditization of ownership could result in new social agents gaining sufficient ownership shares to exert political control over who occupies the board of directors and, therefore, senior management, or even use such political clout to restructure the enterprise by divesting assets, merging assets into other firms, or even transferring enterprise control to another enterprise. These agents could threaten the state nature of the SREs' capitalist class processes. In any event, the publicly traded corporate form opens the door to a wide range of possibilities that did not exist under previous enterprise structures.

For example within those 222 SREs sold to their workforce, workers were given the option of purchasing the right to occupy ownership positions, to become both fundamental producers of and residual claimants to the enterprise SV. The modernist leadership might have introduced worker ownership as a way of legitimizing the reforms as "socialist," given the tendency within Marxism to essentialize ownership: worker ownership could serve the same role as state ownership as *a* sign of socialism. On the other hand, the modernist leadership consistently attempted to create incentives for higher SV and the decision to expand worker ownership can be understood in that context. It was believed that workers would respond to the potential distributive class payments and de jure decision-making authority entitled to them under this arrangement with an increase in work effort (higher productivity and SV generation). There was also the possibility that dividend payments to workers would help finance consumption bundles without an equivalent increase in workers' expectations of total income. If this was the case, then pressures to increase wages and benefits might actually be lessened. By becoming residual claimants to SV, workers might be motivated to cooperate in raising the rate of exploitation, leaving the enterprise in a stronger position to satisfy the larger modernist objective of increased investment in modern technology.

However, workers tend to sell their enterprise shares when offered the opportunity to do so. The sale of enterprise shares by workers, as well as a perceived lack of both worker and managerial responsiveness to this ownership "incentive" would seem to indicate that any incentive effect would be short-lived.[5] Similarly, to the extent worker ownership is a justification for continued use of the adjective "socialist," the tendency of workers to sell their shares would seem to raise a potential ideological problem for the leadership, although it remains to be seen whether or not the CPC vanguard role really does depend critically upon justifying the "socialist" nature of the Chinese economy.

As for the gradual diminution of state ownership, it is important to note that whether state institutions occupy positions of ownership or not, they maintain other positions, as surplus appropriators, providers of political and other processes necessary to capitalist exploitation within SREs, and recipients of distributive class payments in the form of taxes, fees, and other remuneration. Hence the state continues to play a key role in the economy and it can be seen that the strategy of the state releasing ownership to alternative occupants does not imply cutting the dependency relationship between the state and enterprises, only that this relationship is altered. Indeed, it may be possible under the new arrangement for the state to receive more total revenues from these enterprises than was the case when it acted as sole owner. Whether or not this is the case depends upon the magnitude of the SV generated within the firms and the degree to which the state can claim shares of that SV. Certainly it has been the hope of the modernists that the overall result will be to boost state revenues that can be invested in modernization, while simultaneously resulting in more enterprise investment in projects that are also compatible with these modernization plans.

Enterprise restructuring

In order for enterprise directors to secure SV for modernization and to pay the taxes anticipated by the CPC leadership, something needed to be done about to lower enterprise obligations to fund social services that had been part of the feudal reciprocity arrangement (under the danwei system):

> The problem of enterprise-run communities exists universally in China's State Owned Enterprises [*sic*]. In the course of their development over a long period of time, these enterprises accumulated an enormous amount of non-operating assets of a social or welfare service character. Viewed from the nature of these funds, they were invested by the state and should be recorded in the books as state capital and be entitled to after-tax profits distributed by the enterprises. However, from the theoretical point of view, capital funds should be used by the enterprises for the reproduction process. Yet these non-operating assets have not participated in the reproduction process of the enterprises. If they are entitled to profit distribution as state-owned shares, the interests of corporate shares, individually-owned shares and foreign-owned shares are bound to be affected. For this reason, it is necessary to restructure the assets of the former State Owned Enterprises and strip the non-operating assets from the joint stock companies, so that the main production establishment of the enterprises is separated from social burdens. Nevertheless, many State Owned Enterprises have, in the course of restructuring their assets, installed "shell" shareholders. That is, they invest the main assets for production and management (generally accounting for more than 75%, and some even more than 90%, of net assets) into the joint-stock companies, but retain a small part of net assets which are non-operating or in an unhealthy state of operation for the original enterprises, which are basically "shell" enterprises, or "holding companies" converted from the original enterprises.
>
> (Duan 2003: 129–130)

In other words, rather than abandoning feudal era obligations, in the early stages of the commoditization of ownership, the state transformed many SREs into joint stock companies with boards of directors overseeing the assets. In some of these enterprises, the directors moved to segregate the productive assets from the nonproductive by spinning off the productive assets into a separate corporation. The original enterprise retained direct control of the nonproductive assets. The non-state shares of the original joint stock company were then traded for shares of the productive subsidiary. Thus, the corporate entity that was spun-off from the original joint stock company could operate without the burden of the nonproductive assets (such as schools, clinics, housing complexes, etc.) created to meet the old reciprocity arrangement. The original joint stock company, now a solely or mostly state-owned entity once again, was burdened with these nonproductive assets, as well as much of the debt that had been accumulated during the feudal period. This restructuring leaves the state in a weak position *vis-à-vis* the receipt of distributive class payments as owner, because its ownership of the productive assets has both been diluted and made problematic: the original enterprise's directors could complete the spin-off by taking the new subsidiary public, as has happened in numerous cases. The new corporation has minimal (or no) state ownership. The state retains a position as provider of other conditions for the firm's existence and can claim a share of the generated SV, but this claim and the degree of control that the state has over the enterprise's assets have both been reduced by the corporate restructuring:

> As holders of state-owned shares of the joint-stock companies, they are entitled to the profits and interests due to those shares. There is no distinction between these "shell" shareholders and the joint-stock companies in their accounts, while their leading members mutually hold concurrent positions. This practice not only separates the owner of state assets (the State) from a joint-stock company through the use of an unqualified investor ("shell" shareholder) thereby stripping state-owned share of effective control, and providing conditions for the enterprises to make use of restructuring to avoid paying debts (by unloading the debts onto the original enterprises) or to stem and divide profits of state-owned shares, but is also liable to put state shareholders under the control of non-state shareholders in a joint-stock company, or even cause a State Owned Enterprise to become a subsidiary of a joint-stock company.
>
> (Duan 2003: 130)

At the end of the day, the corporate restructuring is posing new problems for state officials in tracking enterprise cash flows, asset dispositions, and debt obligations. The struggle over these aspects of enterprise performance is another of the outputs of the reform process. Enterprise directors will inevitably use their new found clout to resist governmental controls and intrusion and to push public policy in the direction of granting even more latitude to corporations in future. This may ultimately represent another "surprise" for the CPC leadership, which initiated the reform process to spur on the modernization of China, but did so with the full expectation of retaining control over the direction that modernization would take. It becomes increasingly problematic whether the CPC leadership can actually retain this control, as corporations become more autonomous of government, and their structures become more labyrinthine and difficult for government officials to navigate.

6 Agriculture

The perpetual revolution

> The modernization of agriculture is the key to realizing the four modernizations.
>
> (Deng Xiaoping)

The Chinese agricultural sector led the dramatic transition from feudal social relationships. After coming to power, the CPC instituted a historic land reform that ended private feudal relationships in the countryside and fostered the growth of the ancient class process (productive self-employment). However, the transition to the prevalence of productive self-employment was short-lived. During the GLF in the late 1950s, a form of state feudalism was instituted:

> peasants were bound by a strict registration system under the People's Commune on the land which they neither owned nor had control over. They were unable to move freely, because the strict residential registration system coupled with a strict rationing system in an environment of scarcity made it impossible for peasants to make a living in areas other than their own registered residential area. Since the land on which they were bound was publicly owned and managed, peasants were virtually reduced to slaves of the land in the locality... peasants were forced to sacrifice their own interests to support industry and urban residents. They were forced to sell goods and products to the state at discount prices, to plant grain instead of profitable economic crops, and to submit to a set of exchanges that built relative prosperity in the cities while confining peasants to the penurious countryside.
>
> (Chen 1999: 107–108)

The party-state instituted state feudal relationships in order to increase the flow of SV for development of heavy industry and infrastructure. As Mark Selden notes,

> In the high collective years, 1955–1978, rates of accumulation, defined as taxes + public accumulation/net income, ranged, by one informed calculation, from 13.4 to 27.8 percent, among the highest levels in the world... This was the key to China's heavy industrial growth which, together with the building of urban and rural infrastructure, absorbed the agricultural surplus leaving little to improve the livelihood of most rural producers.
>
> (1998: 22)

Initially, the transition to feudal relationships within agriculture (described in the literature as "collectivization") increased output of grain and other agricultural products. Agricultural and urban infrastructure was improved through direct appropriation of feudal surplus labor (compulsory labor). However, farmers who had once been self-employed and in command of their own surplus, became disgruntled with the state feudal arrangement of the commune system and agricultural output fell:

> The whole set of agricultural institutions created significant adverse effects within agriculture. Although agriculture supplied huge quantities of resources for industrial development, farmers' income stagnated. The per capita income of farmers was 133 yuan in 1978, having increased by 1.8 percent annum between 1952 and 1978. Per capita grain output in 1977 was roughly the same as in 1957 and total cotton output remained at the 1965 level . . . Farmers often failed to feed themselves adequately during the prereform period, in part because state purchases were excessive. Famine was widespread in provinces like Anhui, Guizhou, Henan and Ganshu. Agriculture became a severe bottleneck constraining economic development and industrialization. By the end of the 1970s these problems had grown to an unbearable level.
>
> (Huang 1998: 35)

The party-state faced widespread disapproval of its agricultural policies. Rural direct producers frequently opposed official policy and an underground ancient economy of unsanctioned productive self-employment grew in the interstices of the feudal domain. Agents of the party-state were faced with either trying to enforce generally unpopular and unsuccessful policies or officially validating the "experiments" implemented by rural direct producers.[1] Thus, the early economic reforms that led to the ancient class process were a post-facto legalization of practices already established in rural China.

The resurgence of the ancients

Of all the reforms in the post-Mao era, the dismantling of the communes was the most unambiguous assault on the old feudal edifice. As Deng Xiaoping noted in the mid-1970s,

> unless we make a good job of it, we may well hold back the whole of our state construction . . . Industrial development, commercial and other economic activities cannot be founded on the poverty of 80% of the population . . . to develop our industrial sector, we must establish an ideology that is founded on agriculture and that serves agriculture . . . The more industry develops, the more we must put agriculture first.
>
> (Sun and Li 2003: 243)

Thus, the transition from state feudalism began in the agricultural sector where the modernists set in motion a course of economic reform designed to decentralize economic decision making, liberalize market relationships, induce technological innovation, change the mix of class processes in the economy, and raise the level of the aggregate social surplus. The major thrust of reform in the agricultural sector was the restoration of the prevalence of the ancient class process in the form of the household responsibility system. The result was an unleashing of the energies and creative talents of millions of farmers, freed to work as self-employed farmers:

> Among the assumptions shared by the Chinese . . . officials was the belief that rural direct producers allowed to engage in self-exploitation would work more intensively and extensively to create a larger relative and absolute surplus product. It should be understood that this anticipated increased productivity was not based upon "technical" changes in production but upon changes in class processes . . . The Chinese . . . understood the interaction of class and productivity. They understood that the particular manner in which surplus labor was performed and appropriated would affect the aggregate magnitude of new wealth created in the society. By manipulating the form of exploitation . . . they hoped to create the conditions for economic growth.
>
> (Gabriel and Martin 1992: 60)

This early period of reform when rural China made the transition from state feudalism to productive self-employment saw an explosion in agricultural output and related SV. According to Yiping Huang (1998), the average growth rate of agriculture rocketed from 1.9 percent over the period 1952–78 to 7.4 percent during the period 1978–84. Farmers' per capita income increased from 133 yuan in 1978 to 355 yuan in 1984, in nominal terms. The real growth rate of farmers' per capita income was 15 percent per annum between 1978 and 1984. The contribution to China's overall productivity growth from the change in class process from the feudal to the ancient was significant (Table 1).

Although agricultural production in China rose quickly after implementation of the reforms, it was to level off later. Many factors contributed to this decline. The creation of unregulated markets where ancient producers could sell their output contributed to an inflationary environment. In 1985, the State Council, operating under the assumption that inflation might destabilize the economy, imposed regulations on rural markets in an effort to slow price increases for agricultural products.

Table 1 Quantitative assessments of the household responsibility system reform, 1978–84

Study	*Findings*
McMillan *et al.* (1989)	Total productivity growth was 41% from 1978, HRS reform accounted for 78% of this
Lin (1992)	The HRS reform accounted for 46.9% of total output growth from 1978–84 or 96.4% of productivity growth

Source: Adapted from Huang (1998).

These measures negatively affected ancient producers who, for the first time since the reforms were initiated, were caught in a "price scissors" effect where output prices were held down by government price controls even as their input prices continued to rise. In addition, the People's Bank of China (PBC) moved to reduce aggregate demand by tightening credit conditions at the same time that the state council adopted a more austere national budget, placing further downward pressure on spending in rural China. The overall effect was to diminish the total value of the output generated and the SV appropriated by ancient farmers without any relief from preexisting demands upon that SV.

Economic growth is increasingly seen as the primary raison d'etre of the party-state. The CPC has recognized, since before the 1949 Revolution, the need to generate an agricultural surplus to finance modernization, industrialization, and agricultural investment, without squeezing the resources necessary to meet the consumption needs of farm families. As previously indicated, in an effort to solve these problems, the party-state has continuously transformed economic processes in agriculture, political processes shaping rural governance, and cultural processes by which the official ideology of Beijing is transmitted to the rural public. The basic mechanism for capturing a portion (or all of) the agricultural (and rural) surpluses available for investment in industrialization and infrastructure development has changed several times, from taxes on a portion of the surplus generated by ancient farmers after the post-1949 land reform, to the feudal mechanism of direct appropriation of the entire rural surplus during the era of the communes (initiated during the GLF), to the return to taxation of a portion of the surplus generated by ancient farmers and a growing number of capitalist farmers in the post-1978 Reform Era. During the period when productive self-employment was the basis of the prevalent class process, both prior to 1958 and since the post-1978 reforms, the party-state has made use of the so-called scissors effect by which the state's power over input and output prices is used to price agricultural outputs below value and, thereby, to extract an additional portion of the surplus from self-employed farmers. This has resulted in further negative incentives for both self-employed and private capitalist farmers.

Ironically, the combined effect of the price scissors (which, on the output side, has been restricted somewhat by the government's maintenance of only a limited monopsony over agricultural outputs, primarily in rice and other grains) and taxation of a portion of agricultural surpluses of rural direct producers has generally resulted in more surplus resources going to the party-state than the direct appropriation of the entire surplus under the feudal system. In other words, if Y is the surplus that farmers produced when given the power to be the first appropriators of that surplus and Z is the surplus produced by the collective of feudal producers under the commune system, then Y exceeded Z by such a large factor that $\alpha Y > Z$ (where $\alpha =$ the average tax plus scissors rate on the farmers' surplus). In addition, the size of the consumption fund generated by rural direct producers to meet their own family needs, call this X, has grown substantially over the similar consumption fund generated on the communes, call this χ. Thus, $X + Y > \chi + Z$ by a substantial factor, representing the incremental growth in value and incomes

$(X + Y - \chi + Z)$ generated by the shift from feudal relationships (the commune system) to a mixed ancient and capitalist agricultural/rural crafts and industry environment. It has turned out that class process mattered a great deal when it came to the size of the surplus generated by direct producers. Not only did class matter but the impact of this transformation/transition in class processes was measurable. This was a critical lesson learned by the modernists and has shaped their policy approach to not only agriculture but industry as well.

Rural capitalism

The party-state was never committed to the prevalence of the ancient class process in agriculture. As previously indicated, the modernists were concerned with the generation and capture of sufficient SV to finance modernization. Class processes, disappearing in the party's focus on the social relations of production (one aspect of an even larger field of soft technology), was not a concern, particularly because the concept of socialism implied that exploitation was no longer an issue. Nevertheless, there remained some concern, both within the Party and the larger society, that the growing wealth of ancient producers might be somehow antithetical to the mission of the CPC.

Having seen their standard of living rise rapidly over the period of the reforms, ancient producers had found themselves in the enviable position of simultaneously controlling a larger surplus product and enjoying an increasing necessary product. Many economically successful ancient producers invested surplus product in enterprises other than farming. Indeed, the growth of relative wealth among many ancient producers, both rural and urban, had intensified the concern of the Maoists in the CPC that economic reform was fostering economic inequality and placing China on the road to capitalism. This concern was often expressed in comparisons of the growth in incomes for ancient producers with the falling relative standard of living for college professors, professionals, and managers in state enterprises.

Debates over Marxian theory have included a teleological argument that productive self-employment (whether called the ancient class process, individual production, peasant production, petty commodity mode of production or any of a large number of other appellations) leads *necessarily* to capitalism. Lenin made an elaborate argument along these lines in *The Development of Capitalism in Russia* (1960) where he argued that the reemergence and growth of capitalism was an inevitable result of individual producers engaging in productive self-employment.[2] In the 1960s, the ancient class process was out of favor as the Maoists promoted the notion that self-employment represented "seeds of capitalism." It was believed that self-employment inevitably led to the increased polarization of rural incomes, the marginalization of many rural producers and their eventual proletarianization.

The irony is that rather than some teleological logic inscribed in self-employment, capitalism has emerged into prominence in China because of the actions of the avowedly anticapitalist party-state. Exclusive control over the state gave the CPC the power to ban free wage labor contracts, which would have been sufficient to block any *evolution* from productive self-employment to capitalism. Instead, the party-state has supported the expansion of free wage labor markets and the creation of rural industrial capitalist enterprises by relaxing preexisting anticapitalist laws restricting wage labor employment in the countryside. Deng Xiaoping noted that,

> from the present perspective, the solution to the problems of agriculture still lies with the relations of production... As for the most appropriate ultimate form of such production relations, it is probably best to proceed on the premise that whichever form serves most easily and rapidly to restore and develop agricultural production should be adopted; and whichever form the masses want to adopt should similarly be adopted and legitimized.
>
> (Sun and Li 2003: 245)

This reference makes clear that blocking or terminating exploitative class processes ("form of... production relations") is not the objective of the modernists. The "pragmatism" of the modernists leads to the assumption that if the capitalist class process results in higher extraction of surplus (than either productive self-employment or feudalism) then it should be instituted. And this is exactly what the modernist-led party-state has promoted.

The *Four Modernizations* strategy, which originated with Zhou Enlai but is more closely associated with Deng Xiaoping, succeeds on the basis of generating and capturing a relatively large quantum of SV (a significant portion of which must be realized in hard currency to finance the purchase of foreign technology) without regard to the class processes employed. Industrial growth, particularly the rapid increases in surplus generated by the rural-based TVEs, discussed in Chapter 4, but also due to the resurgence of the SREs, discussed in Chapter 5, and the growth in private and joint venture capitalist firms are certainly playing an important role in generating the surplus desired by the modernist leadership for the technological and infrastructure transformation implied by the *Four Modernizations*.

Rural China has followed urban China in moving toward capitalist social relationships, albeit at a slower pace due to the resilience of self-employed farmers. This is particularly exemplified in the rise of the TVEs. As the growth in capitalist employment in agriculture has increased dramatically, so has the degree of unemployment in rural areas. Aubert and Li (2002), in their article on agricultural underemployment and surplus worker migration, argue rural China has seen a rise from 85 million in 1995 to over 135 million surplus workers in 2000 (this concept of surplus workers has gained increasing use as capitalism has become more pervasive in all parts of China).[3] Based on data from the China Statistical Yearbook (2004), one can estimate that the labor force in China approached 740 million in the year 2003, of which a little over 71 percent was employed in the rural areas, mostly in agriculture. This estimate would not include children employed in agricultural work. Some have estimated the total amount of agricultural employment (including children) could be as high as 900 million. The TVEs have been instrumental in employing surplus labor in the countryside. Deng recognized the major contribution made by TVEs in absorbing surplus rural labor on a large scale:

> for a long time now... 70% or 80% of our rural labour force have been tied to the land, with an average of only one or two *mu* land available per person, and most people not even having enough to eat or wear. But once we started the reforms and open policy, and introduced the responsibility system, the numbers of people engaged in farming fell. What about those who were displaced? Ten years of experience has shown that as long as we motivate the grass-roots units and the farmers, and expand the diversified economy and new forms of TVEs, we can solve this problem. The TVEs have absorbed half of the surplus rural labour force.
>
> (Sun and Li 2003: 250)

The potential for new additions to the capitalist labor power market in China are simply astounding. One of the side effects of such a large pool of labor is that in a more competitive, less state regulated and subsidized, labor power market, wages for Chinese workers could fall substantially. Economists for the party-state have the difficult task of navigating public policy between the potential for deflation if deregulation occurs too rapidly and the risk that too many protections could cause Chinese capitalist firms to lose their competitive edge as the nation opens further to external capitalist competition.

Over time as the state has implemented further reforms designed to foster the growth of capitalist production, the growth in agricultural incomes, output, and SV have slowed. Perhaps even more problematically, the amount of arable land is being diminished as new capitalist industrial parks are created on what had been farmland, bringing back an old dilemma for the Chinese authorities:

> China has already lost about a third of its cropland over the past forty years to soil erosion, desertification, energy projects, and, at an accelerating rate since the economic reform, to deforestation and industrial and housing development... The open space for industrial and housing development was and still is in the rural area. Regulations that prohibit the use of arable land for purposes other than agriculture were not effectively enforced due to guanxi politics and corruption. Peasants with money also preferred to build new houses or to look for a higher return by investing in the development of rural industry. There are two consequences. First, China continues to lose agricultural land. Second, investment in agriculture has been at a low ebb, having fallen from 6 percent of all national investment in 1981 to 1 percent in 1993.
>
> (Chen 1999: 109–110)

In a country of about 1.3 billion people, growing enough food is never a minor matter. And, in addition, there is the problem of keeping up the rapid economic growth that has come to be expected by the Chinese population, and which is a necessary, if not sufficient, condition for absorbing the aforementioned surplus population created by the expansion of capitalist labor markets.

In other words, the capitalist economy has developed rapidly but unevenly. Regional disparities and the sharply unequal income distribution between urban and rural China pose a significant challenge to the party-state going forward. Modernization of agriculture is one of the *Four Modernizations*. Technological transformation of agriculture requires bringing new hard and soft technologies to the hinterland. The growth of capitalism in rural China, including the growth of larger capitalist farms, is a two-edged sword. As rural people come to rely upon wage labor employment for their incomes, in the absence of a social safety net, the potential for higher levels of unemployment and related social unrest increase.

Indeed, if agriculture fails to generate a sufficient quantum of SV, it becomes very problematic to continue the current rapid national economic growth, particularly as the demands of a growing urban managerial class seeking to come closer to perceived standards of living of their counterparts in the "advanced" capitalist nations of the West places increased pressure on distributions of the industrial surplus. The modernists recognize the need to create more balanced development of the domestic economy and have taken measures to generate more rapid economic growth in the interior of the country, including the controversial Three Gorges Dam, which will provide some of the energy needed for more rapid industrial growth. Of course, even if this strategy is successful and the interior grows more rapidly, given the current focus on promoting capitalist enterprises, there will be a concomitant growth in demands on this larger capitalist SV by an ever larger contingent of managers and others allied to capitalist exploitation.

The competition over distributed shares of this growing surplus may further intensify, as various recipients fall under the spell of the new culture of conspicuous consumption. As the claimants to portions of the surplus attempt to gain higher amounts, increased pressure will be brought to bear on direct producers, in both agriculture and industry, to produce higher levels of SV. One way to achieve this increase in SV is to raise productivity (in both agriculture and industry) so as to lower the relative cost of meeting the consumption needs of direct producers. Raised productivity can be achieved by utilizing more advanced production techniques and means of production. In other words, the very process of "modernizing," innovating new soft and hard technology and encouraging mass consumerism (which is widely understood as part of the modernization package) creates pressures for more modernization.

Pressures to raise the surplus available for distribution to meet taxes and other social obligations may increase pressures to raise the rate of exploitation in both agriculture and industry. This implies a reduction in that portion of the total value going to meet the consumption needs of direct producers. This risk is particularly acute in agriculture, where many direct producers are still disorganized ancient farmers and an increasing number are wage laborers. In the former case, the pressure may be applied directly to the farmer who is both the performer and appropriator of the surplus labor. It is not unusual for ancient producers, faced with increasing demands on their surplus, to work themselves much harder and/or to extend their workday. However, if these measures are insufficient to meet the increased demands on surplus, the ancient producer may be forced to accept a lower consumption bundle. In the case of increased demand on capitalist SV, the pressure may be to reduce the value of labor power, either in the form of lower relative wage rates or lessened benefits. Agricultural wage laborers are particularly vulnerable because of the relatively low cost of turnover, the abundant "surplus" labor in the countryside, and the relative lack of enforcement of laws designed to protect laborers from mistreatment. If, in the extreme case, the pressures on agricultural surpluses result in a failure to meet the basic consumption needs of the rural population (X falls below some critical threshold φ, which is itself constantly changing and influenced by the same cultural dynamic that raises demands on SV generated in both the ancient and capitalist sectors), the centrifugal forces always present in the Chinese countryside could surface in the form of disruptive protests that threaten the continued CPC control over the state. Chaos is the primary concern of both the CPC leadership and the burgeoning "middle class" that Jiang Zemin referred to as the "new strata," particularly those who have benefited from recent economic growth by receiving residual benefits in the form of distributive payments from the surpluses of TVEs or other industrial capitalist firms.

Thus, the current iteration of the modernists ("the Engineers"), led by Hu Jintao (the new *primus inter pares* within the CPC), must negotiate the next stretch of the river by touching a brand new set of stones (experimental policies and programs) designed to garner an even greater surplus available for their modernization project and to keep the various distributive class agents satisfied. Among the problems that need to be solved: finding the catalyst to increase that portion of the agricultural surplus that goes to investment in more advanced agricultural techniques and related means of production without diminishing the surplus captured for industrial and infrastructure modernization.

WTO and the next great transformation

Given China's membership in WTO, the nation's farmers will be forced to compete with large-scale capitalist agribusiness enterprises with extensive support networks, both public and private. Failure to reorganize agriculture and related institutions to meet this challenge may result in China's farmers losing a large percentage of the urban market for their output to overseas producers. It hasn't happened yet, but that seems to be the result of official foot dragging on compliance with WTO provisions related to agriculture (to the ire of the United States and other nations hoping to crack the domestic Chinese market for agricultural goods). Compliance with WTO provisions may speed up the transition to capitalist agriculture. Larger-scale enterprises typically have more access to private and public funding and support. Thus, capitalist firms may be in a stronger position to obtain financing for new production technologies, seeds, fertilizers, etc. and be able to produce at a lower unit cost and/or with more access to large-scale distribution. Ancient farmers may be priced out of many of the more lucrative markets for agricultural output, although some will survive simply because poor infrastructure guarantees that local markets will continue to meet most agricultural needs. In an environment where money revenues may be critical to survival, it may be difficult for some ancient farmers to continue in business. Given the large numbers of ancient farmers involved, even a relatively small percentage drop in their ranks could swell the ranks of unemployed.

The consequences in rural China of large numbers of ancient farmers being forced out of business could be devastating. The multiplier dynamic that led to higher aggregate demand and more income in the rural sector could reverse, resulting in higher levels of unemployment and generating increased opposition to the party-state. Ironically, as capitalist agribusinesses take market share from ancient producers, perhaps even employing former ancient farmers as low paid wage laborers, total agricultural output and incomes may fall, even as monetized market transactions rise. Thus, the real impact on rural incomes would be understated because GDP mainly captures monetized market transactions, rather than actual output (which include a considerable amount of in-kind production and direct labor services). In any event, lower rural incomes would place new strains on tax revenue collected by the state, as distributive payments from an ailing agricultural sector (and other sectors connected to agriculture) decline, including losses for state wholesalers, who depend on agricultural enterprises for their revenues.

By all indications, a sizable number of rural farmers are already unhappy with both central and local government policies (as well as corruption by local officials that represents an additional drain on the SV generated by self-employed farmers):

> Peasants today are still vulnerable to ad-hoc taxes and fees levied by local officials. For instance, the central government asked local governments to eliminate about 900 such ad-hoc taxes and fees in 1998. But peasants do not have to employ the "weapons of the weak" to deal with these depredations... According to Chinese press reports, at least 830 incidents of rural rebellion involving more than 500 people were recorded in 1993, including twenty-one cases involving crowds of more than 5,000.
>
> (Chen 1999: 108)

The dissatisfaction in the countryside has even resulted in some modest democratization of rural governance. Villages have been granted the right of self-governance through village assemblies and elected representatives in a political structure reminiscent of the New England town hall form of government. It is interesting to note that this form of governance parallels those that prevailed in some ancient social formations in other times and spaces (Gabriel 1989: 135–139). It remains to be seen whether this experiment in democracy will survive or be extended to other realms. However, it is clear that the vestiges of state feudal relationships which resulted in village bosses attempting to reproduce feudal forms of surplus appropriation through the creation of *ad hoc* taxes have caused enough problems that the central government wants to put an end to it.

The central government knows that it is critical that rural direct producers have the wherewithal to invest and this requires their retention of sufficient SV to purchase the appropriate technology to become more competitive and, even more importantly, these rural producers need to meet their own (family) consumption needs or they may feel compelled to revolt against the party-state.

If rural farmers fail to realize sufficient value in sold output to meet the aforementioned þ level of consumption, whether this failure is due to WTO-related competition or other factors, there could be a widespread crisis in rural China. But such an event is the worst-case scenario. The higher probability scenario is for problems to develop gradually, as agricultural incomes fall farther behind industrial incomes, capitalism displaces ancientism in many rural locales, and overall unemployment grows from redundancies in both the rural and urban sectors. Indeed, there seems to be widespread agreement that the level of redundancies in agriculture far exceeds the level in industry (where the long period of feudal relations resulted in SREs that were generally regarded as bloated with redundant workers). In an environment where the memory of feudal obligations (of permanent employment and guaranteed living standards) persists in the imagination of many Chinese citizens, if these rural producers and urban workers join the reserve army of unemployed (an alternative name for "surplus workers"), they could become a tidal force in Chinese politics, culture, and economics. The CPC might be forced to change political course or, even more dramatically, might face a challenge to its authority reminiscent of the clash between Solidarity and the communist party in Poland. Perhaps that is precisely why the government is stalling on implementing WTO provisions related to agriculture, to provide farmers with more time to prepare and hoping to keep acceleration of the unemployment rate and the social impact of overall rising unemployment to a minimum.

Indeed, once WTO-related competition hits the Chinese economy with full force, severe limits will be imposed on the ability of farmers (or the state) to raise agricultural prices (a rise in such prices is often seen as a temporary panacea to agricultural problems – helping to both raise income levels and encourage more productive investment in agriculture) and some prices may even fall. The leadership of the party-state certainly does not want to bear the financial burden of the sort of extensive social safety net (a new iron rice bowl) that might be required to pacify the rural population. After all, ending the iron rice bowl, an expensive drain on the SV available for modernization, was one of the key reasons for the reforms.

What is the solution? The modernists in their technological determinism stress that science is the key to meeting higher productivity goals. Deng Xiaoping noted that

> the development of agriculture depends first on policy, and second on science. There is no limit to developments in science and technology, not to the role that they can play... In the end it may be that science will provide a solution to our agricultural problems.
>
> (Sun and Li 2003: 251)

The best solution, from the modernist perspective, would be for Chinese agriculture to be reorganized on the basis of soft and hard technology that would allow for productivity levels to approach that of Japanese farmers (Fan 1993). This may not be so difficult to fathom, given that current productivity in grain production in China is already comparable to that of American farmers.[4] However, the effects of adopting "advanced" technologies in agriculture are overdetermined by the initial conditions of the agricultural sector:

> Agricultural science and technology have advanced to fairly high levels in China, with some projects ranking among the best in the world and others at the cutting edge of global agrotechnology... Significant results have also been achieved in the development of various forms of rural energy from solar, wind, biological and geothermal sources. The results of such research have reached international standards. But only 30% of the fruits of agricultural research are translated into practical use, compared with 70–80% in developed countries... The main reasons for the slow up-take rate are insufficient funds and staffing to disseminate improvements and the poor quality of the rural workforce... The high rate of illiteracy among China's rural population – approximately 35% (30 percentage points higher than in the USA and Japan) is another major obstacle to developing a rural commodity economy.
>
> (Fang 1993: 282–283)

In addition, these technologies are adopted in the context of specific class processes in agriculture. The same technology would have a different impact when adopted on feudal, ancient, or capitalist farms. The same can be said of the impact of other social and environmental factors. For example, ancient farmers might more readily adopt certain technologies over others or might find that certain technologies, once adopted, might use more resources and therefore reduce the SV generated from commodity production, even though the technology is deemed more "advanced" than those which it replaced. Similarly, capitalist farms might find some technologies better suited to wage laborers than others, even if the preferred technology is less "advanced" than the one promoted by the state. All sorts of factors will influence ancient farmers or capitalist agribusiness managers to make decisions about technological innovation that might seem suboptimal when viewed outside of the context of these factors. Therefore, there is no one-to-one correlation between type of technology and level of productivity.

The modernists were concerned with achieving a number of results in their reorganization of agriculture: higher productivity and more total output, higher SV to finance investment by farmers, and, perhaps most importantly, a higher quantum of SV going to the state from agricultural enterprises. In pursuit of these objectives, the state council took measures to reform the Chinese economy. The test of their success is whether or not a higher outflow of SV from agriculture to finance modernization of industry and infrastructure (mostly in urban areas) is achieved. Today and for the entire reform era, the percentage of social investment going to agriculture has been a fraction of the amount of surplus generated in that sector (and less than 2 percent of the total). According to Fan (1993: 287), "If agriculture's share of national investment were to be brought in line with its share of national income, farm investment would have to rise to over 300 billion yuan (at 1994 prices), or ten times its current level." It's a catch-22. In order to raise agricultural productivity SV would need to be transferred to agriculture (presumably from industry) which would result in a slowdown in the modernization of industry (with the concomitant slowdown in productivity improvements and "competitiveness" in that sector).

Based on the current trajectory of the modernists' agricultural development plans, the future of agriculture is toward capitalist agricultural firms engaged in large-scale, relatively capital intensive production. As an important social aspect of the OECD nations, capitalism is viewed as an element of "modernity." Thus, the promotion of capitalism is integrally connected to the promotion of those technologies favored by the current leadership. According to Sun and Li (2003: 251) science and technology will aid in the "transformation of traditional agriculture into a modern farm system." The "modern farm system" would include not only tractors and expensive fertilizers, but also the deployment of wage laborers to carry out agricultural work. Indeed, it is anticipated that the trend toward capitalist agriculture will continue until that sector is controlled by vertically and horizontally integrated agribusiness conglomerates engaged in a wide range of production and research activities, including production, biotechnology research, and marketing (both domestic and international in scope).[5] Ironically, while WTO related competition will take its toll, resulting in the "creative destruction" of some ancient and capitalist enterprises in agriculture and industry, the trend toward conglomeration will be reinforced and accelerated by these same processes.

Moreover as capitalism becomes prevalent in both rural and urban China, in agriculture and industry, the dynamics of governance will be transformed. The central, provincial, and local governments will come to depend on shares of capitalist SV and other revenue flows linked to the development of capitalism (such as income taxes on wage laborers and managers) and by this process be more likely to become captive to the needs of capitalism.

7 Finance capital

Reforming the capital markets

In their quest to modernize China, one of the objectives of the current leadership is the transition of financial institutions that had been integral to the bureaucracy into relatively autonomous firms operating on the basis of hard budget constraints, with managers innovating the sort of loan and credit evaluation technology prevalent in banks and other financial enterprises of the OECD nations. In order to create the conditions for a transition from state feudalism to state and private capitalism, reform of the financial sector does not simply require changing existing financial institutions, but also entails the development of new financial institutions, such as the stock market, insurance companies, and a wide range of other financial enterprises. The construction of the stock exchange building in Shanghai, a beautiful glass and steel structure built in the shape of the Chinese symbol for rice, is reflective of this commitment, for as Deng Xiaoping noted, "Experience tells us that whoever has grain has everything." Just as rice has been the basic life sustenance for the Chinese people, so the financial markets symbolize for the modernists the role of financial relationships (and financial instruments, including money) in sustaining the Chinese economy. The financial markets are a medium through which power can be wielded to control assets and ultimately people.

Money is the historical starting point for the financial system. Money, in all its manifestations, as medium of exchange, store of value, and mechanism for allocating appropriated value, is an instrument for social control. Humans, exercising creative and physical abilities, create objects of value from the environment and the technology that was produced by previous labor. These fruits of labor embody value and are the substance that is allocated and reallocated within society by a variety of social mechanisms, including money, shaping all of the political, cultural, economic, and environmental processes that comprise the social formation. Money is the predicate of savings, which is the raw material (store of value) upon which financial institutions are grounded. The relatively high rate of savings in the Chinese social formation has been and continues to be an important factor overdetermining the availability of productive capital.

In most instances, the power to create money is vested in banking institutions and directly linked to the banking institution's ability to attract savings to its possession. China, like many other countries, operates on a fractional banking model, which means the money creating potential of the banking system is directly related to the level of savings (in the form of currency deposits) in the system and the required reserve ratio determined by the central bank, in this case the People's Bank of China. The state, by granting to specific institutions the social right to act as banks in creating money (in the form of demand deposit accounts and, increasing, lines of credit), selects which institutions are vested with this particular power to allocate and reallocate value, in all its myriad forms, including the form of productive capital. It is in the form of productive capital that money directly enters into the social formation as an instrument in the creation and reproduction of a particular type of exploitation. The reshaping of financial institutions, relationships, and instruments is a critical moment in reshaping the class processes in the social formation. Thus, this reshaping of finance has been a critical element in the transition from feudalism to capitalism. In China this has taken the form of expanding the money creating powers of banks, relaxing restrictions on savings and other banking deposits, including restrictions on interest payments and foreign currency accounts, allowing a wider array of institutions to attain bank status, reducing the degree of political interference in provision of debt capital, and gradually opening the banking system to competitive conditions that include foreign financial firms.

The initial condition of these financial reforms was the financial landscape under the state feudal regime. This landscape was divided into formal and informal financial sectors. The formal sector was considerably larger with institutions possessing money creating powers granted by the state and a highly bureaucratized process of financial intermediation. The informal sector was populated largely by ancient moneylenders, revolving loan associations, money houses, and lending based on ties of lineage. The informal sector functioned without state sanction and lending and credit tended to be on a cash basis, in the manner of revolving loan arrangements. This revolving loan aspect to informal lending provided an important condition for the survival and growth of the ancient class process, but was only peripheral to the dominant state feudal system. Indeed, the withholding from these informal financial institutions of official sanction was an important condition for the reproduction of the feudal order because it denied non-feudal direct producers relatively unproblematic access to loanable funds. The formal financial sector, on the other hand, was part of the feudal bureaucracy, supported the reproduction of feudal exploitation, and played an important coordinating role between various component enterprises and agencies of the bureaucracy.

The feudal banking system

Prior to the reforms, the state-owned and controlled banking system, an integral part of the feudal bureaucracy, played an important role in reproducing feudal relationships, including feudal exploitation and reproduction of a system of loyalty and vassalage among distributive class agents linked by the receipt of payments flowing from state appropriated feudal SV. The banking system transferred feudal capital to managers in state enterprises to satisfy administratively mandated costs of production. As Raphael Shen (2000: 170) points out, "Unlike its role in market-based economies, money played a passive role in China before reform. Money served more as units of accounting than a medium of exchange, since exchange activities for the most part were plan directed as well." The banks merely moved money between various accounts to meet the financial obligations of the enterprises:

> The largest share of nominal money supply was in transfer accounts held by the SREs. Transfer money was a liquid asset to the SREs, although it was not readily transferable to cash form. Three forms of transfer money existed: budgetary allocation from the state, bank credits to SREs, and the SREs' retained earnings. A budget allocation was given to an SRE for plan-designated investments. This was a grant charging no interest and requiring no repayment on the principal. Bank credits, on the other hand, were loans extended to an SRE as short- or medium-term working capital. The loan was simply credited to the SRE's account as transferred money for transaction purposes. Unlike direct budget allocations, both principal and interest were payable when due. The SRE's retained earnings constituted the third source of transfer money in the banking system. With the exception of a few adjustment and partial reform periods before 1978, the SREs had little retained earnings to show, because all surplus values automatically went to the state.
>
> (Shen 2000: 170–171)

The objective of state planners was to provide a necessary condition for the creation of surplus value which could then be distributed to reproduce the bureaucracy and certain social conditions for the continued rule of the CPC, including meeting the demands of the feudal reciprocity arrangement, and fostering modernization and economic growth. Bank managers, as agents (vassals) in a feudal hierarchy and recipients of feudal surplus value, were rewarded on the basis of their loyalty to the State Council (and the larger party-state) and not on the basis of making profitable loans. Loyalty was demonstrated by following orders, making loans to the firms that were designated for the receipt of such funds in the state plan. Thus, under the feudal arrangement, ER_f, the expected value of the loan as an asset, could be less than P_f, the net present value of the principle extended by the bank, to the SRE, much less $P_f + R_f$, the net present value of the principle plus interest over the duration of the loan, and the enterprise and bank managers continued their relationship without negative consequences to either. Under the feudal system it was inconsequential to the banks where in the bureaucracy value was being created (and in what magnitude) and, besides, the banks had no control over where in the bureaucracy they could lend:

> More than 90 per cent of total financial assets were concentrated in the PBC [People's Bank of China]. The PBC did not formulate monetary policy. Credit policy was dictated by the State Council vis-à-vis plan objectives. Financial flows were the proper domain of the central planners, not the PBC

> management. The PBC was thus a conduit of financial flows as well as an instrument of central control ensuring compliance with the financial control figures dictated by the plan.
>
> (Shen 2000: 170)

The state could cover the costs to the overall system by shifting resources around within the bureaucracy. Feudal culture and social relationships shaped the national plans adopted by the State Council, which included allocations of feudal capital to various enterprises within the bureaucracy, and fostered lending decisions on the basis of the same ties of personal and political loyalty that influenced the survival, promotion, and other rewards (and punishments) of bank and enterprise managers. Managing for success in state feudal China had more to do with maintaining the goodwill of one's liege lords in the hierarchy and adjusting budgets to reflect past allocations (regardless of actual capital requirements) than with making value enhancing management decisions or repaying loans:

> firms with the best political connections, rather than those offering the highest potential return on investment, attracted the bulk of scarce capital... In order to guarantee continued levels of investment in future years, firms made sure they consumed fully the current year's allocation, regardless of need. Firms habitually overestimated their capital requirements simply to ensure that, if output targets were increased in the future, necessary capital would always be on hand.
>
> (Steinfeld 1998: 68)

The internal workings of the feudal bureaucracy were such that there was no incentive to lower costs and significant incentives to raise them. The SREs used the banking system as a sugar daddy precisely because the rules of the feudal bureaucracy made this the rational management response. The result was that a substantial share of the surplus value generated within the state feudal system was trapped inside the bureaucracy and could not be made available for the scale of investment in infrastructure and new technology required to achieve the overarching objectives of modernization and rapid economic growth. The reforms were specifically aimed at dismantling the feudal financial allocation mechanism by which surplus value was simply shifted around within the bureaucracy. An important part of this reform would be the restructuring of state banks, transforming them from instruments within this feudal financial allocation machinery to commercial banks focused on profitability. It was anticipated that banks subject to hard budget constraints and, therefore, focused on profitability would carry out due diligence in evaluating loans. Loans to enterprises would, under that scenario, be evaluated on the basis of the borrower's ability to generate sufficient cash flow to meet commitments, including commitments to repay the borrowed principle and make the required interest payments. In effect, the restructured banks were expected to encourage behavior from SRE directors and managers that would cultivate value creation. The modernist leaders anticipated that these new modes of lending coupled with hard budget constraints would result in pressure on SRE management, who remained dependent on the banks for money capital, to make value enhancing (if not value maximizing) decisions in order to generate sufficient surplus value to meet various distributive class payments, including interest due to the banks.

The modernist view that reform of the financial system is necessary for further economic development is simply a variation on the classical Marxist theme that the forces and relations of production must be compatible. From the standpoint of the modernists, the highly centralized system of the state feudal period was incompatible with the low level of development of the productive forces in China. Similarly, the modernists viewed the role of the state as a direct appropriator of surplus value as incompatible with existing productive forces. The evidence for these incompatibilities was the failure, under the previous system, to secure the SV necessary for modernization and economic growth. Thus, the modernist reforms were designed to produce a restructured state, including the creation of a firewall between banks and other agencies of the state bureaucracy and allowing these relatively autonomous banks to become integral institutions in a newly capitalist financial system, which was deemed compatible with China's current level of development. The financial system and the enterprises it supported would be autonomous from the state bureaucracy because this was deemed appropriate to a social formation that was only in the early stages of capitalist development. The state bureaucracy would largely, though not entirely, give up the role of direct appropriator of SV and become a "modern" state acting primarily as regulator of "the market economy" via indicative planning, monetary, and fiscal policies.

One of the first steps in this transformation, in the 1970s, was reduction in budgetary appropriations to the SREs, requiring them to fund investment through bank loans (Gao Shangquan and Chi 1997; Gao Shumei and Schaffer 2000: 76). In theory, if SRE management had to finance capital spending from loans then the requirement to meet interest and principle payments would push managers to be more concerned about value enhancement. In other words, by inducing SRE managers to enter into loan contracts with the banks, with payments out of SV due at specified time intervals, it was expected that those managers would develop strategies for generating sufficient SV to meet these new claims. For example, SRE managers could innovate technologies (hard and soft) that would raise the rate of exploitation within the SREs, generating more SV per worker hour. Any strategy that raised the level of SRE SV would likely reduce the need for subsidies from the central government. Reducing subsidies was particularly critical if the central government was to shift resources toward its modernization and economic growth objectives. Thus, the modernists believed that changing the relationship between the SREs and the banks into one where the former had to meet claims from the latter out of SV would move the nation further along the path toward modernization.

Like stones dropped into the sea

The plans of the modernist leadership and the requirements of WTO may be synchronous when it comes to transforming the financial system into one that more closely resembles that of the OECD countries. The banks are expected, over the coming years, to become more competitive, both with each other and with the increasing numbers of foreign banks that will be allowed to operate in China. Banks that had previously catered to the needs of a captive SRE sector will now have to service a wide range of capitalist firms (locally controlled SREs and TVEs, joint venture and privately owned and controlled enterprises), and consumers, especially in light of the WTO provision requiring China to open up its financial services market to foreign competition in January 2007.

In yet another sign of the rise of modernist Marxism, the State Council has adopted an idealized model of commercial banking as grounded in a nonpolitical relationship of lending and borrowing, driven by *rational* profit motives and devoid of the personal and political ties of loyalty and obedience observed in the state feudal system. However, banks in China, like banks everywhere, are complex institutions (comprised of complex individuals) shaped by a range of processes (including political ones) and legacies. Among the legacies that must be dealt with in the Chinese banking system are the loans that were products of a feudal structure of loyalty and reciprocity, a system that was always unambiguously political, cultural, *and* economic, rather than the sort of abstract commercial loans (made purely on the basis of economic profit) imagined in the idealized commercial banking system. One of the most serious concerns of top management in China's commercial banks (both those older specialized banks that are being commercialized and newer commercial banks that have never been anything else) was dealing with their portfolio of NPL. The worse offenders were and still are the SREs, whose financial performance (measured in terms of interest coverage ratios and the ratio of debt to total assets) deteriorated in the 1990s after these firms, already changed from state feudal to state capitalist enterprises, were further transformed into autonomous (though still largely state owned) capitalist enterprises operating in an environment of intensified market competition.

The state-owned commercial banks, otherwise known as the "Big Four" (Bank of China, Industrial and Commercial Bank of China, China Construction Bank, and Agriculture Bank) had been closely linked to the SREs in the state feudal bureaucracy. Political processes related to the workings of the state feudal bureaucracy were always present in banking decisions. The early reforms were supposed to minimize, if not eliminate, the role of politics in lending. Nevertheless, the early reforms did not (and could not) insulate bank managers from the effect of political processes but, rather, changed the nature of the political processes that linked external institutions to the banks:

> During the reform period, decentralization granted local governments a greater control over state banks' local branches. The greater autonomy of local governments, combined with quantitative credit control, has given rise to political pressure, corruption and collusive behavior between banks, governments and enterprises. Local governments pressure local banks to lend to subsidiary SREs and TVEs and support local projects to promote local development. The expected economic value of these projects alone presumably would not justify this lending, and hence the recipients of these loans will

> often not be in a position to service or repay them. Furthermore, when SOEs run into financial difficulties, whether because they are over-indebted or because of other reasons, local governments and enterprises lobby the authorities to direct banks to rescue firms by injecting new loans – a case of the soft budget constraint. To the extent that these loans will not actually be repaid, they can be seen as providing in effect a flow of quasi-fiscal subsidies to enterprises.
>
> (Gao Shumei and Schaffer 2000: 77)

In other words, the pressures of intra-bureaucratic political processes may have been reduced by the early reforms but the gradual decentralization of decision making that accompanied the disintegration of the feudal hierarchy brought new extra-bureaucratic political pressures that shaped lending practices in ways incompatible with the idealized commercial banking model. Bank managers did not become commercial lenders purely focused on evaluating the net present value of the loans they issued; rather they were, among other things, interested in satisfying the local government leaders whose powers had been enhanced by decentralization. In this and other regards, bank managers were no different from the SRE managers taking their loans. Both were overdetermined by their histories within the feudal bureaucracy and by extant political processes that could be used to hinder, if not terminate, their careers. The continued creation of bad loans was not the result of irrational behavior (although there is always the possibility of such behavior), but of rational responses to an existing social environment. Nevertheless, the modernist leadership was determined to change this social environment to encourage bankers and borrowers to behave like the agents in the idealized commercial banking model. The first step in this direction originated with the PBC, the central bank, which began tightening credit conditions in the early 1990s in the hope of slowing the acceleration of nonperforming loans.

It is estimated that there is almost $200 billion in bad loans in the Chinese banking system (Bottelier 2004).[1] The State Council avoided a credit squeeze, which could have triggered a sharp slowdown in economic growth, by creating a fund to buy some of the bad loans from the banks. The state then resold the debt through four asset management companies that were established in 1999. Third party purchasers of the NPLs then negotiated with the debtor firms to receive at least partial payment: secured through either asset sales or by renegotiation of the timing and/or amount of cash payments. This solution had the following consequences:

1. many debtor SREs were forced to negotiate claims on appropriated SV with parties that had not been participants in or conditioned by the reciprocity arrangements of the old feudal structure;
2. the state effectively signaled a change in the meaning of lending and borrowing from some sort of grant akin to feudal period allocations of capital via the banks to real obligations of debtor firms to meet interest and principal payments;

3 the banks were given a fresh start free from the NPL legacy that was one of the outcomes of the feudal financial allocation mechanism. The ability of China's banks to compete effectively in an environment of increased competition, particularly from richly capitalized foreign banks, would seem to depend, at least in part, on bank managers adopting a stronger system for evaluating credit worthiness and less of a predilection for reproducing the relationships with SREs that had been forged in the state feudal period. Nevertheless, experts believe that the state-owned banks have continued and will continue to issue preferential policy loans to the SRE sector.

(Gao Shangquan and Chi 1997: 137; Chen *et al.* 2000: 11–12)

The obstacles to reform

It should be clear from the earlier discussion that the bonds of loyalty forged in the feudal bureaucracy, within which banks and SREs were component parts, are under stress as directors and managers in banks and SREs adjust to the logic of capitalist social relations. Whereas feudal surplus labor (in all its forms) was appropriated and distributed with little or no regard to the profitability of individual units within the bureaucracy, capitalist SV is secured within relatively autonomous industrial enterprises and shares of that SV must now be secured by the banks through enforceable loan contracts. Hard budget constraints, deregulation, and increased competition will oblige banks to improve collection of interest and principal from the SREs in order to avoid insolvency.

The State Council wants more SV generated within the SRE sector, with higher shares flowing to the state to finance modernization. However, if the money pipeline from the banks to the debt laden SREs is closed or even severely restricted then the generation of capitalist surplus value within the SRE sector could be sharply curtailed. This negative impact of the reforms might be avoided if bank officials could identify those SREs where additional finance capital might help in a restructuring that results in higher levels of SV, including shares of SV flowing to the bank to pay interest. The same process would allow bank officials to deny loans to that fraction of SREs where additional funds would only add to NPLs.

However, one of the obstacles to this scenario is that bank managers do not have the banking technology or experience to judge credit risk. They have no history of doing fundamental analysis of capitalist firms or of judging the fluctuations in profitability, demand, and supply conditions in an economy where competition over market shares is not only present but increasing. US bank managers are experienced in this regard and yet make serious mistakes all the time.

Hard budget constraints and competitive conditions in the market for loanable funds are not always enough to discipline bankers in their lending. The US savings and loan crisis of the 1980s occurred in an environment of privately owned and controlled financial institutions in a competitive financial market which had undergone extensive deregulation. Deregulated Savings and Loans (S&Ls) engaged in highly speculative lending resulting in huge nonperforming loans.

A similar crisis followed in the early 1990s in the commercial banking sector, in part, because of excessive lending to the commercial real estate sector. The resolution of the crisis resulted in a sizable credit tightening in the US macro economy and substantial costs to US taxpayers. In other words, these are examples of financial institutions operating in an environment that comes close to the ideal imagined by neoclassical and other modernist theorists.[2] And yet, these institutions were still subject to tremendous credit risk and sectoral (if not economy-wide) crisis.

Deregulation and greater bank autonomy can have unanticipated side effects. There have been a number of high profile corruption cases: $500 million stolen by a group of employees from the Bank of China; 80 million *yuan* embezzled from a bank customer's account by a former chief loan officer at the Shanghai branch of Citic Industrial Bank; the sentencing to jail for fifteen years of Zhu Xiaohua, a senior financial official and former protégé of former prime minister Zhu Rongji, for accepting $500,000 in bribes' (*People's Daily* 2002). As Nicholas Lardy notes:

> losses caused by fraud, corruption, and other lending irregularities in Chinese banks may be similar to those associated with crony capitalism in Indonesia . . . The People's Bank of China, . . . in 1996 acknowledged that some banks had lent funds without recording them in their account books, and that some nonbank financial institutions created false assets to cover up the black holes in their balance sheets caused by large financial losses.
>
> (2000: 28–29)

The theft of bank funds reduces the capital available for investment in capitalist (and other) enterprises. Unless it is assumed that the thieves will invest the funds in ways that spur economic growth and modernization, then corruption makes it more difficult to meet the objectives of the party-state. To remedy this problem, in 2003 the State Council created the Central Huijin Investment Co., to supervise investment transactions of the state banks (Lo 2004).

These problems are part of a larger principal–agent problem in state-owned banks and enterprises. The Chinese government, as principal/owner, needs to encourage agents working in these more autonomous banks and enterprises to act so as to meet the state's objectives, particularly securing SV that might be, in part, channeled into state projects designed to foster further modernization and economic growth. The separation of the SREs and banks from feudal era reciprocity arrangements, wherein all components of the state bureaucracy were protected from the consequences of negative cash flows, was supposed to have this effect. However, the Meiji Restoration-style dismantling of feudal bonds (wherein the State Council was the first appropriator of feudal surplus labor performed in state enterprises and could directly command lending behavior within the banks) embodied new risks to the state's ability to secure SV, both by shifting the power to appropriate and distribute SV of thousands of SREs away from the central authorities and by granting autonomous bank officials the power to direct the flow of finance capital. Thus, the State Council needed to guard against the potential for short-term crises resulting from the restructuring (and loss of feudal protections against bank or SRE insolvency).

The State Council has been particularly concerned that insufficient capital and NPLs might encourage more autonomous bank officials to sharply curtail lending to the SREs, triggering an economic slowdown that might accelerate the already problematic growth in unemployment. In an effort to resolve this contradiction, the state has conducted several bank recapitalizations as part of bail out packages and has continued to exert influence on bank officials to issue loans to finance favored enterprises and projects. These interventions created new contradictions:

> Once they have made policy loans directed from above, bank officials have nothing to lose by simply loaning the rest of their available capital to the highest bidder, regardless of the bidder's creditworthiness. After all, in the unlikely chance that the loan is repaid, the bank will make a handsome profit; in the more likely event of default, the bank can always be bailed out by the central state... as long as the commercial banking sector serves as the chosen vehicle for pumping in SOE "policy" loans, the central state cannot credibly threaten to stop bailing out insolvent banks. The government, in effect, loses the few levers it has to force ostensibly "commercial" banks actually to operate on a commercial basis.
>
> (Steinfeld 1998: 71)

Unfortunately, the idealized meaning behind the term "commercial basis" (some sort of pure economic calculation unhindered by political, cultural, and environmental considerations) has no real world corollary and bank officials continue to act on the basis of past experience. In fact, the state-owned banks increased lending after their recapitalization in late 2003 (Cheng and Hulme 2004). This is not surprising. The banks have received contradictory messages from the State Council. At the same time the banks have been charged to reduce NPLs, they have also been encouraged to increase loans and deposits so as to gain market share before the aforementioned 2007 date when foreign banks will be allowed to compete in the Chinese market for financial services on an equal footing. And the PBC and the China Banking Regulatory Commission have directed the banks to improve loan quality and to tighten lending in fixed-asset investments. Perhaps not surprisingly bank officials have sifted through all this noise and acted in accordance with their past experience by increasing lending to SREs and local government infrastructure projects.

While the SREs still benefit from governmental interference in the bank lending process, capitalist firms not controlled by the central authorities (including many TVEs and most private capitalist firms) and virtually all ancient proprietorships have been largely excluded from the financial resources of the relatively well capitalized state banks, putting them at a competitive disadvantage *vis-à-vis* the SOEs. These firms have been forced to seek loanable funds through interpersonal lending, or the considerably less well-capitalized banking cooperatives, illegal credit associations, and/or from loan sharks.

The informal sector

In the early years of the post-1978 transition to capitalism, the state experimented with "policy" loans to non-state firms, although the requirements of these loans made them very difficult to obtain and/or problematic to meet enterprise needs. However, as Susan Young notes:

> Such official sources of funding remained extremely limited, however, and often ill-suited to the circumstances and requirements of individual businesses. Bank loans were short term, usually for three to six months, and the guarantor generally had to be a state or collective unit of reasonable standing. It was often impossible, particularly in the early years after 1978, when suspicion of and opposition to private business was widespread, for an individual operator to obtain such a guarantor.
>
> (1995: 83)

Association with private enterprises (capitalist or ancient) was considered culturally taboo, and, as a result, the number of possible lenders to non-state enterprises was limited to those willing and able to go against cultural norms. Policy loans were created by the party-state as part of a strategy to favor enterprises whose operations matched the priorities of the central and local governments. The legacy of the feudal bureaucracy and its impact upon the behavior of bank officials was a serious barrier to expanding bank loans beyond the SRE sector, at least in the short term. Changes in bank technology do not necessarily help the situation. Standard operating procedure in OECD-based banks would include some evaluation of the loan risk. However, risk is not an objective phenomenon. Bank officials perceive loans to firms outside the SRE sector, and particularly smaller scale enterprises, as high risk, almost by definition. The perceived risk to lending to ancient producers would be considered off the charts. Prejudices against rural people are one of the determinants of a reluctance to lend to rural TVEs, even though they typically have the strong backing of their community government. Ironically, the public policy and lending legacy of the feudal bureaucracy does raise the risk to ancient producers and private capitalist firms. In addition to the difficulty these firms have in obtaining money capital, they continue to be discriminated against by the public sector in terms of access to supplies, land and building infrastructure, and energy. In a further irony, one of the ways that private capitalist enterprises and ancient producers may solve their supply problems is through guanxi (another legacy of the interpersonal ties of feudalism), cultivating a network of contacts often by the exchange of expensive favors or gifts (Young 1989: 59–60). However, TVE directors, private capitalists, and ancient producers are understood by the bankers as possessing relatively little to offer in a relationship of reciprocity, particularly relative to the vast resources and reciprocity networks of the SREs, especially those privileged SREs that remain part of the central government bureaucracy, and sources of formal sector funding still remains an acute problem for these enterprises. Thus, those outside of the SRE sector have had to turn to the informal sector for loanable funds.

Private capitalists and ancient producers, cut off from the state banks, can use their appropriated SV as a means for securing funding from informal sector financiers: a varied group including family members, friends, credit associations, and loan sharks. Kellee Tsai (2002) in *Back Alley Banking*, having conducted the most extensive fieldwork on this issue, at least as it relates to small-scale private capitalists and ancient producers ("micro-entrepreneurs") discusses the impact that informal finance has made to the development of enterprises outside the SRE sector since the late 1970s. As Tsai argues, the use of informal finance to foster the development of small-scale private capitalist enterprises and ancient proprietorships contradicts one version of the modernist teleology (including the neoclassical version) wherein economic growth (and, in classical Marxian terms, the advance of capitalist class relationships) can only happen within a context of legal rules that clearly define private ownership, use, and transfer of assets:

> When consistently enforced, according to this view, property rights reduce the uncertainty and transaction costs of market exchanges, and provide economic actors with the information and incentives to maximize efficiency. Consequently, some explain the persistence of Third World underdevelopment by its lack of formal property rights... In China, however, there *has* been a dramatic expansion of private economic activity. Financial entrepreneurs, private businesses, and discriminating consumers are accumulating, exhibiting, and trading their assets, both formal and informal. That this is occurring despite the nebulous nature of private property rights presents a challenge to conventional theories of capitalist growth.
>
> (Tsai 2002: 3–4)

Tsai's research on the dynamic role of informal finance, in an environment where certain essentialized conditions for transition to capitalism are absent, supports a post-structuralist rethinking of this transition. Furthermore, she demonstrates that the innovation of informal financial relationships and institutions comes directly out of the absence of conditions normally perceived as detrimental to "entrepreneurship" and economic growth, further challenging the teleological narratives of both classical Marxism and neoclassical theory.

Her work on informal finance focuses on three aspects: its existence despite government regulations against private money lending; its variation in form among localities; and the variation among non-state capitalist firms and ancient proprietorships in their use and access to informal finance. While overdetermination would argue that informal finance is shaped by the entire matrix of social and environmental processes occurring within the Chinese social formation, Tsai argues for a limited and specific vector of factors that determine the existence and variation of informal finance. For instance, Tsai (2002: 5) argues that whether informal finance thrives in a particular locality is wholly dependent on "local governments' orientation toward private businesses and, hence, their degree of tolerance for the unusual institutional camouflage that private financial intermediaries often have to wear." Although she acknowledges that other factors have influenced the existence and nature of the informal sector, it is her contention that the power of local governments is *the* determining factor:

> Ultimately, individual staff of the state decide whether and how to enforce specific regulations, collect fees and taxes, and issue licenses. Policies are not implemented uniformly because individual agencies and bureaucrats are not implementing them uniformly. And more important, an integral part of their decision-making calculus in policy implementation stems from their interaction with local economic actors. Entrepreneurs can offer material, employment, and social incentives to their state-appointed regulators... local governmental policies toward private businesses are central in mediating the proliferation or restriction of informal finance... Even in areas where a substantial portion of the population is employed in the state sector, local officials may implicitly permit the innovative provision of private credit.
>
> (Tsai 2002: 17–18, 48)

Second, Tsai argues that forms of informal finance vary within localities due to political competition between governmental agents in the changing regulatory environments. As she contends:

> Within the sphere of informal finance,... there is no compelling reason why institutions that remain underground would become alike. In fact, it is plausible that financial institutional diversity will persist as long as structurally induced competition exists in the broader political environment... Rather than delimiting the range of possible organizational forms, interbureaucratic and central–local competitive dynamics may actually spawn greater institutional diversity.
>
> (Tsai 2002: 262)

Once again, Tsai posits political processes as an ultimate determinant of variation in the forms of informal finance available to non-SRE enterprises. Implicit in her analysis of the political dynamics is recognition of yet another legacy of the hierarchy of feudal relationships and fiefdoms of the immediate past. This legacy influences the ways in which laws are interpreted, contracts understood and enforced, and the shape of financial relationships, even in an environment where feudal surplus appropriation and distribution has ceased to act as one of the bonds holding social agents together.

Lastly, Tsai makes the fascinating argument that ancient producers and small-scale private capitalist enterprises have access to different kinds of informal finance (and, more generally, have different experiences in social relationships) because of differences in socially constructed identities:

> Women in the coastal south who dominate rotating credit associations, migrant peddlers in an industrial center who rely on native-place networks for short-term credit needs, and former Communist Party officials who run private finance companies are all private entrepreneurs, but it would be simplistic to

> view them as sharing similar identities, resources, and interests... financing practices vary with their gender, residential origin (local or migrant), length of time in business, and strength of local political ties.
>
> (Tsai 2002: 19)

Tsai is here celebrating the complex identity of individuals within the Chinese social formation in a manner that some would define as postmodern (understood as implicit critique of the modernist view of humans as homogeneous, simplistically determined beings that underlies both classical Marxism and neoclassical economic theory). This postmodern critique underlies her rethinking the financial relationships in China as influenced by identity, particularly gender identity, even as she also falls back into a more structuralist essentialism of politics as determinant, in the last instance, of financial relationships (and, more broadly, of social change). Tsai's survey results provide evidence that a sizable percentage of the small-scale private capitalists and ancient producers were women and that there is a gender aspect of financial relationships which has influenced the complex processes and institutions of the post-1978 Chinese social formation (2002: 105, 109). For example, to the extent the banks and other formal institutions refuse to extend loans to small-scale non-state capitalist firms and ancient direct proprietorships because of a perception of these enterprises as gendered feminine *vis-à-vis* SOEs perceived as gendered male enterprises, then China might be more likely to develop a form of capitalism that favors the larger scale (masculine) version of capitalism over smaller scale (perhaps more competitive but also perceived as more feminine) capitalism and ancientism. However, as Tsai points out, the gendered aspect of financial relationships can also generate institutional innovation. The same structural and cultural barriers to women gaining access to capital from the formal sector (banks and credit cooperatives) has led to a preponderance of female participation in mutual aid societies and rotating credit associations (Tsai 2002: 104–109). The presence of these alternative (feminine/nurturing) institutions, as well as successes among entrepreneurial women in the private capitalist and ancient sectors, might act as a catalyst for changes (away from a masculine identity) in the gendered nature of the SREs and banks. The strong feminine influence upon the informal sector and the masculine dominance of the formal sector may need to be overcome to the extent modernity is understood as a more gender neutral condition. Indeed, the classical Marxist concept of socialism, which continues to play a foundational role in the CPC, has always been defined in terms of a protective and nurturing (feminine) state and aggressively competitive (masculine) economy. The yin-yang balance between the informal and formal sectors has shaped the trajectory of social and environmental processes in the reform period and will likely continue to impact development of a post-WTO Chinese financial sector and social formation. Perhaps new reforms will erode the firewall of restrictions, masculine dominance, and feudal legacy separating formal institutions from the informal relationships that developed to meet the financing needs of economic agents less favored by the state sector.

The blurring of the lines between the clientele of the formal and informal has already begun. What Tsai describes as "back alley banking" does not simply impact the non-state capitalist and ancient sectors. The SREs (like their kin from the previous state feudal arrangements, the TVEs) may be forced, on occasion, to seek loans from the informal sector because of harder budget constraints and less automatic loan rollovers (and stricter terms) from the banks. As the reform process has advanced, conditions have been created whereby managers in these state capitalist enterprises often do not have access to sufficient formal sector financing to meet their rapidly growing need for capital. Financial sector reforms will need to resolve this contradiction, perhaps by further blurring the lines between the formal and informal sectors, just as overall reforms (including the trend toward corporatization) are doing the same for the distinction between SREs, TVEs, and other types of capitalist enterprises. The social dynamic set in motion by the transition from state feudalism to state and private capitalism is one in which a wide network of social relationships is being forged on the basis of links to capitalist SV flows from capitalist enterprises of varying sizes and with distinct histories, state and private, but all participating in shaping the dynamics of change within the Chinese social formation.

Informal lending processes are intertwined in this transition. The complex ties of dependency between informal lenders and private capitalist enterprises have created a new class of recipients of distributed capitalist SV: informal lenders providing financing to these enterprises in return for shares of SV. Many informal lenders are relatives or friends who receive large shares of distributed capitalist SV in the form of interest payments. Tsai recounts the story of a Mr Wan who decided to leave farming and open a mini-arcade. He borrowed 40,000 yuan at 24 percent annual interest from relatives in order to start his business. His monthly distribution of SV to relatives totals 800 yuan (2002: 70). These informal lenders are likely to support the reform process insofar as it secures their position as recipients of capitalist SV: the support structure for the growth of capitalist relationships expands as such ties of dependency are formed.

However, the reforms may resolve the contradictions of the financial system in ways that are not favorable for the informal lenders. The State Council wants the state banks to expand their sources of cash flow. The state banks can do this, in part, by expanding their clientele beyond the traditional link with the SREs in order to capture flows of distributed capitalist (and, perhaps, even ancient) SV that are now going to informal lenders. China's membership in WTO has further opened the lending market to international competitors, creating even more potential competition for both formal and informal domestic lenders. Distributive flows of SV to informal lenders from privately owned firms, TVEs, and ancient proprietorships will therefore likely slow as a result of the reforms. Nevertheless, Tsai is optimistic that the informal financial sector will not suffer in an environment where identity and firm size continue to play a role in lending:

> To the extent that an economically active portion of the population (small businesses, or enterprises run by minorities or women) is structurally restricted from access to official sources of credit, informal finance is likely to continue... the substitution effect between formal and informal sources of

> finance is imperfect because they are not functionally equivalent. In financially repressed environments, formal bank credit may offer borrowers lower interest rates than the curb, but commercial bank loans generally entail complex application procedures, collateral or legal guarantees, and fixed repayment schedules. These conditions are usually more relaxed among informal creditors at the price of higher interest rates – or none at all... Regardless of purely monetary considerations, however, sometimes informal finance is simply more convenient in locally and personally defined terms.
>
> (Tsai 2002: 262–263)

Tsai's optimism is supported by the fact that any thorough examination of financial relationships in almost any nation will uncover informal institutions and relationships, both those within and outside of the law. This is just further evidence of the complexity of social formations. The transition from the prevalence of feudal exploitation to that of capitalist exploitation is not a smooth, orderly process of progression, but a messy, disorderly transformation, birth, and demise of a wide range of social processes and institutions. In this sense the financial sector is no different from other sectors in the economy.

The stock market

Financial market reform has not simply been focused on freeing the banks from the feudal bureaucracy. There has also been a concerted effort to expand the sources of future capital (including hard currency denominated capital) beyond the market in loanable funds. The development of a market in equity and other derivative securities has been a priority for the State Council because such markets are not only potential sources of capital but are perceived as signs of modernity.

Thus, the fact that the Chinese stock markets have so far not proven to be very effective in either providing sizable amounts of investment capital to firms or in disciplining the management of listed firms (Naughton 2000: 160) may be of far less importance than the fact that these markets have attracted a great deal of publicity and excitement among both domestic and foreign observers (and portfolio managers) and because the Shanghai and Shenzhen exchanges have, perhaps more than any other institution, come to symbolize the growth of capitalism in China. It is important to recognize that stock markets are both economic and cultural institutions. As an economic institution, the stock market provides a market for commoditizing ownership and raising capital. This latter economic function is limited, as firms usually raise money only once through this channel in the form of an initial public offering (IPO). It is relatively rare for firms to dip back into the stock market for additional funding through secondary or tertiary offerings as this negatively affects shareholders and stock valuations (spreading out/diluting ownership over more shares). Instead, the market for seasoned shares provides current owners with a ready means for rebalancing their portfolio of ownership shares and other securities. Ownership has become a fluid commodity, insulating owners of publicly traded corporations, including capitalist firms and/or firms dependent upon the receipt of distributed shares of capitalist SV appropriated elsewhere, from the sort of rigid association with a specific enterprise that is associated with private ownership. Thus, owners of publicly traded capitalist corporations are not wedded to the firms in their portfolios. Modernist Marxism, Chinese-style, has embraced the commoditization of ownership as a necessary factor in the current stage in development. The traditional belief that socialism requires state ownership may appear rather archaic when viewed in the context of publicly owned corporations. This is a point that will be returned to later on. As a cultural institution, the stock markets provide a way by which owners and creditors can send signals to both each other and to firm management, generating changes in behavior that influences internal and external relationships, corporate strategies, and the magnitude and distributions of SV. The owners may not be wedded to any particular firm in their portfolio, but this does not imply disinterest. To the extent these owners care about actual or potential capital gains (the possibility or reality of selling shares at higher share prices than they originally paid), then they must be concerned about the factors that determine share prices. Share prices are influenced by a wide range of factors, including profitability (which is influenced by the magnitude of SV generated within the firm), firm reputation, the ability of the firm to effectively compete for output markets, and general economic conditions. On the other hand, a firm's share price is one of the factors shaping these same factors that influence the stock price. Thus, a high share price may enhance the firm's reputation. A strong reputation may positively influence the ability of firm managers to secure loans from bankers, as well as their ability to enter into a wide range of other relationships critical to securing conditions for continued capitalist exploitation. The ability to secure these relationships may positively effect SV generation and profitability, which in turn may cause the firm's share price to go up.

And national stock markets can act as barometers of rentiers' perception of the relative riskiness of capitalist social formations, providing a signal to transnational corporations about which social formations are best suited for FDI. This signaling mechanism creates an incentive for the Chinese government to deepen those reforms that are preferred by rentiers and managers in the transnationals.

However, there is also a degree to which trading in the Chinese stock markets, including the Hong Kong exchange, reflects the mentality of day traders and other speculators. The level of liquidity in the Chinese stock markets is such that short-term changes in sentiment can have much larger impacts on day-to-day stock price valuation than might be the case in more liquid stock markets with higher percentages of trading by institutional investors. Nevertheless, this has not been a major problem in the Chinese stock markets and as liquidity increases the signaling aspect of prices may, except during rare market bubbles or panics, become dominant over short-term trading noise (where noise is here understood to be the effect of all those motivations for buying and selling other than overdetermined evaluations by rentiers of the fair price of stock shares, including trading based on rumors, data from time series or astrological data, and/or analyst recommendations).

Despite the fact that the State Council began the process of converting SREs to joint stock corporations in 1984, only a fraction has been allowed to issue publicly traded securities (with the hope that those favored firms would be able to raise more money in an environment where the supply of new stock was limited) and those firms have raised far less capital (particularly capital denominated in US and Hong Kong dollars) than had been anticipated. The relative lack of enthusiasm for these IPOs is influenced by a wide range of factors. Certainly the demand for IPOs of these corporations is influenced by the fact that the state retains control over them, in terms of ownership (a majority of the total shares of listed companies remains under the control of the central government and related holders of legal-person shares), in terms of SV appropriation and first distribution, and in terms of the political power to change the rules of corporate governance. This gives the Chinese state (governed by the CPC and still self-described as socialist) extraordinary power to simultaneously set the rules governing residual claims to the SV generated within SREs, as well as the rules for the deployment of investable funds, and direct control over how those rules are followed in practice.

Publicly traded SREs, state-owned *and* state controlled (at least in terms of value flows), represent a bit of a contradiction. The State Council has mandated that senior management in these firms have greater autonomy in shaping corporate strategies (and have created incentives, such as bonus pay, for them to take such strategies seriously), yet the state bureaucracy maintains ultimate control over the SV generated within such enterprises. Shares of these firms trade actively and are understood to provide some sort of information about the market value of the SRE's portfolio of investments (properly calculated with risk taken into account), yet these firms are part of a political and economic structure whose boundaries are very difficult to pin down – the state bureaucracy appears, in many ways, to spill into the firm and vice versa. Some of these ambiguities may disappear if the State Council gives up control over the SV appropriation and first distribution within these firms (placing fixed and impermeable boundaries between the state bureaucracy and the SREs). It could do this without relinquishing majority ownership. There are countless variations on stock shares and the rights that such shares confer. In any event, if the state were to give up its role as SV appropriator, this would undoubtedly influence the market value of these firms. But other questions would arise. Would the state bureaucracy adjust to simply being one among many claimants to the SV of more autonomous capitalist enterprises? How would minority shareholders' rights be protected? Currently those who buy shares of SREs have virtually no power to influence the internal value flows (including residual claims to SV, such as dividends) and strategies of these firms, much less the political outcome of struggles over corporate governance in China.

The contemporary Chinese version of capitalism is one where the minority owners are incredibly weak and the single majority owner has extraordinary powers. In other words, in the legislation and adjudication of corporate governance in China, there is no rule of law autonomous from the executive authorities within the central government. There is no independent judiciary. There is an innate conflict of interest when the entity solely responsible for creating, changing, and enforcing the rules of corporate governance is the majority owner of corporate assets, appropriator and first distributor of SV, and primary claimant to the SV generated by those assets, particularly in the context of minority claimants. This creates a serious political risk to portfolio investors in China, but perhaps is not much different from similar risks to portfolio investors in other capitalist financial markets (such as Japan) where minority ownership rights are weak.

Chinese shareholders may not be particularly concerned with this aspect of the financial system. In the recent past, there was no stock market and very few tradeable financial instruments. The primary asset held by Chinese citizens was their bank savings accounts at the state banks. These accounts paid very low rates of interest. The possibility of diversifying their holdings over a wide range of assets, including shares in publicly traded SREs is very attractive compared to this past circumstance. This is particularly the case given the high gloss marketing of stock market investment in the global mass media and the increasingly easy access to such media by Chinese citizens. The popularity of stock market investment may also be an important component in the modernist strategy of reform because expanding the number of Chinese citizens "playing" the stock market simultaneously expands the number of such citizens with a direct stake in further reforms that raise the value of their equity. To the extent such reforms are the same ones the modernists have targeted as creating conditions for modernization, then the expansion in stock market ownership may be an excellent tool for expanding popular support for the larger modernist project.

The perception that the Chinese stock exchanges are a big experiment may finally be fading. Global portfolio investors are always a fickle bunch, but they are currently interested in China. It doesn't hurt that China has become the leading site of FDI and the Chinese economy has continued to be one of the fastest growing. A quarter century of nearly double digit growth is very hard to ignore. The modernist leadership should not be faulted for taking advantage of the circumstances by opening the door wider to foreign investors, both direct and portfolio. The modernization project required hard currency funding and, at least for the moment, there appears to be no shortage of hard currency denominated financial capital to be invested in China.

To the extent that market participants believe that the party-state will continue to reform the Chinese economy in the direction of an OECD like capitalist social formation there will be no shortage of portfolio investors wanting to participate. The money flowing into China creates opportunities for further expansion in productive capital: more capitalist exploitation. It also creates the potential for speculative bubbles. The Shanghai real estate market may be a prime example of such a bubble. One of the possible sources of derailment of the modernist train is the bursting of one of these bubbles. Financial markets can be both a source of economic growth and social stability and a source of economic collapse and social crisis.

Perhaps it is concern over such possibilities that has driven the State Council to occasionally demonstrate that its vanguard party/bureaucratic roots remain well entrenched:

> Whenever the government wants to redirect the economy, which it frequently does, it often resorts to drastic, non-market based measures, such as a decree to halt bank lending overnight. [Also]... there may be greater uncertainty about the fundamentals specific to individual firms. The disclosure requirement is less detailed and less well enforced relative to the U.S. and Hong Kong. Less publicly available information in China may translate into more volatile assessment of corporate fundamentals.
>
> (Wei 2000: 222)

These sorts of actions remind portfolio investors of the uncertainties of Chinese capitalism. More uncertainty about the state's future course of actions is likely to lead to less liquidity in Chinese financial markets and those who do get involved in the stock market will be less interested in evaluating their stock purchases on the basis of the long-term cash flow generating ability of companies, but instead take an attitude akin to that of Internet stock investors of the late 1990s in the United States – buying on momentum and whim. Technical analysis is very popular in China, in part, because stock buying and selling is seen as a complicated gambling exercise in which money is made by correctly predicting the waves of optimism and pessimism of other buyers and not by selecting companies that, in the long term, will generate more cash flow. Of course, even those who believe Chinese stock markets and pro-capitalist reforms are here to stay will be influenced in their portfolio management by these waves of optimism and pessimism of the other buyers and sellers. The result is more volatility in the Chinese exchanges than would be the case if these markets were believed to be permanent.

Financial markets and the vision of modernity

At the Fifteenth National Congress in October 1997 the CPC reaffirmed its commitment to the shareholding corporate structure (gufenzhi jingji) as the model for separating corporate management responsibilities and ownership rights. The CPC also passed a new Securities Law that was widely supported by the new financial industry in China. The party-state leadership viewed these reforms and the consequent further development of financial markets as another step forward toward a "modern" China. In pragmatic terms, the hope was to simultaneously reduce agency costs by using the financial markets as an early warning signal for troubles in the most favored SREs, provide a means (external to the state) for raising the capital needed to modernize these SREs, and to bring millions of Chinese into direct allegiance with the new capitalist system, as shareowners benefiting indirectly from the appropriation and, where dividends are paid, directly from the distribution of capitalist SV. The Chinese rentier, an unrecognized member of Jiang Zemin's "new social strata" (of agents allied to Chinese capitalism), is connected to capital's circuit within the capitalist mode of production via commoditized shares (equity) in publicly traded capitalist firms: firms oriented around the exploitation of Chinese wage laborers, whose surplus labor generates the value that is divided into profit and interest, among other payments, upon which share valuations depend. The commoditization of ownership within a public market (open to anyone with sufficient capital to participate) acts as a means for making the reproduction of a private relationship (between the firm's appropriators and productive workers) social: successful exploitation of the firm's workers becomes in the interest of all those shareowners, as well as bondholders, connected to the firm via the financial markets. In this sense, financial markets serve a similar role in capitalism as white supremacist racism served in ante-bellum American slavery. In American slavery, white supremacist racism provided a cultural mechanism for convincing many socially categorized as white citizens to support the slave system because it was seen as reproducing their social status as superior to those categorized as nonwhite. It was via this mechanism that the private exploitation of the slave by the slave master was socialized, made into a relationship that a wide range of citizens, not directly involved, felt a stake in. The pre-1978 state feudal system did not need to produce such a mechanism of indirect allegiance: most Chinese citizens were directly involved in the feudal system, either as performers of surplus labor or as members of the bureaucracy whose livelihoods were secured via the distribution of the fruits that came from that surplus labor or both.

In that vein, it must not be forgotten that the State Council initiated the transition to capitalism in order to satisfy the economic growth and modernization objectives of the party-state leadership, objectives that required larger amounts of SV flowing into various state projects, and broad based support for these objectives. It was not the intention of the State Council to create a system wherein powers over SV were dispersed in ways that might threaten these objectives. Thus, it is not surprising that the result of the reforms would be a Chinese version of capitalism where minority owners have extremely limited channels of influence over publicly traded SREs, particularly over the distribution of SV. The Chinese version of capitalism was created to address the contradictions facing the Chinese party-state coming out of the feudal period, including low levels of economic growth, a perceived lack of motivation among either workers or managers to take seriously the creation of greater value within state enterprises, a general perception of backwardness, and the growing gap in military capabilities between China and its potential adversaries, particularly the United States. The resolution to these contradictions would require creating an environment where financial and productive capital were both motivated to act in ways that generated more SV and directed this SV to "modernization" – to reducing the perceived gap between China and the OECD.

8 Globalization and Chinese capitalism

The postrevolutionary transition of China from state feudalism to state and private capitalism has been largely implemented by the state feudal bureaucracy itself, as part of a strategy to achieve the objective of modernization. The idea of modernization is an expression of a version of Marxian theory that has gained dominance within the CPC since the death of Mao Zedong. The modernist vision at the core of this version of Marxism is grounded in technological determinism. Technology (the forces of production) is understood as the driving force (determinant) of social transformation (the social relations of production). Thus, in more than one sense, the Chinese transition from feudalism to capitalism has much in common with the Japanese transition under the Meiji Restoration, which was similarly focused upon technological improvement and implemented from the top levels of the feudal hierarchy based upon the notion that technological transformation would necessarily constitute the type of social progress desired.

The transition in China was designed by the CPC leadership to achieve the "modernization" of industry, agriculture, research and development, and the military (the *Four Modernizations*). This technological transformation in the means of production and consumption in Chinese society was and still is *the* top priority of the modernist Marxists who have risen to dominance within the CPC. Indeed, the modernists have made the continued adoption of more advanced technology (similar to technologies common within the OECD universe of nations) a cornerstone of their economic development strategy, and achieving equal status with the United States and European Union, a cornerstone of their international relations strategy. These strategies have won them the support of the leadership within the PLA (traditionally a swing faction within the CPC), which seems to share their technological determinism, and local officials, whose dissatisfaction with the highly centralized power structure of the state feudal period had served as one of the catalysts for the modernist victory over the Maoists. Thus, an important condition for the modernists to maintain control over the Party is widespread acceptance of a technologically determinist version of Marxian theory by Party members and others in Chinese society. Thus, the story of the economic reforms is not simply an economic one but also a political and cultural story, as well. The modernists were able to take advantage of the power vacuum left after Mao's death, as well as the widespread discontent with Maoist political strategies, particularly the GPCR, to generate widespread acceptance of the notion that adopting new technologies *by whatever means necessary* constitutes successful socialism. Success (or the legitimation of CPC rule) is manifest in the Three Gorges Dam, the Shanghai magnetic levitation Train, new skyscrapers and airports, a proliferation of automobiles and cell phones, the launching of Chinese made rockets carrying Chinese made satellites, as well as thousands of smaller scale innovations of new technology.

The combination of capitalism and competition over input and output markets facilitates the innovation of these new technologies in a variety of ways. Capitalism is based upon a temporary contractual relationship between employer and employee: both parties have options to terminate the contract. This allows for much greater flexibility for the firm management in deciding on the composition of the labor force. The flexibility of employment under capitalist social relations provides management in these capitalist firms with the freedom to tailor the labor force (and the soft technology of industrial organization) to different hard technology choices. If firm management is given the political autonomy to make investment decisions in the context of competition over output markets, they may seek technology (both hard and soft) that creates advantages over competing firms (or reduce advantages achieved by those competing firms).

The decentralization of the appropriation and distribution of SV to local governments, where it is easier to monitor firm performance, has, in the context of increasing competition, reinforced this dynamic. Local officials, and the enterprise directors and managers within the various state capitalist enterprises, as well as private capitalist directors and managers, typically share the technological determinism that prevails within the CPC, whether or not they are party members, and compete in an environment where certain technological choices are viewed as necessary to achieve "professionalism" and competitiveness. Thus, the tendency is to use some of the SV under their control to acquire and innovate these favored technologies. Jiang Zemin, the first of the new generation of "engineers" to lead the nation, quietly carried out a campaign to transform the internal membership within the CPC (a policy that began with Deng Xiaoping) to reinforce the dominance of the modernist worldview, recruiting new party members from management and professional ranks of the new economy. Jiang even provided a name for this category of citizens, who he would include in the "majority of the people" that, under his *Three Represents*, were recognized as constituents of the CPC. They were called the "New Social Strata." By calling them "new" he disconnected them from past exploitative social arrangements and gave them the patina of modernity.

Elements of the "New Social Strata" were expected to help make the reforms a success, particularly the directors and managers in SREs. To encourage this increasingly autonomous group of managers to engage in SV generating innovation, the economic reforms reduced or eliminated the rules that protected SREs from competition over input and output markets. Competition among these enterprises was designed to motivate directors and managers to use SV to invest in new technologies because of real or imagined benefits to the productivity of the wage laborers employed, making it possible (so long as wage increases are held below productivity gains) to lower the cost of firm output and provide pricing flexibility. Similarly, new technologies have allowed workers to produce products that have improved quality and/or marketing characteristics necessary to generate sales in a competitive environment. Chinese firms are currently producing a wide range of products, some with quite sophisticated components, for the domestic and foreign markets. To the extent the technology directors and managers seek to innovate must be acquired from foreign transnationals, the need to obtain hard currency is created. Under modernist leadership, it has been imperative that the party-state use public policy to reshape social rules such that enterprise managers can acquire these foreign technologies, including fostering conditions that make hard currency available. The party-state has fulfilled its obligations in this regard, promoting the growth of export-oriented capitalist enterprises that generate SV in the form of hard currency in an environment of new rules that grant firm managers the freedom to use this hard-currency-denominated SV to purchase technology from foreign transnationals and/or enter into joint venture agreements that include arrangements for technology transfer. As Chinese capitalism integrates into global capitalism, another channel for acquiring desired technologies is to use hard-currency-denominated SV to directly acquire either patents or the firms holding the patents. Each perceived step forward on the path to the most advanced technology available on the planet is, in the modernist Marxist vision, a step closer to the telos.

This technologically driven path is completely consistent with the internal logic of modernist Marxism. It is not, as some have charged, a form of anti-Marxian Marxism. For that to be the case there would need to be a general understanding of both the meaning of "socialism" and the specific landmarks of the closely related path from capitalism to communism (socialism being a "way station" on that path). No such consensus exists. The modernist vision of a technologically driven transition and the serendipitous path from state feudalism to capitalism have come together to form the content of socialism with Chinese characteristics.

The existence of forms of exploitation in post-1949 China, even the uncovering of feudal exploitation in the context of communist party rule, does not negate socialism. Socialism is, perhaps, the most protean of all the "isms." It has always been a shape shifter, capable of taking on many forms. In the post-modern moment of modernist Marxism when socialism with Chinese characteristics was born, the concept became even more malleable. Socialism with Chinese characteristics is a way of defining socialism as whatever type of social formation arises out of CPC rule. After all, the CPC remains the steward of the transition from capitalism to communism.

Thus, Zhou Enlai's *Four Modernizations* and Jiang Zemin's "Well-off Society," all point in the same direction: the path toward telos is delineated by technological sign posts, not class analysis. Deng Xiaoping's "black or white cat analogy" was a succinct statement of the public policy logic favored by the modernists for achieving movement along the path: do whatever works and whatever works are consistent with socialism. Thus, in fostering social relationships, including capitalist exploitation, that stimulates the desired technological innovation/modernization, the CPC is fulfilling its mission. It is through this technological innovation that the Chinese leadership hopes to move the Chinese social formation into a dominant position in the global capitalist economy and polity, displacing (if not necessarily replacing) the United States as the global hegemonic power. What could possibly be a stronger sign of movement closer to the telos?

The concept of modernization has been a recurrent theme within internal CPC debates over Marxian theory and public policy. However, technological determinism is not new to Marxian debates. One variant of classical Marxian theory has long held technology (the forces of production) at the center of a deterministic causality. The concept of modernization embodies the classical notion of technological progress and determination: hard and soft technologies are understood as advancing along a linear path from primitive to modern. It is not possible, in this conception, to create a communist society without the requisite level of technological development. Socialism becomes, in this technological determinist framework, the outcome of a communist party led government guiding the social formation along this technological path. Any notion of the party as advocate for nonexploitative class processes is either subordinated to the technological imperative (since it is deemed impossible to create a nonexploitative society without the requisite hard technology) or lost entirely. Each stage in the teleological development of human society is understood as the outcome of an appropriate level of technological development. The technology of contemporary industrial organization is generally understood, in this framework, as consistent with capitalist class processes. Thus, the advance of capitalist appropriation and distribution of SV is understood as a necessary means for innovating more advanced hard and soft technology. If the new forms of hard technology are progressive (in this teleology), then capitalism is similarly viewed as a progressive force completely in accord with the socialist (and communist) mission of the Party and the government it leads.

Rather than viewing capitalism as antithetical to socialism (or the pursuit of communism at some unspecified future date), the modernists view capitalism as a necessary form of social organization on the road to communism (a nonexploitative society). Capitalism is understood as a relatively advanced system of exploitation (in comparison to feudalism or slavery) that has built into its logic the flexibility and rapid response to competitive challenges required for the acquisition of hard-currency-denominated SV. And the acquisition of hard-currency-denominated SV is required for the Chinese social formation to advance along the teleological/technological path.

The particular variant form of capitalism adopted in China is also instrumental in this process. First, capitalist labor markets were established, creating the conditions by which Chinese workers could be gradually weaned from the protective confines of the feudal danwei and commune systems, where lifetime employment and social security had been guaranteed, to the impermanence and uncertainties of capitalist employment. As part of this first step, the communes were abolished, counties, townships, and villages reestablished in the countryside, and the former commune industrial enterprises became the community government controlled TVEs. Second, state capitalism was decentralized, with thousands of SREs transferred into local control, and restrictions on private capitalism were lifted. During this stage the level of competition within the new capitalist economy expanded, creating further incentives for capitalist firms to innovate new technologies. Third, domestic capitalists (both state and private) were forced to compete with international capitalists, as the Chinese government connected the Chinese economy more closely to the global capitalist system. Only through such a connection could the enormous surplus labor potential of Chinese workers and farmers be translated, through foreign exports and FDI, into SV in US dollars, Japanese yen, and euros (the hard currency necessary to acquire the desired advanced technologies).

The popularity of technological determinism within the CPC, partly shaped by its long history within orthodox Marxism, made it possible for the modernists to convince others within the Party to approve the economic reforms that have paved the way for the transition to capitalism. It was widely understood that the technology necessary for modernization was that which prevailed within the OECD universe of nations and could be acquired only through connecting the Chinese social formation to the global transnational enterprises that owned that technology. During the early reform era, the primary nexus joining China to the global capitalist system was contractual and market exchange relationships between Chinese SREs and foreign transnationals, including joint venture arrangements that allowed for the sharing of capitalist SV. This nexus was gradually expanded to allow greater foreign participation in the Chinese economy, as well as more autonomy for and decentralized control of the SREs and TVEs. The success of the reforms was manifest in the rapid expansion of FDI in China and the acquisition by Chinese firms and other institutions of hard currency for the purchase of advanced technology (and, increasingly, of foreign patents and firms) in the global marketplace.

The continued predominance, within the CPC, of modernist Marxism provides a critical condition for the continued expansion of capitalism within China and the deepening of the nexus connecting the Chinese social formation to foreign transnational enterprises. In this context, whether the transition to capitalism is consistent with the original stated mission of the Party (to achieve communism) may be beside the point. First, as previous chapters have demonstrated, class analysis cannot provide evidence that prior CPC policies were consistent with a transition to communism (having first effected the post-revolution displacement of private feudalism and private capitalism with ancientism and then restoring feudalism in a state variant form). Second, the concept of socialism as a transitional stage to communism is so open-ended that almost any social formation could be declared socialist. Socialism with Chinese characteristics, if anything, further blurs the definition and allows the CPC to claim that current policies are, indeed, moving China closer to communism. And third, the CPC hedged by restating its mission (at least in the "short term"), under former President Jiang Zemin, as "building the well off society" (xia gang she hui). Building the well-off society is simply another way of stating the objective of modernization. The well-off society appears to be nothing more than a society where advanced technology (from an orthodox engineering perspective) is available to and has been widely adopted by businesses, individual households, and the government (which implies the attainment of a certain level of discretionary income by these economic agents in order to secure this technology through market exchanges). If the well-off society is simply the short-term mission of the CPC, then there is insufficient evidence to claim that the modernists have explicitly broken with the mission of building a nonexploitative (communist) society. However, the fact that technological criteria have displaced class analysis as gauge for progress along the teleological path, a major point of contention between the modernists and Maoists, is a break with the class entry point of Marx and connects the dominant Chinese Marxian framework more closely with the technological determinism at the heart of European modernism than with the concerns that Marx (and many others since) articulated.

The displacement of the *class* entry point by a *technology* entry point and the related technological mission of the CPC are directly related to the measurable (and dramatic) rise in Chinese exports and in FDI. These quantitatively measurable phenomena, related to the goal of modernization, are the standards by which the CPC leadership (and others) determines reform policy success or failure. No attempt is made to directly measure the relative rise and fall of participation in class processes or the value generated within various class processes.

Thus, the rise in capitalism is not considered problematic, anymore than the earlier establishment of state feudalism was considered problematic for the continued monopolization of state power by the CPC. "Socialism with Chinese characteristics" is not only a success in the aforementioned quantitative terms but is also considered a justification for the CPC "vanguard" role in Chinese society going forward. The CPC leadership can justify the promotion of capitalist social relations by the argument that the party continues to guide these developments in the direction of the telos, by way of the well-off society. In this sense and ironically, modernist Marxism, and its underlying technological determinism, is a condition for both the expansion of capitalism *and* the continued hegemonic power of the CPC within China. As a further irony, these three factors, modernist (technological determinist) Marxian theory, the expansion of domestic capitalism, and the hegemonic power of the CPC may be conditions for the integration of the Chinese social formation into the global capitalist system.

Quantitative measures of the success of the reform are also reflective of this increasing integration of the Chinese economy with the global capitalist economy, with implications for domestic and global political and cultural development. Since the economic reforms began in 1978, foreign trade between China and the rest of the world has grown dramatically. In 2004, exports had nearly reached $600 billion (Hong Kong Trade Development Council 2005). Capitalist SV distributions worldwide are increasingly dependent upon the production and first appropriation of SV within China, with approximately half of China's exports generated by transnational firm activities in China. Domestic markets for consumer goods are rapidly developing, showing every indication of becoming, within as little as another generation, at least as important as the United States as a mass market for global suppliers of everything from computers, cell phones, and other electronic goods to automobiles, refrigerators, and other consumer durables. China is already at least as important as the United States in terms of incremental growth in imports, which has certainly not escaped the attention of senior managers at transnationals. The best way for these managers to meet their growth targets, to realize the SV embodied in enterprise products, is to develop an effective strategy for selling goods into these fast growing Chinese markets. In East Asia, China is already becoming a more important trading partner than the United States for a number of countries, including South Korea.

In other words, China is rapidly becoming a critical component in global capitalism. Consequently, China's economic institutions have accumulated massive hard currency (primarily US dollar) reserves – $609.9 billion by the end of 2004, second largest reserves after Japan (Hong Kong Trade Development Council 2005). As discussed, the accumulation of these hard currency reserves simultaneously serves to advance the technology acquisition and innovation objectives of the CPC *and* has global political ramifications. China has become an important participant in a wide range of global markets, including markets for advanced technology (both in hard and soft forms) and for hard currency loans to governments and transnational firms. The larger the role that Chinese institutions play in these markets, particularly the market for US and EU government bonds, the greater the bargaining clout for the Chinese leadership and Chinese firms in the dealings with the United States and the European Union. The recent rapid growth in US government deficits has served to intensify the interdependence of the United States and China, moving the relationship between these two former and potentially future adversaries into uncharted political and economic terrain.

Indeed, China's foreign exchange earnings from the United States are substantial. The trade imbalance between China and the United States is larger in absolute terms than any such imbalance between China and any other country and between the United States and any other country. China's trade surplus now accounts for 3 percent of GDP. China recently surpassed the United States as the world's top recipient of FDI (another potential source of advanced technology transfer and hard currency earnings). China is rapidly becoming the world's biggest "low-cost" manufacturer, flooding the global marketplace with relatively cheap electronics and appliances. Taiwanese firms have led the way in developing manufacturing (mostly reprocessing) plants on the mainland, taking advantage of the relatively low wages and high productivity (very high rates of exploitation, in Marxian terms). As already indicated, a substantial percentage of China's exports are the fruits of foreign firm production in China (rather than indigenous Chinese firms). This has led some to label China "the world's sweatshop."

Thus, the modernists' decision to transition China into a capitalist economy closely linked to foreign transnational firms has simultaneously met their goal of securing advanced technology *and* created a new source of SV for these transnational firms. China had long been lusted after by transnational directors and managers eager to gain customers in the world's most populous domestic economy and to exploit China's relatively low cost workforce. If the current trajectory of economic reform continues then the consumption of Chinese labor power and the realization of SV in Chinese markets will become increasingly important conditions for growth of global capitalism. The modernist-led CPC has made investing in China all the more attractive by adopting the most liberal FDI rules in any of East Asia's major economies, far more open than the rules in Japan and South Korea. In the domestic Chinese economy, local incomes have become increasingly dependent upon the reproduction and expansion of capitalist SV, which in turn, depends upon economic liberalization. The legitimacy of the CPC has become closely linked to continued economic growth: this growth being manifest in both rising incomes and visible technological innovation. To the extent that growth has become dependent upon the actions of domestic and foreign capitalist firms, government policy has become captive to the needs of these firms.

Three Represents: Marxism for the new Chinese capitalism

Former President Jiang Zemin's *Three Represents* was officially adopted as a new component in the ideology of the CPC, alongside Mao Zedong Thought and Deng Xiaoping Theory. One can think of it as an upgrade to CPC software, CPC 3.0, if you will. Whereas, Mao Zedong Thought was grounded in class struggle and contradiction, Deng Xiaoping Theory was grounded in the modernist vision of technologically driven transcendence and experimentation. Jiang Zemin's *Three Represents* starts with the same modernist premise as Deng Xiaoping Theory but then carries out a subtle but powerful shift in the rationale for CPC public policy. Deng Xiaoping Theory made Zhou Enlai's concept of *Four Modernizations* the central public policy mission of the party – the target result of a deterministic Marxian algorithm in which the continual adoption of advanced technology were the stepping stones. While Deng Xiaoping Theory formed the basis for "socialism with Chinese characteristics," Jiang Zemin's *Three Represents* is a blueprint for "modernizing" the communist party itself, for transforming it into a more "bourgeois" party. While Mao wanted to fight a continual revolution against the forces that would block the movement toward a nonexploitative telos and Deng wanted to "liberalize" the party by focusing its activities on modernization, Jiang, as the first of the "engineers" to take over the presidency (Hu is the second), wanted to completely change the nature of the communist party. Deng Xiaoping never rejected the notion that the CPC was the representative of the working people of the nation: peasants and urban proletariat. The *Three Represents*, on the other hand, displaces this notion of the party as representing the working people in favor of the notion of the party as representative of a majority of the people, advanced technology, and advanced culture. There is no reference in the *Three Represents* to class structures, relations, or transformation.

The rise of the "engineers," Jiang and Hu, as well as the other "technocratic" leaders who have populated their administrations, such as former premier Zhou

Rongji and present premier Wen Jiabao, is a logical consequence of the dominance of modernist Marxism within the CPC. The seeming abandonment of a primary theoretical foundation of CPC rule, its role as vanguard for the working people, is shaped by the rise of these "engineers" and their Deng inspired pragmatism. If the CPC version of Marxism becomes so dominated by its technological determinism notions of class structure, relations, and/or process are not merely displaced from the center but completely marginalized, then what is to distinguish this Marxism from other modernist ideologies? And if the CPC leadership abandons the notion of representing the working people, then what is the justification for its monopoly hold on the state? Perhaps the CPC is simply taking a cue from Lee Kuan Yew's successful transformation of his own version of socialism. The CPC has, in many ways, come to resemble the People's Action Party in Singapore, which has served as the steward of a dramatic economic success story, complete with all the technological trappings that the modernists in China so desire. The PAP has held onto power in Singapore purely on the basis of this successful economic performance, with no need for any sort of vanguard party justification. Maybe that is what the "engineers" have in mind for the CPC.

On the other hand, this would be a very risky strategy. President Hu Jintao has already indicated that he may diverge from Jiang Zemin's radical pragmatism. President Hu has even made speeches praising Mao. Perhaps this is an indication that the leadership recognizes the continuing need for ideological justification for their monopoly hold on power. Economic success, measured in standard OECD terms, may not be enough.

Nevertheless, the shift in party allegiances indicated by the first of the *Three Represents* – the party represents the majority of the people – may already be too ingrained in the party, given the internal changes in party composition that began with Deng and speeded up under Jiang. The "majority of the people" notion makes it easier to promote technocrats with no worker credentials within the party and that is precisely what has been taking place. These changes to the CPC may prove particularly important as China becomes more closely integrated into global capitalism. The metamorphosis of the CPC into a party that produces policies supportive of the growth of domestic and foreign capitalist firms has been fostered by the rise of technocrats (who do not simply place the acquisition of advanced technology at a higher priority than class transformation, but appear completely disinterested in such class transformation).

The second of the *Three Represents*, stating that the Party represents "advanced culture," acknowledged the interdependence of hard and soft technology: soft technology being embodied in culture and producing the social relationships that organize the nexus connecting human beings to each other and to hard technology. The broad concept of culture employed in the *Three Represents*, culture as a form of technology that exists on a similar linear scale to material technology, can be used to justify CPC support for pro-capitalist policies. The social relationships of capitalism are necessarily a component of the techno-cultural gestalt in the OECD nations. The *Three Represents* makes it the responsibility of the CPC to support "advanced culture," understood as those sociocultural processes consistent with advanced technology. It follows from this that the capitalist social relationships prevalent in the OECD would be perceived as a necessary part of techno-cultural gestalt that makes the OECD the epitome of modernity.

The last of the *Three Represents*, stating that the Party represents advanced technology, is the direct link between the "engineers" and Zhou Enlai's *Four Modernizations*, as well as the reform period policies identified with Deng Xiaoping. This expression of modernist/technocratic rule is, perhaps, the least problematic of the so-called represents. It rests on the position that technological transformation should be the primary objective (if not mission) of the CPC. This is important for political, as well as economic, reasons. The modernists rule on the basis of a coalition of factions within the CPC, linked to some degree by a common interest in the current structural transformations underway. For instance, the PLA elements within the Party understand the drive to advanced technology as meaning they will eventually gain access to the same sort of weaponry available to the American military, the sole basis for American military superiority. This provides a strong basis for PLA support for the modernist agenda. Similarly, CPC members who are primarily interested in the industrial sector understand the drive for advanced technology as meaning that Chinese firms will be able to innovate the latest production technologies, with a concomitant rise in gross domestic output and national income (an expectation that has certainly been fulfilled by past results of the reforms). Municipal and local party officials have been pleased with the dramatic transformations in infrastructure, as well as the aforementioned decentralization of SV appropriation into their control, and certainly recognize the modernization objective as benefiting them on the local level which further such public investments.

As has already been indicated, this focus on technology is not new for the CPC. Technological advance, not revolutionary changes in class processes, has been and continues to be the most persistent defining mission of the CPC. Jiang Zemin's *Three Represents* simply reinforces this prevailing ideology of technological determinism within the CPC by completely abandoning any reference to class. Whether or not President Hu or future leaders find it necessary to return to references to class processes, to signal their intellectual connection to Mao or other less modernist Marxists, it seems likely that technological determinism will continue to play a critical part in the formation of public policy in China for some time to come.

Missing the point about modernist Marxism?

The modernist vision is not lacking in either logic or empirical support. Whereas the Maoists might be more prone to placing economic growth at a lower priority than transforming class relations, the modernists set out to transform the technological foundation of Chinese society and there is little doubt that they have succeeded. From a class analytical perspective, this has occurred, in no small part, as the consequence of a state orchestrated transition from one form exploitation, the feudal form, to another, the capitalist form. From Marxian perspectives, this can be viewed as good, bad, or neutral. Marxists who believe that the forces of production ultimately determine the relations of production and agree with the modernists that the "advanced" technology pushing the social formation forward along a predetermined teleological path can be unambiguously identified are likely to applaud the efforts of China's leadership. Marxists who agree with the defeated Maoists that the path to communism requires continuous struggle against exploitative class processes and for the construction of nonexploitative ones (or the conditions for such) are likely to be unhappy with the modernist approach, despite the resultant economic growth.

At the end of the day, agreement or disagreement with the modernist leadership misses the point (or at least, *a* point). The Chinese social formation is undergoing one of the most dramatic transformations in human history and it is happening in the present. It will change the planet in every imaginable (and many unimaginable, at present) ways. The struggle between the modernists and the Maoists, the various social structures that came out of the struggle, the interaction of the Chinese social formation with the rest of the world, and much more, have created this moment in human history. It is a grand experiment under way and ripe for analysis, both Marxian and otherwise. A great deal can be learned from this transformation and it is important not to miss the moment. Thus, it is somewhat surprising that there is not more analytical (as opposed to mostly polemical) attention accorded to this transition within the Marxian literature. And not only analytical attention to the economic and political processes shaping and coming out of the transition, but also attention to the cultural processes – to the rise of modernist Marxism, Chinese style. There seems to be a tendency to dismiss not only Jiang Zemin and his *Three Represents*, but also Deng Xiaoping and Zhou Enlai. The path that China has taken cannot be disconnected from the intellectual output of these theorists or the debates they participated in within the CPC. Modernist Marxism and its underlying technological determinism did not simply contribute to the transition in China, it is integrally intertwined in that transition, and the effects of the transition may include elevating the importance of this version of Marxian theory in the years to come, and in ways not currently comprehended. This is all the more likely if the Chinese social formation continues on its current path of close integration with global capitalism. The cultural changes this integration will generate will not flow only in one direction – from the "advanced" capitalist nations to China – but Chinese cultural products, including modernist Marxism, are likely to penetrate the cultural barriers of the world beyond China's borders with a depth and frequency closely correlated to the path of globalization.

This may be particularly important in less industrialized and debt ridden nations, where disenchantment with "Western" solutions is pervasive. The modernist Marxism of China may prove to be an attractive alternative, albeit one those local leaders may find difficult, if not impossible, to adapt to their local circumstances. China's growing influence among these nations may be quite timely. The rapid transformation underway in China has resulted in a dramatic increase in the consumption of raw materials and a number of large Chinese SREs are rapidly morphing into transnational superorganisms with operations spanning the globe in search of opportunities to tap into local sources of needed material inputs or other commodities in high demand back home. There are a large number of nations possessing coveted inputs and with governments alienated, to some extent, from the United States and other "Western" nations. The perception that the United States is governed by imperialists (if not outright crusaders) only widens the opening for the growing Chinese transnational sector.

China, globalization, and the rise of cybersuperorganisms

It is in this context that we can observe that twenty-first century globalization is the latest stage in a process of shrinking economic and cultural distance and decentering capitalism, interrupted at certain intervals by world wars, political isolationism, and failed attempts to create competing political-economic power centers (such as the CMEA). The social technic of the transnational corporation (within which political, economic, and cultural power is increasingly congealed) has been the primary catalyst for this transformation. Transnationals have become geographically decentered cybersuperorganisms with internal and external elements connected by increasingly complex computer/internet/telecommunication/financial/legal networks. These "high technology" networks facilitate rapid communication and determinate lines of control between operating and related units directly inside the corporate structure of the transnational and quasi-independent firms connected via outsourcing arrangements for production, design, and testing spread around the globe. They also facilitate similar connections between the transnational and various local and multinational governmental bodies, providing the mechanisms by which globalization is programmed to serve the interests of transnational growth.

The transnational cybersuperorganism is comprised of a culturally diverse population of cyberorganically linked workers and managers, with subordinate linkages to external political, cultural, and economic agents (such as managers of government regulatory agencies, trustees of think tanks dependent upon contributions from transnationals or related parties, directors of quasi-independent corporations dependent upon contractual receipts of cash flow from transnationals, spouses, children, and other relatives and friends). The ability to rapidly transmit commands and communicate information across geographic space has become increasingly sophisticated, with the quantity and quality of data transmission rapidly approaching the boundaries of virtual presence, where corporate employees can interact across geographic space in ways that had previously only been possible by physical travel. These advances in communication technology coupled with computer assisted design and manufacturing, have made it possible to disperse the production process across greater geographic space without losing centralized control. Managers, attorneys, and sales personnel within these cybersuperorganisms use the same technology to facilitate rapid consummation of agreements as commercial relationships routinely cross international (and currency) boundaries. These cybersuperorganisms can be structured as private or state capitalist enterprises, financial or nonfinancial enterprises, industrial or nonindustrial enterprises, the entire panoply of economic activities. They can be joined in conglomerates across various sectors of the global economy or operate as specialists in the global economic sea.

The transnational firm qua cybersuperorganism is the nuclear force transforming the meaning of community and citizenship – the OECD nation states have, to a significant extent, been captured by the transnationals. Transnationals control significant aspects of the culture producing machinery, either directly (oligopolistic control over major mass media production and distribution) or indirectly (such as via their advertising budgets, vendor, and clientelist relationships), and increasingly command the webs of communication technology (broadband, private corporate communications networks, data collection, storage and processing networks, including effective control over information on both citizens and firms, etc.) necessary to the new cyber social formation. By developing patron–client relationships with political leaders and other government officials (including promises of corporate life after political death/dormancy), these cybersuperorganisms, whether themselves part of state bureaucracies or operating as private enterprises, connect their power centers directly to the agencies of the state and direct the flow of public policy in the interest of further enhancing the economic, political, cultural, and environmental hegemony of the transnational collective. This dynamic process has been exported to Russia, Eastern Europe, and other emerging competitive capitalist spaces. The interconnectivity of input and output markets, global trading agreements, and changing technology (internet, cell phones, satellites, etc.) that allows for rapid and seamless global communication results in the decentering of both production and exchange relationships, even as political power is simultaneously decentralized and recentered within the corporate executive offices and board rooms.

China has yet to be fully incorporated into this process. By maintaining state capitalism, even in its current relatively decentralized form, the Chinese government remains relatively autonomous and plays a significant leadership role in shaping corporate behavior within the political boundaries of the People's Republic. Government ministries, under the leadership of the State Council, continue to exercise regulatory control over the expansion of factories and other construction, even when SREs and TVEs have been placed under local control. This continuing hegemony of the central government allows for the continued formulation of policies that do not always serve the interests of the transnationals *or* local firms (although this does not necessarily distinguish Chinese capitalism from the variant forms of capitalism in the European Community or North America, where there are often occasions where local or national interests conflict with the specific interests of transnational firms – in many ways, it is still more a matter of degree of autonomous political control by governments, rather than a matter of kind of control).

Nevertheless, there are signs of transformation along "Western" political lines, in that the relative power balance may be shifting away from the central government and toward a rapidly transforming collective of capitalist firms, including those under local authority, private domestic capitalists, and foreign capitalist transnationals. Local officials, who were instrumental in the rise to power of the modernist leadership, now operate both inside the corporate sphere and as public officials, regularly interacting with managers of transnationals and others outside the traditional power structure. Their growing economic clout and political autonomy has both fueled the rising level of corruption in the Chinese economy and threatens to further erode the powers of the center.

Central government officials, who escaped the unmanageable requirements of comprehensive command planning, now find themselves having difficulty managing the complex flows of influence and revenues from a wide array of enterprises. Regulating this complexity is not easy or straightforward. Often the transnationals have the political savvy and sophisticated structure of influence construction and manipulation to shape public policy, even in a nation as relatively autonomous as China. These influences have been manifest in a variety of ways, including significant changes to the taxation system: foreign transnationals have extracted tax breaks and other subsidies that give them competitive advantages over domestic firms and add to the generation of SV flows to finance their cybersuperorganism.

WTO

Perhaps most importantly, the modernist leadership signed onto the WTO, which is a critical mechanism for extending and protecting the political rights of transnational capitalism against the parochial interests of local citizenries. Some have argued that the Chinese leadership was simply too weak to resist the push by the American government to join WTO and, by doing so, open the Chinese economy to American firms and farmers. This argument implies that the potential negative consequences on Chinese firms and farmers are not something the Chinese administration would have accepted if not for external pressure. WTO comes with a long laundry list of strings attached, binding agreements that force "sovereign" governments to change their economic rules of the game. Given the current mono-superpower status of the United States, it is not difficult to conclude that the growing pervasiveness of these supranational rules of the economic game must be in the interest of American firms and farmers. After all, WTO is the only international agreement where the US government has actually conceded direct and binding judicial authority to an outside body.

On first glance, such external intrusions upon the sovereignty of the Chinese government would seem to be something to be avoided, particularly given Chinese sentiment about such external coercion (and very much active memories of "Western" imperialism in China). Indeed, there is opposition within the party to the growing role of foreigners in Chinese economic life, especially from the Left. But perhaps it is precisely this continued struggle within the CPC over policy, even if relatively muted, that was the reason for the modernists pushing so hard for WTO. They recognized that the long-term struggle within the party between themselves and the Left (including the remaining Maoists) may be in a relatively quiet period but is hardly over. The modernists have used WTO as a mechanism for forcing more rapid and deeper pro-capitalist changes in China's economic rules over the objections of the Leftist minority. In other words, WTO provided a convenient tool for keeping the Left in check within the CPC and institutionalizing reform.

In addition, WTO provided the current leadership with a fall guy for the problems that developing a competitive capitalist economy, linked to the expanding global capitalist economy, have produced. Restructuring of SREs has resulted in a rapid increase in unemployment, street demonstrations, and sabotage. The rise of the Shanghai "engineers" to leadership of the Party has resulted in a less "peasant friendly" administration. The shift from policies that might be described as pro-ancient (favoring productive self-employment) in rural China to policies designed to guarantee relatively low food prices and the expansion in larger scale capitalist enterprises, even in agriculture, coupled with all too frequent corruption at the village level, has sparked farmer protests. The potential for even more wide-scale antigovernment demonstrations increases with each new set of plant closings and layoffs and the increasing inequality between "town and countryside," regions, and between individuals in different "class positions." The fact that membership in WTO was promoted as crucial to continued economic prosperity in China and that the United States and the European Union were seen as forcing China to make major concessions provided the modernists with the raw material for blame shifting. They blame the growing unemployment and other economic ills on the United States and European Union, saying that they (the modernist leadership) had little choice but to cave into the demands, even if it cost many Chinese their jobs. Those who argue that the Americans coerced the Chinese leadership into joining WTO are, in this scenario, playing exactly the tune that the modernists want to hear. However, the modernist-led government had already moved to decisively end the old lifetime employment system (a key component of state feudalism) and melted down the iron rice bowl of social welfare and social security (both part of the feudal reciprocity arrangement and a "sign" of Chinese socialism, Maoist style). The Chinese government's role in shaping the current transition to competitive capitalism may be obscured by the rapid penetration of the Chinese domestic economy by foreign-based transnational firms as WTO provisions are implemented, resulting in sharp tariff reductions and the fall of the Great Wall of nontariff barriers. These policy decisions do not so much reflect the clout of foreign firms as the aggressive strategy of China's modernist leadership in seeking to attract foreign firms into specific locations within China and to encourage technological diffusion. The *Four Modernizations* required this diffusion and so China's leaders were consciously trying to find ways to attract ideas and hard technology into the country. The advance of China to the status of top recipient of FDI is one indication of the success of this strategy (between 1991 and 1996, FDI grew by an astounding average rate of 60 percent per annum). Transnational firms from Hong Kong, Taiwan, Japan, South Korea, Germany, the United States, Sweden, etc. have transported advanced technology (both in material technics, the hardware of technological development, and in the structure of industrial organization, the software of technological development) into mainland China, in many cases sharing the technology with SREs through joint ventures or other forms of cooperative arrangements, but in all cases working closely with local, provincial, and often national political leaders.

The decentering of political power in China

A clearer sign that political power is becoming increasingly decentered, with capitalist firms gaining more influence over public policies can be seen in the growing clout of domestic capitalists. The same dynamic that brought foreign transnationals favorable treatment in the tax code was employed by domestic capitalists to alter this situation. In 1994, the Chinese government moved to satisfy the complaints of executives in domestic firms, including local officials speaking on behalf of their RSCE conglomerates, that the tax code favored foreign firms by adopting a new uniform taxation system designed to tax all firms, foreign and domestic, at the same corporate tax rate of 33 percent and value added tax rate of 17 percent. But the most dramatic example of the growing clout of domestic capitalists has been the aforementioned expansion in CPC membership. Recognizing that the Party's old constituencies, the farmers and urban wage laborers, may become disenchanted with the reforms as rural incomes stagnate and unemployment rises, the leadership has broadened (if not outright changed) its base of support to include agents linked to the growth of capitalism.

The party continues to recruit more members from the ranks of capitalist "entrepreneurs" and managers in both state-owned and private capitalist firms.[1] This would further dilute the strength of the Left within the Party and build a foundation for even more dramatic reforms in future. It will also create the basis for the party-state being "captured" to serve the interests of a narrow constituency more focused on the appropriation of SV than broader social development. The process of changing the "class composition" of the CPC is shaped, in part, by the growing power and influence of indigenous capitalist firms, both state and private. The distributive payments of SV from these capitalist firms, as well as the power these firms hold over the magnitude and income of wage laborers spreads their influence throughout various levels of government and the larger social formation. Local government involvement in this growth of capitalism creates a context within which these public officials loyalties become complexly divided between commercial and social interests. It may be only a matter of time before non-Chinese based transnationals, producing increasing amounts of SV, hiring ever more wage laborers within China, paying tax revenues to various levels of government, and hiring relatively well paid managerial personnel from among China's educated elite, who have been increasingly exposed to the hardware and software deployed by foreign transnational firms in the realization of SV (the quantum matter of economic and social transformation), capture their own elements within the CPC (perhaps this would necessitate a fourth "represent") to a significant enough extent to shape and/or reshape public policy.

Thus, it may simply be that Jiang Zemin was a pioneer in translating this change in political dynamics into ideological form with his doctrine of the *Three Represents*, but the policy of opening the Party to the managerial elite within domestic capitalist firms, as well as other professionals and private entrepreneurs critical to the development of a state and private capitalist (and, to a lesser extent, ancient) economy, may have already been baked in the reform cake, so to speak. The "engineers" have, therefore, moved to decidedly alter the demographics of the CPC in accord with changes that have already occurred in the linkages between the political apparatuses of the party-state and the growing private capitalist sector. Thus, Jiang Zemin and Hu Jintao, and their policies, can also be understood as shaped by the very dynamics that the reforms set in motion.

It is not surprising then that the *Three Represents* unleashed a fierce struggle within the CPC that seems to have been won by Jiang and carried forward by new president Hu Jintao.[2] Thus, the nature of the internecine struggles over policy within the CPC may be significantly different in the future from the past struggles between the modernists and Maoists. The basic Left versus Right struggle may be displaced by various struggles between politicians linked to different economic constituencies. The divisions will not be simply between domestic versus foreign or state versus private capitalist firms. Foreign manufacturers seeking easy access to domestic Chinese markets or low-cost labor in China (including low-cost skilled technical and managerial talent), either through direct operations, joint ventures, mergers with or acquisitions of Chinese firms, or through subcontractors may cultivate their own group of loyal politicos within the CPC and local governments. This will be all the more likely if corporatization should eventually make it easier for foreign transnationals to become majority/controlling owners of domestic enterprises, inheriting a complex web of financial relationships and personal ties.

Similarly, foreign banks, insurance firms, and other financial institutions may capture their own clique within the CPC. Foreign telecoms may do the same. These cliques may struggle on the same side for certain policies and be in opposition on other policies. Similarly, politicians linked to domestic textile firms may ally with politicians more closely linked to foreign wholesalers or retailers of clothing in support of certain policies. The undemocratic nature of the CPC-dominated state may actually foster this sort of pro-capitalist clientalism. The democratization of local politics has already opened the door to increased use of economic influence to shape policy outcomes. And when and if the Chinese state moves to broaden the democratization process, the power of capitalist firms over citizens' lives and over which politicians are funded may be such that the policy choices might not be significantly altered (in the sense of promoting capitalist development and integration with the global capitalist economy) from those under the present less democratic political arrangements. On the other hand, the aforementioned local democratization may actually work to reinforce the status quo than to change it. Public officials at the local level have access to both political and economic power and are likely to use it to promote their own reelection and the reproduction of their broader socioeconomic power. In this instance, politicians under democratic rules are more likely to work against opening up the local economy to outside capitalist enterprises, including (or especially) foreign transnationals. The fusion of local government and capitalist enterprises gives local officials considerable economic clout, particularly in an environment where the central government frets over rising unemployment and the potential for social unrest. The decentralization of control over value flows placed the levers of employment creating (or destroying) investment decisions, to a significant extent, under the control of local officials. The central government is walking a tightrope as it attempts to keep economic growth going without losing further authority to these local politico-economic forces, as well as to private domestic capitalists, and transnationals. Each and every one of these economic entities is in a position to put pressure on the central government and, therefore, on the CPC.

China connects to the transnational grid

The race is on to shape the next phase in the economic reforms. It is a game of strategy. In this regard, the transnationals *may* be at an advantage over competing interests. The basic mechanism for connecting political bureaucracies to the transnational networks, that is, distributive class payments and the use of communications technology to transmit information, requests, and commands is the same under democratic institutional relationships as it is under the less democratic CPC arrangements. Indeed, even the mechanism of capital strikes (where transnationals refuse, *en masse*, to invest in a nation where the home government refuses to cooperate) might be no less effective under the latter arrangement than the former. A severe drop in FDI (which has become increasingly important to Chinese economic growth and has always been an important factor in modernization), for example, might arguably pose an even larger threat to the CPC under the current political structure than to democratically elected politicians. Either arrangement poses serious problems for those who would favor more local control over public policies (including policies shaping the quality of the natural environment, employment, infrastructure, and so on), although the more democratic the political processes shaping public policy the more likely citizens will be in a position to exert the primacy of policies that would not be favored by the transnationals (or the bureaucracy).

In the world of WTO and cybercommunications, it has become relatively easy for top-level managers of transnational corporations to transmit information (e.g. commands and plans) and move financial resources across distant geographic space. In addition, it has become easier to process information on both economic and political transactions. The ability to connect "local" politicians to transnational headquarters should facilitate increasing corporate influence over political policy. In this case, local would include national level politicians. A carefully constructed politico-economic strategy for a transnational corporation might include developing close links to political leaders in Beijing, Shanghai, in various provincial locations, and among particularly strong community government RSCEs, as part of their overall plan for managing production and market conditions *and* political risks. Given the degree of influence wielded by community, municipal, and provincial governments over policies emanating from the center and the openings created by WTO, it may be relatively easy for transnationals to create key connections between themselves and Chinese institutions such that influence over future reforms, as well as current policy implementation and regulation, can be exerted.

The impediments to closing the political distance between transnational headquarters and Beijing (as well as the various local nodes of political influence within China) are now mostly linguistic and cultural, though the spread of OECD (mostly US) culture and American English is eroding this barrier. New cybertechnics, especially the Internet and satellite communication, provide the mechanisms for linking transnational elements across vast geographic space and for incorporating political agencies into the transnational cybersuperorganism. But the grid of communication and influence is not one-way. The more transnationals integrate China into their operations, the more important China becomes to those transnationals. Local, municipal, and national leaders in China may be influenced by their relationships with transnationals, as well as with domestic firms, but they may also increasingly be in a position to influence those transnationals, as well, both explicitly and implicitly. For example, every transnational that sets up operations in China is faced with the need to integrate domestic personnel. These Chinese employees bring some of their own culture with them into the transnational and, over time, this cultural influence will permeate throughout the corporate culture, albeit transformed by the corporate culture itself.

The future of Chinese capitalism

The financial fragilities created by a growing public debt (particularly when one includes the debt owed to state-owned banks by SREs), rising unemployment (which is likely to worsen as a result of the increased competition resulting from WTO), and the difficulties in maintaining legitimacy based on traditional views of citizenship rights under "socialism" are likely to push the CPC into the arms of corporate patrons (both domestic and foreign).[3] This is not guaranteed. China is still primarily state (not private) capitalist and the Chinese state is still a strong state, even if not as strong as the state that Chris Bramall (2000) had in mind when he described the "suppression of growth-retarding interest groups" as "one of the main achievements of the Maoist era." In particular, one should not underestimate the continuing influence of the senior leadership of the PLA which has not yet lost its clout within the Party. The PLA leadership's support for the modernist agenda could weaken if social unrest becomes a more serious issue. Outside of China the network of close ties between transnationals and political institutions does not go unchallenged. Indeed, there is a continuing struggle by grassroots organizations of citizens to regain popular democratic control over public policy, if not to completely sever the lines of transmission connecting transnational power centers to government agencies and legislative bodies. Nevertheless, opening up the CPC to a larger number of capitalist managers and others dependent upon capitalist SV for their livelihood (either directly or indirectly), as well as private capitalists, linking China to international markets (and cultures) via WTO, sending capitalist transnationals to locate new sources of strategic inputs and SV in the less industrialized world, and reorienting the Chinese economy toward market determined levels of employment and income (including growth in export-oriented manufacturing) creates connections between the Chinese state, domestic and transnational firms, and international agencies that will be difficult to challenge, much less sever, in the future. As more and more Chinese citizens work for foreign firms (or domestic firms whose livelihood is linked to foreign markets and/or firms) and political leaders depend on such firms for distributed SV (either for public or personal well being), it will become less likely that Leftist (much less Maoist) political policies would gain much acceptance within either the CPC or the general public.

At the same time, the growth of Chinese capitalism brings with it the increased potential for social unrest, particularly in the context of a reduction in the central government's provision of social services (another aspect of the reforms). Millions of Chinese are now without access to good quality healthcare. A social security system is still in the planning phase, even as the elderly find it increasingly difficult to obtain services that had once been considered a right of citizenship. Young people are becoming increasingly unhappy with what they see as a culture of corruption and selfishness. Photos of Mao are once again starting to proliferate and President Hu tries to capitalize with speeches that speak affectionately about Mao's commitment to social justice. The form of competitive capitalism being promoted by the modernists is a new world for the Chinese population to inhabit. To make matters worse, many of those most likely to adapt to these changes, the better educated and technically trained workers – those most needed by Chinese firms hoping to effectively compete against foreign firms in both domestic and foreign markets – are taking advantage of the opening up of the Chinese economy by joining foreign firms at pay levels well in excess of salaries in similar Chinese firms. This results in a subtle but continuous erosion of Chinese competitiveness from within. The problem will only worsen under WTO. Finally, the assumption on the part of the Party leadership that the legitimacy of their continued rule rests on economic growth may prove overly simplistic. It could turn out that the contours of this new world are not recognized as consistent with the ideals of the People's Republic. If that should turn out to be so, a serious crisis of legitimacy (of continued one-party rule by the CPC) could already be in progress. If WTO should exacerbate the problems that competitive capitalism have already generated – for example, by causing rural incomes to fall, rather than simply stagnate, as cheap American agricultural goods cross the Pacific and enter Chinese cities – then all bets are off. Calling upon the citizenry of China to recognize the logical necessity of participating in WTO and reorganizing Chinese society according to the global dictates of the "West" may not be sufficient to resolve the crisis in favor of the CPC leadership.

But this does not mean the end of Chinese capitalism. If that were to occur, it is more likely to be the product of the combined effect of grassroots political movements, democratization, and community control over the appropriation and distribution of SV. The fact remains that community governments have not yet given up their control over value flows and, in the past, have been able to push the central government in unexpected public policy directions. This could happen again. On the other hand, corporatization could ultimately spell the end of community government control over industrial enterprises. Privatization could become the next phase of Chinese capitalism. This seems more likely than a movement toward nonexploitative class processes. But no matter what happens in the future, the Chinese social formation has already been sufficiently transformed and linked to the global economy (with dependencies running in both directions) that the genie cannot be put back in the bottle. Whether under CPC rule or some other political form, the likelihood is that China will become the next great superpower on the planet.

The question is, how will this development reshape the internal dynamics of a global capitalist system that increasingly dominates local politics, economics, and culture?

Glossary

Ancient class process (ancientism) Nonexploitative class process distinguished by a direct producer's position as sole appropriator/distributor of their surplus labor.

Capitalist class process (capitalism) Exploitative class process distinguished by human beings selling their potential to do labor (their labor power) in a "market" with enough potential buyers to allow some modicum of choice of employer.

Communist class process (communism) Nonexploitative class process distinguished by collective appropriation and distribution of surplus labor by its performers (direct producers).

Cybersuperorganism Superorganism within which computer technology has connected the various units, including human beings, with relatively instantaneous means of communications and control. The ultimate cyber-superorganism would approximate to the Borg in the fictional Star Trek universe.

Direct producers Those who perform surplus labor.

Distributive (subsumed) class process Initial distribution of the fruits of appropriated surplus labor.

Exploitation Appropriation of surplus labor by someone other than the direct producer.

Feudal class process (feudalism) Exploitative class process distinguished by the production and appropriation of surplus on the basis of socially constituted ties of obligation of direct producers to the service of a specific feudal appropriator qua lord. Feudal obligation presents the direct producer with a socially determined limitation on his or her ability to perform labor.

Fundamental class process Performance and appropriation of surplus labor.

Hard technology Material artifact(s).

Labor power Potential to perform productive labor.

Labor power market Site of the buying and selling of labor power.

Maoists Those who are committed to the ideology of Mao, specifically the notion of class struggle as critical to achieving communism.

Market Site of buying and selling.

Modernist One who conceives of society as progressing along a linear path of stages from primitive to advanced.

Modernist Marxist Modernists who conceive of communism as being the historical end point of society.

Necessary labor Amount of labor power a direct producer needs to expend to produce the goods and services necessary to satisfy her/his standard of living.

Post-structuralism A breaking with the enterprise of creating deterministic grand narratives.

Privatization To shift the position of surplus appropriation to private (non-state) agents.

Rural state capitalist enterprise (RSCE) Superorganic entity comprised of a community government and the TVEs whose surplus it appropriates and distributes.

Slave class process (slavery) Exploitative class process distinguished by the ability of an appropriator to exploit direct producers as conditioned by the direct producers' status as chattel (living capital).

Social contract Relationship between citizens and their government involving expectations that have been shaped historically regarding the behavior, rights, and entitlements of citizens.

Soft technology Social organization by which material artifacts are used.

State capitalism Variant form of capitalism where the social location of surplus production and appropriation occurs within or under the control of a state bureaucracy or its constituent agencies.

State-run enterprises (SREs) Urban enterprises run by the state.

Superorganic Social entity/institution comprised of a relatively large number of human beings acting as a single entity, for example, a corporation.

Surplus labor Labor power that is expended beyond what the direct producer needs to satisfy his/her standard of living.

Surplus product Surplus labor in product form.

Surplus value Surplus labor in value form.

Technological determinist One who believes that technology is *the* determinant of other social processes.

Technology Useful artifacts of human culture.

Township and village enterprise Rural capitalist enterprises affiliated with township and village governments.

Value of labor power Socially determined value of a direct producer's labor power.

Notes

1 Theory matters

1 The Marxian theory which serves as our means of theoretical production (and which, like all theories, is in a state of constant transformation), is based upon the concepts and critical reading of Marx forged into a unified theoretical framework by Stephen A. Resnick, Richard D. Wolff, and the other members of the school of Marxian thought they have founded. This school of Marxian thought, distinguished in part by a theoretical vocabulary borrowed and modified from the French philosopher Louis Althusser, is most closely associated in the current period with the Association of Economic and Social Analysis (AESA) based at the University of Massachusetts, Amherst, and the AESA's journal, Rethinking Marxism. See their detailed theoretical work, Resnick and Wolff (1987) *Knowledge and Class: A Marxian Critique of Political Economy*, Chicago, IL: University of Chicago Press and a second work that contrasts this particular version of Marxian theory to neoclassical theory, *Economics: Marxian Versus Neoclassical*, Baltimore, MD: Johns Hopkins Press.

2 Freud used the concept "overdetermination" in his analysis of dreams to refer to the way in which the content of dreams was not simplistically determined by a finite set of life-events, but was, rather, the product of the totality or gestalt of life experiences, including the state of mind of the dreamer at the moment of revealing the dream. Thus, in the interpretation (or reading) of an individual's dreams, the meaning is always partially understood and necessarily open to further interpretation. See Freud, S. (1950) *The Interpretation of Dreams*, trans. A.A. Brill, New York: Modern Library. Louis Althusser (1970: 87–128) borrows and then transforms this term in order to construct an understanding of his reading of Marx, in particular as a means of producing an understanding of Marx's radical epistemological and ontological break from essentialist discourse. See Althusser's essay, "Contradiction and Overdetermination," in *For Marx*, trans. Ben Brewster, New York: Vintage.

Resnick and Wolff further transform the Althusserian concept of overdetermination as part of their ongoing reading of Marx and production of new knowledge of the effectivity of class upon other social and natural processes and vice versa. Like Althusser, Resnick and Wolff use the term overdetermination to differentiate the unique epistemological and ontological position of Marx from essentialist epistemological and ontological positions. One of the consequences of Resnick and Wolff's theoretical production and their transformation of the concept of overdetermination is the displacement of notions of static objects of analysis with the concept of process. In this concept of process, the overdetermined, and thus ever changing, nature of all social and natural phenomena is given conceptual clarity. The ontological roots of this conception may be traced as far back as the Greek philosopher Heraclitus and certain Daoist philosophers in China, for whom the universe was conceptualized as always in flux and the product of the overdetermined contradictions produced in the interplay of its constituent processes. We follow Resnick and Wolff in the use of the terms overdetermination and process as unambiguously anti-essentialist notions of how knowledge is produced and how all social and natural phenomena exist and interact. See Resnick and Wolff (1987: 1–37).

3 See Resnick and Wolff's discussion of alternative views of class, ontology, etc. in both *Knowledge and Class* (1987) and *Class Theory and History* (2002).

4 "The ancient form of the fundamental class process is characterized by a type of private appropriation of surplus labor that unites the production and appropriation of surplus labor on an individualized basis. This unity is conceptualized as the fusion within the direct producer qua ancient of the roles of private producer and private appropriator of surplus labor. This unified production and appropriation of surplus labor in a single human being constitutes self-exploitation" (Gabriel 1990), See dissertation for elaboration of the theory.

5 Neil C. Hughes (2002: 8) makes a short note of this in his book, *Smashing the Iron Rice Bowl*, Armonk, NY: M.E. Sharpe. At the Fourteenth Communist Party Congress in October 1992, then party secretary-general Jiang Zemin announced the adoption of market competition as official policy under the ideological banner of a socialist market economy with Chinese characteristics. In a footnote referring to World Bank's publication, *Updating Economic Memorandum: Managing Rapid Growth and Transition*, p. 30, the Chinese constitution was amended in March 1993 by the party's Central Committee to include the concept of a socialist market economy, and the concept of a planned economy under public ownership was deleted.

2 Social contracts and the rural–urban divide: the nexus of the Maoist and modernist visions

1 As a philosophical idea, the social contract has been influenced primarily by Thomas Hobbes, John Locke, and Jean-Jacques Rousseau. See footnotes 1 and 2 in Tang and Parish (2000: 3) for notes on the social contract as applied to "socialist" and "post-socialist" societies.

2 See Laaksonen (1988) *Management in China during and after Mao* for a discussion of how culture has shaped the management and structure of the CPC as well as other organizations in China.

5 State capitalism in urban China: the case of the SREs

1 Excerpts from talks given in Wuchang, Shenzhen, Zhuhai, and Shanghai, January 18–February 21, 1992: http://english.peopledaily.com.cn/dengxp/vol3/text/d1200.html (accessed December 10, 2004).

2 This experiment was extended, in modified form, to first 100 then 300 additional enterprises in 1980, and further expanded the same year to 403 enterprises in a more radical form whereby "factories were allowed to 'manage independently', pay tax, rather than profit, to the state and assume full responsibility for profit and losses" (Cheung *et al.* 1998: 385). The results were perceived a success – as determined by increases in output, productivity, profit, and tax paid to the state, 29.9, 12.72, 29.2, and 23.34 percent, respectively – and the reforms were subsequently dubbed the "Sichuan experience" and recommended for national use (Cheung *et al.* 1998: 385; Ming 2000: 49). This marked the central government's decision to shift the site of surplus appropriation to within each enterprise. The enterprise general manager, an appointed official/vassal of the state bureaucracy, was responsible for distributing revenues to the State Council based on a fixed tax rate. General managers, and later boards of directors were given greater autonomy. The statistical outcomes of "Sichuan experience" signaled to the modernist-Marxist CPC leadership that decentralizing enterprise authority could achieve their objectives.

In May 1979, the State Economic Commission, the Ministry of Finance, and four other departments conducted experiments in the expansion of decision-making powers to enterprises in Tianjin and Shanghai. These early reforms were supported by the workers and management, and many more enterprises took matters into their own hands and followed the example of the Sichuan, Tianjin, and Shanghai enterprises. In July 1979, the State Council made these experiments official and called for their expansion to other locales and the enterprises therein (Zhou 2000: 15–27). In accord with the "Sichuan experience," urban industrial enterprises, and more precisely senior management of these enterprises, have on a wide scale been granted the authority, by the State Council, to "produce, price, and sell extra products after the quota [specified in the state plan] had been met..." and to "hire and fire [allocate and de-allocate labor power] within state guidelines..." and to "determine rewards and punishments based on performance [production of surplus value]" (Li 1999: 56). Although the reforms were varied in their application, there is also strong evidence that the decentralization of surplus appropriation has not been completely implemented. In many cases, the State Council or its bureaus have continued to determine investments and other surplus value distributions within central state controlled enterprises and a similar dynamic occurs within municipal and locally controlled enterprises. Either way, these enterprises remain within the boundaries of state control (whether central or local levels of the state) and are state capitalist in nature.

3 There is evidence that surplus appropriation occurs internally within the SRE, by its board of directors. However, the preponderance of the evidence indicates that this is an illusion – that the State Council or its appointed bureaus retain control over the distributions, and therefore is the appropriating superorganic body. From a class standpoint this is irrelevant, since either way the enterprise is state capitalist, given that the directors are selected by the state bureaucracy and the form of exploitation is unambiguously capitalist. Nevertheless, the continuing struggle over the site of the appropriation, even if it is between state governed bodies, is an important determinants of the enterprise's behavior and of the interaction of the enterprise with the larger social formation.
4 "AMCs are normally not supposed to take over new NPLs [non-performing loans] (as declared after 1996) and to concentrate on old loans that are difficult to recover" (OECD 2002: 179).
5 See OECD (2002: 184) the reselling of worker shares is discussed in greater detail in the reducing social costs section.

6 Agriculture: the perpetual revolution

1 I interviewed direct producers in the Xishuangbanna Prefecture, Yunnan Province, November 1983, after the start of the nongye shengchan zeren zhi reforms but prior to the dismantling of the communes. A number of producers admitted that there was some shirking under the feudal form of production. Work slowdowns under the commune system appeared to be relatively frequent and motivated by discontent with the system in general as well as specific gripes with local officials.
2 For a critique of this view of the relationship of productive self-employment and capitalist exploitation, see Gabriel (1989) Ancients: A Marxian Theory of Self-Exploitation, PhD dissertation, University of Massachusetts and Gabriel (1990) "Ancients: A Marxian Theory of Self-Exploitation," *Rethinking Marxism*, 3(1): 85–106.
3 Capitalist firms in China, as elsewhere, tend to employ far fewer workers per investment outlay than enterprises of self-employed producers or family-based enterprises (whatever the class process underlying the family enterprise). This is indicated by the relatively low employment elasticity of investment in capitalism. Thus, when capitalist firms make up a larger share of investment spending in China, then employment growth slows. It is likely that this trend will both increase the unemployment rate over time and make it increasingly difficult to absorb unemployed workers for any given amount of

overall investment spending in the Chinese economy. The potential for this leading to social unrest is of no small importance in analyzing the stability of Chinese society going forward.

4 Fan Gang (1993: 290) also suggests in terms of increasing grain supply:

> As for specific measures, apart from increasing grain imports through different channels, we could also consider the establishment of our own grain bases in countries, such as Russia or Brazil, where the man–land ratio is low. The associated costs would be considerably less than those involved in trying to increase output on our own land. Economic liberalization in China is under way and our economic strength and market development require that we consider problems of resource allocation from a broad international perspective. Of course it is possible for Chinese people to "support themselves." But this does not necessarily mean that we must grow our own grain. We can use our own money to buy the grain that we need. Nor does it mean that we have to use our limited arable land base to grow our own grain. Just as Western countries have set up enterprises throughout the world in order to support themselves, so China's grain can be grown in various different parts of the world.

5 See Chen (1999: 72):

> It was emphasized in the Resolution on Agriculture and Many Important Issues of Rural Work passed by the Third Plenum of the Fifteenth CCP Central Committee on October 14, 1998, that China must develop a collective-ownership-dominated, variegated economic system in the countryside. If China can find in the village conglomerate a structure for promoting economic growth and maintaining social and political stability, the path and form represented by the village conglomerate would have significant implications for China.

Also, Research Group for Fixed Capital Investment (1993: 277):

> We must carefully regulate the relationship between raising agriculture's production capacity and raising the production capacity of individual industries related to agricultural production. We must also improve external conditions for agricultural construction and ensure a high degree of coordination within overall agricultural production capacity. The Eighth Plenary Session of the Thirteenth Party Congress stressed the need to raise agriculture's overall production capacity. Accordingly, we must increase the output capacity of crop farming, forestry, livestock, fishing, and subsidiaries. We must also expand the production and supply of capital goods for agriculture and extend capacity at every stage of the production process. This is a more complex process than merely strengthening agricultural construction and increasing fixed capital investment in farming. That is, we must also strengthen other industries and services that are related to agricultural production – including building facilities for agro industry, transportation, communications, energy resources, commerce, supply and marketing, education, technology, information, private and public finance, etc. All of this will help ensure that overall production capacity is both comprehensive and coordinated.

7 Finance capital: reforming the capital markets

1 It has been estimated that from 20 to 30 percent of the loan portfolios of state banks are nonperforming and 50 percent or more of these nonperforming loans may be unrecoverable.

2 See OECD's report *China in the World Economy* (2002: 245–247) for other examples of banking crisis in deregulated and liberalized banking sectors in thirteen OECD countries.

8 Globalization and Chinese capitalism

1 Li Changchun, a member of the Standing Committee of the CPC Central Committee Political Bureau, describes the new philosophy governing the CPC, the *Three Represents*, as putting forth the principle that "the CPC must always represent the most advanced productivity and culture in China as well as the fundamental interests of the maximal majority of the Chinese people" (Xinhuanet 2003). The shift of the CPC in representing "the interests of the maximal majority of the Chinese people" has actually been a way to open up the Party to greater influence by the managerial and professional elites who have benefited enormously from the economic reforms but, until recently, remained somewhat alienated from the Party. Jiang Zemin, and now Hu Jintao, is transforming the CPC into what Marx might have described as a "bourgeois" party, with workers and peasants fading into the background and the urban elite rising to prominence within the Party ranks and leadership.

2 The victory of the pro-capitalist wing of the CPC and the leadership of the Engineers faction of Jiang Zemin and Hu Jintao is being solidified at this point. The Central Committee of the CPC has proposed amending the 1982 constitution by adding the *Three Represents* into the document as one of the guiding principles of the nation and recognized as "heritage and further development of Marxism, Leninism, Mao Zedong Thought and Deng Xiaoping Theory" according to Wang Zhaoguo, vice chairman of the National People's Congress Standing Committee. Wang explained this to National People's Congress (NPC) representatives in his capacity as a member of the Political Bureau of the CPC Central Committee. See People's Daily Online http://english.peopledaily.com.cn/200403/08/eng20040308_136881.shtml (accessed June 10, 2004).

3 Ironically, the growth in autonomy of domestic firms (which have been transformed from state-run enterprises to merely state-owned or privatized enterprises) simultaneously takes away the central and provincial government's powers to guarantee employment to millions of Chinese workers but also makes these governments more vulnerable to the decisions of newly autonomous managers in these enterprises precisely because it is now the managers who control the allocation of employment (and other inputs). As firm managers (and boards of directors) gain greater control over the number of employed and unemployed in Chinese society, they also gain greater influence over the public authorities who must learn to respond to the concerns of these managers or face the prospect of social instability (or greater social instability) when firms increase lay-offs or refuse to invest. At the extreme, capitalist managers and directors can threaten capital strikes, refusing to invest and forcing a sharp fall in aggregate demand, if the government authorities do not satisfy their demands. See He Qinglian's 1998 text *Xiandaihua de Xianjing* (China's Pitfall) for a discussion of the impact of granting firms more autonomy over investments and hiring practices (rising unemployment and poverty, increased inequality, etc.).

Bibliography

Althusser, L. (1970) *For Marx*, New York: Vintage.

Aubert, C. and Li, X. (2002) "Agricultural Underemployment and Rural Migration in China: Facts and Figures," *China Perspectives*, 41: 47–58.

Baxandall, R., Ewen, E., Gordon, L., Ehrenreich, J. and B., Gordon, D., Greenbaum, J., Rosenberg, N., Stevenson, G., Weinbaum, B., Bridges, A., and Weiss, D. (eds) (1976) *Technology, the Labor Process and the Working Class*, New York: Monthly Review Press.

Becker, J. (2000) *The Chinese*, New York: Oxford University Press.

Bettelheim, C. (1978) *China Since Mao*, New York: Monthly Review Press.

Bloch, M. (1961) *Feudal Society*, Chicago, IL: University of Chicago Press.

Bottelier, P. (2004) "China's Domestic Capital Markets and Interactions with International Capital Markets," Paper Presented at US–China Commission Hearing, April 16, 2004. Online. Available: http://www.uscc.gov/hearings/2004hearings/written_testimonies/04_04_16wrts/bottelier.htm (accessed July 10, 2004).

Bramall, C. (2000) *Sources of Chinese Economic Growth: 1978–1996*, New York: Oxford University Press.

Brook, T. (ed.) (1989) *The Asiatic Mode of Production in China*, Armonk, NY: M.E. Sharpe.

Brown, G. (2003) "China's Factory Floors: An Industrial Hygienist's View," *International Journal of Occupational Environmental Health*, 9: 326–339.

Chakrabarti, A. and Cullenberg, S. (2003) *Transition and Development in India*, London: Routledge.

Chan, A. (1998) "Labor Standards and Human Rights: The Case of Chinese Workers Under Market Socialism," *Human Rights Quarterly*, 20(4): 886–904.

Chan, A. and Zhu, X. (2003) "Disciplinary Labor Regimes in Chinese Factories," *Critical Asian Studies*, 35(4): 559–584.

Chang, C., McCall, B., and Wang, Y. (2000) "Incentive Contracting versus Ownership Reforms: Evidence from China's Township and Village Enterprises," Working Paper no. 365, Carlson School of Management, University of Minnesota.

Chang, K. (2001) "The WTO, Labor Standards, and the Safeguarding of Laborers' Rights and Interests," *The Chinese Economy*, 34(6): 57–86.

Che, J. and Qian, Y. (1998) "Institutional Environment, Community Government, and Corporate Governance: Understanding China's Township–Village Enterprises," *Journal of Law, Economics, and Organization*, 14(1): 1–23.

Chen, B., Dietrich, J.K., and Feng, Y. (eds) (2000) *Financial Market Reform in China: Progress, Problems, and Prospects*, Boulder, CO: Westview Press.

Chen, W. (1999) *The Political Economy of Rural Development in China, 1978–1999*, Westport, CT: Praeger Publishers.

Cheng, I. and Hulme, V. (2004) "Time To Regroup: China Must Use 2004 to Put its Growth on a Solid Foundation," *China Business Review*, May 2004. Online. Available: http://www.chinabusinessreview.com/public/0405/hulme.html (accessed August 20, 2004).

Cheung, P.T.Y., Chung, J.H., and Lin, Z. (eds) (1998) *Provincial Strategies of Economic Reform in Post-Mao China: Leadership, Politics, and Implementation*, Armonk, NY: M.E. Sharpe.

China Statistical Yearbook (2004) Beijing: China Statistical Publishing House.

Chow, C. (2004) "Workers Protest at Low Wages, Long Hours," *South China Morning Post*, October 7.

CPC White Paper (2004) "China's Employment Situation and Policies," Information Office of the State Council of the People's Republic of China, Beijing: China. Online. Available: http://www.china.org.cn/e-white/20040426/4.htm (accessed December 10, 2004).

Critchley, J.S. (1978) *Feudalism*, Boston, MA: G. Allen & Unwin.

Deng, X. (1984) "Build Socialism with a Specifically Chinese Character," speech given June 13. Online. Available http://english.peopledaily.com.cn/dengxp/vol3/text/c1220.html (accessed December 26, 2004).

—— (1985) "There is no Fundamental Contradiction between Socialism and a Market Economy," speech given October 23. Online. Available: http://english.peopledaily.com.cn/dengxp/vol3/text/c1480.html (accessed February 13, 2005).

—— (1992) "Excerpts from Talks Given in Wuchang, Shenzhen, Zhuhai and Shanghai," January 18–February 21. Online. Available: http://english.peopledaily.com.cn/dengxp/vol3/text/d1200.html (accessed December 10, 2004).

Dennis, C. (2004) "Mental Health: Asia's Tigers Get the Blues," *Nature*, 429: 696–698. Online. Available: http://www.nature.com/news/2004/040614/pf/429696a_pf.html (accessed February 12, 2005).

Dobb, M. (1978) "A Further Comment," in R. Hilton (ed.) *The Transition From Feudalism to Capitalism*, London: Verso.

Doyal, L. and Pennell, I. (1979) *The Political Economy of Health*, London: Pluto Press.

Duan, Y. (2003) "The Question of Assets and Property Rights in the Transformation of State Owned Enterprises to the Shareholding System," in C. Howe, Y.Y. Kueh, and R. Ash (eds) *China's Economic Reforms: A Study with Documents*, London: Routledge Curzon.

Edin, M. (1998) "Why do Chinese Local Cadres Promote Growth? Institutional Incentives and Constraints of Local Cadres," *Forum for Development Studies*, 98(1): 97–127.

Ehrenreich, J. and B. (1976) "Work and Consciousness," in R. Baxandall, E. Ewen, L. Gordon, J. and B. Ehrenreich, D. Gordon, J. Greenbaum, N. Rosenberg, G. Stevenson, B. Weinbaum, A. Bridges, and D. Weiss (eds) *Technology, the Labor Process and the Working Class*, New York: Monthly Review Press.

Einhorn, B. (2004) "Suicide: China's Great Wall of Silence," *BusinessWeek*, November 2, 2004. Online. Available: http://yahoo.businessweek.com (accessed February 10, 2005).

Fairbank, J.K. and Goldman, M. (1998) *China: A New History*, Cambridge, MA: Harvard University Press.

Fallows, J. (1994) *Looking at the Sun: The Rise of the New East Asian Economic and Political System*, New York: Random House.

Fan, G. (1993) "Short-term Policies and Long-term Strategies for Solving China's Grain Supply Problems," in C. Howe, Y.Y. Kueh, and R. Ash (eds) *China's Economic Reform: A Study With Documents*, London: RoutledgeCurzon.

Fang, Y. (1993) "China Throws Itself Into International Competition: Agriculture Faces A New Challenge," in C. Howe, Y.Y. Kueh, and R. Ash (eds) *China's Economic Reform: A Study With Documents*, London: RoutledgeCurzon.

Findlay, C. and Watson, A. (eds) (1999) *Food Security and Economic Reform: The Challenges Facing China's Grain Marketing System*, New York: St. Martin's Press.

Fleisher, B. and Yang, D.T. (2003) "China's Labor Market," paper presented at the Stanford Center for International Development Conference on China's Market Reforms, Stanford University, September 19–20, 2003.

Fourquin, G. (1976) *Lordship and Feudalism in the Middle Ages*, New York: Pica Press.

Freud, S. (1950) *The Interpretation of Dreams*, trans. A.A. Brill, New York: Modern Library.

Friedman, E., Pickowicz, P.G., and Selden, M. (1991) *Chinese Village, Socialist State*, New Haven, CT: Yale University.

Gabriel, S. (1989) "Ancients: A Marxian Theory of Self-Exploitation," PhD dissertation, University of Massachusetts, Amherst.

—— (1990) "Ancients: A Marxian Theory of Self-Exploitation," *Rethinking Marxism*, 3(1): 85–106.

Gabriel, S. and Martin, M.F. (1992) "China: The Ancient Road to Communism?," *Rethinking Marxism*, 5(1): 56–77.

Gabriel, S. and Todorova, E. (2003) "Racism and Capitalist Accumulation: An Overdetermined Nexus," *Critical Sociology*, 29(1): 29–46.

Gaetano, A.M. (2004) "Filial Daughters, Modern Women: Migrant Domestic Workers in Post-Mao Beijing," in A.M. Gaetano and T. Jacka (eds) *On the Move: Women in Rural-to-Urban Migration in Contemporary China*, New York: Columbia University Press.

Gao, Shangquan and Chi, F. (eds) (1997) *Rapid Economic Development in China and Controlling Inflation*, Beijing: Foreign Languages Press.

Gao, Shumei and Schaffer, M.E. (2000) "Financial Discipline in the Enterprise Sector in Transition Countries: How Does China Compare?," in S. Cook, S. Yao, and J. Zhuang (eds) *The Chinese Economy Under Transition*, New York: St. Martin's Press.

Genicot, L. (1990) *Rural Communities in the Medieval West*, Baltimore, MD: Johns Hopkins University Press.

Gibson-Graham, J.K. and O'Neill, P. (2001) "Exploring a New Class Politics of the Enterprise," in J.K. Gibson-Graham, S. Resnick, and R. Wolff (eds) *Re/Presenting Class: Essays in Postmodern Marxism*, Durham, NC: Duke University Press.

Gu, S. (1999) *China's Industrial Technology: Market Reform and Organizational Change*, London: Routledge.

Hart-Landsberg, M. and Burkett, P. (2004) "China and Socialism: Market Reforms and Class Struggle," *Monthly Review*, July–August, 56(3).

Harvie, C. (ed.) (2000) *Contemporary Developments and Issues in China's Economic Transition*, New York: St. Martin's Press.

He, Q. (1998) *Zhongguo de xianjing (China's Pitfall)*, Hong Kong: Mingjing chubanshe.

Hilton, R. (ed.) (1978) "Introduction," in *The Transition From Feudalism to Capitalism*, London: Verso.

Hong Kong Trade Development Council (2005) "Market Profile on Chinese Mainland." Online. Available: http://www.tdctrade.com/main/china.htm (accessed March 12, 2005).

Hope, N., Yang, T.D., and Li, M.Y. (eds) (2003) "Agenda for Future Research," in *How Far Across the River?: Chinese Policy Reform at the Millennium*, Stanford, CA: Stanford University Press.

Howard, P. (1988) *Breaking the Iron Rice Bowl*, Armonk, NY: M.E. Sharpe.

Howe, C., Kueh, Y.Y., and Ash, R. (eds) (2003) *China's Economic Reform: A Study with Documents*, New York: RoutledgeCurzon.

Hsieh, C. and Lu, M. (eds) (2004) *Changing China: A Geographic Appraisal*, Boulder, CO: Westview Press.

Huang, Y. (1998) *Agricultural Reform in China: Getting Institutions Right*, Cambridge: Cambridge University Press.

Hughes, N.C. (2002) *China's Economic Challenge: Smashing the Iron Rice Bowl*, Armonk, NY: M.E. Sharpe.

Hussain, A. (2003) "Social Welfare in China in the Context of Three Transitions," in N. Hope, D.T. Yang, and M.Y. Li (eds) *How Far Across the River?: Chinese Policy Reform at the Millennium*, Stanford, CA: Stanford University Press.

Iredale, R. (2000) "China's Labour Migration Since 1978," in C. Harvie (ed.) *Contemporary Developments and Issues in China's Economic Transition*, New York: St. Martin's Press.

Jacka, T. (1997) *Women's Work in Rural China: Change and Continuity in an Era of Reform*, New York: Cambridge University Press.

Jefferson, G.H. and Singh, I. (1999) *Enterprise Reform in China: Ownership, Transition, and Performance*, New York: Oxford University Press.

Johnson, T. (2004) "Large-scale Local Protests Erupting More Often in China's Hinterlands," Knight Ridder. Online. Available: http://www.chinalaborwatch.org (accessed November 10, 2004).

Knight, J. and Song, L. (1999) *The Rural–Urban Divide*, New York: Oxford University Press.

Korzec, M. (1992) *Labour and the Failure of Reform in China*, London: Macmillan Press.

Kurtenbach, E. (2004) "South China Faces Shortage of Migrant Labor," *Washington Post*, September 9.

Laaksonen, O. (1988) *Management in China During and After Mao in Enterprises, Government, and Party*, New York: Walter de Gruyter.

Lardy, N. (2000) "China and the Asian Financial Contagion," in B. Chen, J.K. Dietrich, and Y. Feng (eds) *Financial Market Reform in China: Progress, Problems, and Prospects*, Boulder, CO: Westview Press.

Lee, M.K. (2000) *Chinese Occupational Welfare in Market Transition*, New York: St. Martin's Press.

Lefebvre, G., Procacci, G., Merrington, J., Hill, C., Hobsbawn, E., Dobb, M., Sweezy, P., Takahashi, K. (1978) *The Transition From Feudalism to Capitalism*, London: Verso.

Lenin, V.I. (1960) *Collected Works*, Moscow: International Publishers.

Lewis, W.A. (1955) *The Theory of Economic Growth*, Homewood, IL: Richard D. Irwin.

Li, S. (1999) "Institutional Change and Firm Performance," in A. Nathan, Z. Hong, and S. Smith (eds) *Dilemmas of Reform in Jiang Zemin's China*, Boulder, CO: Lynne Rienner Publishers.

Li, Y. (2000) "Institutional Analysis and Innovation of Labor Relations in China," *Social Sciences in China*, 21(1): 29–35.

Lin, J.Y. (1992) "Rural Reforms and Agricultural Growth in China," *American Economic Review*, 82: 34–51.

Lin, Y. (2001) *Between Politics and Markets: Firms, Competition, and Institutional Change in Post-Mao China*, New York: Cambridge University Press.

Lippit, V. (1987) *The Economic Development of China*, Armonk, NY: M.E. Sharpe.

Liu, G. (1999) "Questions Related to the Reform of Small and Medium-sized Enterprises in China," *Social Sciences in China*, 20(1): 5–15.

Liu, Yingqiu (2003) "Development of Private Entrepreneurship in China: Process, Problems, and Countermeasures," Research Report, The Mansfield Center for

Pacific Affairs, Washington, DC. Online. Available: http://www.mcpa.org/programs/entrepreneurship_china.pdf (accessed January 20, 2005).

Liu, Yongren (2003) "Some Tentative Ideas on the Reform of China's Labour System," in C. Howe, Y.Y. Kueh, and R. Ash (eds) *China's Economic Reform: A Study with Documents*, London: Routledge Curzon.

Lo, Chi (2004) "Bank Reform: How Much Time Does China Have?," *China Business Review*. Online. Available: http://www.chinabusinessreview.com/public/0403/chilo.html (accessed June 30, 2004).

McIntyre, R.J. (1999) "Building Real Markets Under Conditions of Policy Chaos: Russian Regional Strategies and Chinese Precedents," paper presented at American Economic Association Meetings, New York, January 5, 1999. Online. Available: http://www.ecaar.org/Articles/mcintyre.pdf (accessed December 10, 2004).

McMillan, J., Whalley, J., and Zhu, L. (1989) "The Impact of China's Economic Reforms on Agricultural Productivity Growth," *Journal of Political Economy*, 97: 781–807.

Marx, K. (1977) *Capital: A Critique of Political Economy, Vol.1*, trans. B. Fowkes, New York: Vintage.

Meisner, M. (1970) "Yenan Communism and the Rise of the Chinese People's Republic," in J.B. Crowley (ed.) *Modern East Asia: Essays in Interpretation*, New York: Harcourt, Brace and World, Inc.

Meng, X. (2000) *Labour Market Reform in China*, New York: Cambridge University Press.

Milgrom, P. and Roberts, J. (1992) *Economics, Organizations, and Management*, Englewood Cliffs, NJ: Prentice-Hall.

Ming, X. (2000) *The Dual Development State: Developmental Strategy and Institutional Arrangements for China's Transition*, Brookfield, MA: Ashgate.

Mok, K. (2000) *Social and Political Development in Post-Reform China*, New York: St. Martin's Press.

Nathan, A.J., Hong, Z., and Smith, S.R. (eds) (1999) *Dilemmas of Reform in Jiang Zemin's China*, Boulder, CO: Lynne Rienner Publishers.

Naughton, B. (2000) "Financial Development and Macroeconomic Stability in China," in B. Chen, J.K. Dietrich, and Y. Feng (eds) *Financial Market Reform in China: Progress, Problems, and Prospects*, Boulder, CO: Westview Press.

Nee, V. and Stark, D. (eds) (1989) *Remaking the Economic Institutions of Socialism: China and Eastern Europe*, Stanford, CA: Stanford University Press.

Nolan, P. and Wang, X. (2000) "Reorganizing Amid Turbulence: China's Large-Scale Industry," in S. Cook, S. Yao, and J. Zhuang (eds) *The Chinese Economy Under Transition*, New York: St. Martin's Press.

OECD (2002) *China in the World Economy: The Domestic Policy Challenges*, Paris: OECD.

Oi, J.C. (1999) *Rural China Takes Off: Institutional Foundations of Economic Reform*, Berkeley, CA: University of California Press.

—— (2003) "Bending Without Breaking: The Adaptability of Chinese Political Institutions," in N. Hope, D. Yang, and M. Li (eds) *How Far Across the River? Chinese Policy Reform at the Millenium*, Stanford, CA: Stanford University Press.

Oi, J.C. and Walder, A.G. (eds) (1999) *Property Rights and Economic Reform in China*, Stanford, CA: Stanford University Press.

O'Leary, G. (2000) "Labour Market Developments," in C. Harvie (ed.) *Contemporary Developments and Issues in China's Economic Transition*, New York: St. Martin's Press.

People's Daily (2002) "Ex-Bank Chair Sentenced to 15-Year Imprisonment," October 11. Online. Available: http://english.people.com.cn/200210/11/eng20021011_104846.shtml (accessed August 20, 2004).

Perry, E.J. and Wong, C. (1985) *The Political Economy of Reform in Post-Mao China*, Cambridge, MA: The Council on East Asian Studies/Harvard University.

Pringle, T.E. and Frost, S.D. (2003) "The Absence of Rigor and the Failure of Implementation: Occupational Health and Safety in China," *International Journal of Occupational and Environmental Health*, 9: 309–316.

Qian, Y. (2001) "Government Control in Corporate Governance as a Transitional Institution: Lessons from China," in J.E. Stiglitz and S. Yusuf (eds) *Rethinking the East Asian Miracle*, New York: Oxford University Press.

—— (2003) "How Reform Worked in China," in D. Rodrik (ed.) *In Search of Prosperity: Analytic Narratives on Economic Growth*, Princeton, NJ: Princeton University Press.

Research Group for Fixed Capital Investment in Agriculture (1993) "A Brief Overview of China's Strategy for Fixed Capital Investment in Agriculture," in C. Howe, Y.Y. Kueh, and R. Ash (eds) *China's Economic Reform: A Study With Documents*, London: Routledge Curzon.

Resnick, S.A. and Wolff, R.D. (1987) *Knowledge and Class: A Marxian Critique of Political Economy*, Chicago, IL: University of Chicago Press.

—— (2002) *Class Theory and History*, New York: Routledge.

Reynolds, B.L. (1987) *Reform in China: Challenges and Choices*, Armonk, NY: M.E. Sharpe.

Riskin, C., Zhao, R., and Li, S. (eds) (2001) *China's Retreat from Equality: Income Distribution and Economic Transition*, Armonk, NY: M.E. Sharpe.

Roberts, D. and Kynge, J. (2003) "How Cheap Labour, Foreign Investment and Rapid Industrialisation are Creating a New Workshop of the World," *Financial Times*, February 4, 2003.

Santoro, M.A. (2000) *Profits and Principles: Global Capitalism and Human Rights in China*, Ithaca, NY: Cornell University Press.

Schnitzer, M.C. (2000) *Comparative Economic Systems*, Columbus, OH: South-Western College Publishing.

Schram, S. (ed.) (1974) *Chairman Mao Talks to the People: Talks and Letters, 1956–1971*, New York: Random House.

Schumacher, E.F. (1973) *Small is Beautiful*, New York: Harper & Row.

Selden, M. (1988) *The Political Economy of Chinese Socialism*, Armonk, NY: M.E. Sharpe.

—— (1998) "Household, Cooperative, and State in the Remaking of China's Countryside," in E. Vermeer, F. Pieke, and W.L. Chong (eds) *Cooperative and Collective in China's Rural Development: Between State and Private Interests*, Armonk, NY: M.E. Sharpe.

Sheehan, J. (1998) *Chinese Workers: A New History*, New York: Routledge.

Shen, R. (2000) *China's Economic Reform: An Experiment in Pragmatic Socialism*, Westport, CT: Praeger Publishers.

Shi, Y. (1998) *Chinese Firms and Technology in the Reform Era*, New York: Routledge.

South China Morning Post (2004) "Spoiled Rice Used to Feed Migrant Workers," July 1, 2004. Online. Available: http://www.chinastudygroup.org (accessed July 1, 2004).

Spence, J.D. (1999) *The Search for Modern China*, New York: W.W. Norton.

Steinfeld, E.S. (1998) *Forging Reform in China: The Fate of State-Owned Industry*, New York: Cambridge University Press.

Stiglitz, J.E. and Yusuf, S. (2001) *Rethinking the East Asian Miracle*, New York: Oxford University Press.

Sun, L. (2001) "Economics of China's Joint-Stock Co-operatives," Discussion Paper no. 2001/24, United Nations University/WIDER.

Sun, Z. and Li, S. (2003) "Learning from Comrade Deng Xiaoping's Exposition of Agricultural Problems," in C. Howe, Y.Y. Kueh, and R. Ash (eds) *China's Economic Reform: A Study with Documents*, London: Routledge Curzon.

Sweezy, P. (1970) *The Theory of Capitalist Development*, New York: Monthly Review Press.

—— (1978) "A Critique," in R. Hilton (ed.) *The Transition From Feudalism to Capitalism*, London: Verso.

Sweezy, P. and Bettelheim, C. (1971) *On the Transition to Socialism*, New York: Monthly Review Press.

Takahashi, K. (1978) "A Contribution to the Discussion," in *The Transition From Feudalism to Capitalism*, London: Verso.

Tang, C. (1998) "Sexual Harassment: The Dual Status of and Discrimination Against Female Migrant Workers in Urban Areas," *Social Sciences in China*, 19(3): 64–71.

Tang, W. and Parish, W.L. (2000) *Changing Urban Life Under Reform: The Changing Social Contract*, New York: Cambridge University Press.

Todaro, M.P. (1977) *Economics for a Developing World: An Introduction to Principles, Problems and Policies for Development*, London: Longman.

Tsai, K.S. (2002) *Back-Alley Banking: Private Entrepreneurs in China*, Ithaca, NY: Cornell University Press.

US–China Business Council (2003) *Economic Forecast 2004*. Online. Available: http://www.uschina.org/statistics/2004economyforecast.html (accessed July 10, 2004).

Vermeer, E.B., Pieke, F.N., and Chong, W.L. (eds) (1998) *Cooperative and Collective in China's Rural Development: Between State and Private Interests*, Armonk, NY: M.E. Sharpe.

Wei, S. (2000) "Noise Trading in the Chinese Stock Market," in B. Chen, J.K. Dietrich, and Y. Feng (eds) *Financial Market Reform in China: Progress, Problems, and Prospects*, Boulder, CO: Westview Press.

Wei, S., Wen, G.J., and Zhou, H. (eds) (2002) *The Globalization of the Chinese Economy*, Northampton, MA: Edward Elgar Publishing.

Weston, T.B. (2000) "China's Labor Woes: Will the Workers Crash the Party?," in T.B. Weston and L.M. Jensen (eds) *Beyond the Headlines*, Lanham, MD: Rowman & Littlefield Publishers.

Whiting, S.H. (2001) *Power and Wealth in Rural China: The Political Economy of Institutional Change*, New York: Cambridge University Press.

Wolf, C., Jr, Yeh, K.C., Zycher, B., Eberstadt, N., and Lee, S. (2003) *Fault Lines in China's Economic Terrain*, Santa Monica, CA: Rand.

Wolff, R.D. and Resnick, S.A. (1987b) *Economics: Marxian versus Neoclassical*, Baltimore, MD: Johns Hopkins University Press.

World Bank (1993) *China Updating Economic Memorandum: Managing Rapid Growth and Transition*.

Xinhuanet (2003) " 'Three Represents' is Marxism for Contemporary China: Official," September 23. Online. Available: http://news.xinhuanet.com/english/2003–09/24/content_1095983.htm (accessed January 24, 2004).

—— (2004) "Better Conditions for Farmers Laboring in Cities," October 27. Online. Available: http://www.chinaview.cn (accessed October 27, 2004).

Yeung, H.W. and Olds, K. (2000) *Globalization of Chinese Business Firms*, New York: St. Martin's Press.

You, J. (1998) *China's Enterprise Reform: Changing State/Society Relations after Mao*, London: Routledge.

Young, S. (1989) "Policy, Practice, and the Private Sector in China," *The Australian Journal of Chinese Affairs*, 21: 57–80.

—— (1995) *Private Business and Economic Reform in China*, Armonk, NY: M.E. Sharpe.

Yusuf, S. (2003) *Innovative East Asia: The Future of Growth*, New York: Oxford University Press.

Zhang, L., De Brauw, A., and Rozelle, S. (2004) "China's Rural Labor Market Development and its Gender Implications," *China Economic Review*, 15: 230–247.

Zhen, T. (2004) "From Peasant Women to Bar Hostesses: Gender and Modernity in Post-Mao Dalian," in M.A. Gaetano and T. Jacka (eds) *On The Move: Women in Rural-to-Urban Migration in Contemporary China*, New York: Columbia University Press.

Zheng, S. (1997) *Party vs. State in Post-1949 China: The Institutional Dilemma*, New York: Cambridge University Press.

Zhou, C. (2001) "The WTO and China's Labor Standards," *The Chinese Economy*, 34(6): 32–56.

Zhou, S. (2000) "A Review of the Reform in Chinese State-owned Enterprises Over the Last Twenty Years," *Social Sciences in China*, 21(1): 14–28.

Index